CANADA AND THE AMERICAN CIVIL WAR
PRELUDE TO WAR

MARK VINET

WADEM PUBLISHING
Canada Civil War Association
North American Historical Institute

http://www.geocities.com/markvinet

Canadian Cataloguing in Publication Data

Vinet, Mark, 1964-
    Canada and the American Civil War: Prelude to War

ISBN 0-9688320-0-8

1. United States–History–1815-1861. 2. United States–History–Civil War, 1861-1865–Participation, Canadian. 3. Canada–History–1841-1867. 4. Canadians–United States–History–19th century. 5. Canada–Relations–United States. 6. United States–Relations–Canada. 7. United States–Foreign relations–1861-1865. I. Title.

FC249.V55 2001   973.7'11   C00-901733-X
F1029.U6V55 2001

Artwork: www.proudproductions.com
Printed in Canada

For any additional information contact:

Mark Vinet / Canada Civil War Association
WADEM PUBLISHING / North American Historical Institute
117 Bellevue Street
Vaudreuil-Sur-Le-Lac, Quebec, Canada, J7V-8P3
Telephone: 450-510-1102 / 514-951-6762 / 450-371-1803
Fax: 450-510-1095
E-mail: vinet@hotmail.com
http://www.geocities.com/markvinet

AUTHOR

Historian, author, lawyer Mark Vinet was born in 1964 in the city of Sorel near Montreal in the province of Quebec, Canada. He shares a bicultural English and French ancestry and is fluently bilingual in both languages. He is founder of the North American Historical Institute and the Canada Civil War Association, which presents a series of lectures by Mark Vinet on Canada and the American Civil War. He is presently writing his second book entitled *THE ROAD TO SECESSION: Canada and the American Civil War.*

DEDICATION

This book is dedicated to my parents.

My father, Claude Vinet, who carries the proud family name of a mid-seventeenth century French immigrant to the North American colony of New France.

My mother, Judith Wade, who as a young girl immigrated with her family from England to Canada after World War II.

The stage was thus set for a young French Catholic man to meet a young English Protestant woman while playing tennis in Valleyfield, a small town west of Montreal. They first spoke the language of love and in their small way contributed to the merging of two wonderful cultures. I shall always love, respect, and cherish them both.

ACKNOWLEDGMENTS

I wish to thank the many authors, scholars, curators and friends who helped me with my research for this book. My gratitude is extended to all those who warmly greeted and assisted me on my numerous field and research trips throughout North America and Europe.

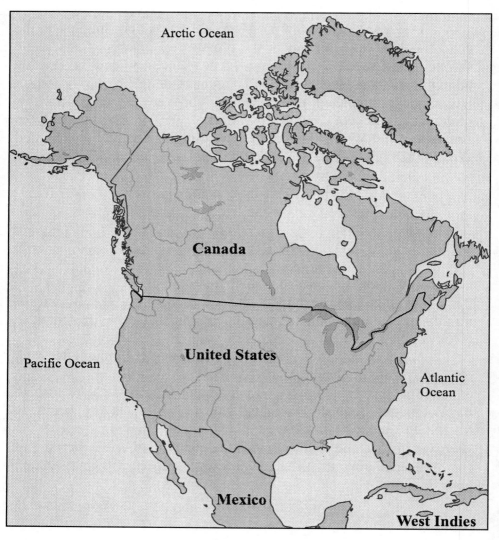

Map of North America

CONTENTS

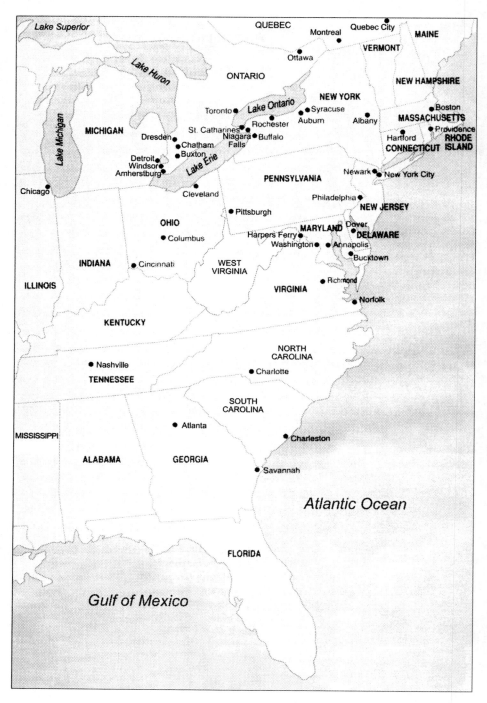

Map of Eastern-Central North America

LIST OF MAPS, PHOTOGRAPHS, & ILLUSTRATIONS

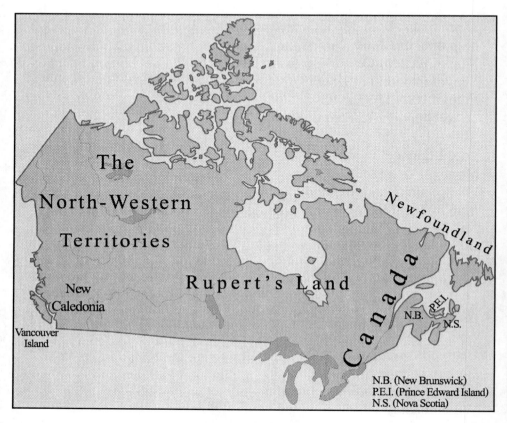

Map of Canada 1849

INTRODUCTION

In April 1861, troops of the new Confederate States of America opened fire on Union-occupied fort Sumter and launched a bloody four-year war that killed at least six hundred and twenty thousand men, including thousands of Canadians who fought in the War.

In accordance with Britain's foreign policy towards the War, Canada was officially neutral. This, however, did not prevent approximately fifty thousand Canadian-born soldiers from serving in both armies. Four Canadians attained the rank of brigadier-general and twenty-nine were awarded the Congressional Medal of Honor. Throughout the War, Canadian public opinion was divided for various reasons, including religion, language, culture, economic class, and moral background. The Civil War was the culmination of the reciprocal, sometimes parallel, but often intertwining influence of both the United States and Canada on each other's historical, territorial, political, economic, and social development. Following the War – two new nations emerged.

PRELUDE TO WAR is the first in a series of books dealing with Canada and the American Civil War by Canadian author and historian Mark Vinet. It offers an in-depth study of the fiery issues that led to the War and dramatically unveils how both countries, as neighbors, dealt with the contentious issues of Sectionalism, Slavery, Slave Rebellions, Abolitionism, and the Underground Railroad.

To better appreciate the contents of this book, certain specific terminology and abbreviations should be noted. Although some terminology and abbreviations are standard, others are custom-made and delivered by the author. The author believes that voluntary and conscious unorthodox use of the written language for the purpose of effect or emphasis is refreshing and stimulating.

In this book, the word "Canada" refers to the ensemble of colonies, provinces, and territories within Canada's present-day borders. The word "Canadian" refers to its inhabitants. The word "Aboriginal" collectively refers to North America's original native inhabitants often called Indians, Native Indians, or Native Americans. The terms "Black", "Colored" or "Negroes" refer to people with dark skin of African decent. When individual states, colonies, provinces, counties, districts, regions, or territories are referred to, the complete spelling or standard abbreviations are used. The word "Quebec" refers to the territory of New France, Canada East, or Lower Canada. "Ontario" refers to Canada West or Upper Canada. The word "Maritimes" refers to the area including Nova Scotia, New Brunswick, Prince Edward Island, and Newfoundland. "United States", "America", "U.S.", and "USA" all refer to the Republic of the United States of America. The word "American" refers to its inhabitants. The word "Americas" includes the North and South American continents as well as the group of islands referred to as the Caribbean or West Indies. When referring to the American Civil War, other terms are occasionally used such as: Civil War; War; War between the States; War for Southern Independence; War of Succession; War between the North and the South; War of the Rebellion; Great Rebellion; and, War of Northern Aggression. The abbreviation "CSA" refers to the Confederate States of America. The term "Union" refers to the United States of America.

Throughout this work, concise birth and death information is often provided following the names of historical figures. The birth or death date is followed firstly by the village, town, or city, and secondly by the state, province, region, district, or county, and finally, by the country or nation. For example: William Lloyd Garrison [1805, Newburyport, Massachusetts, USA; 1879, New York City, New York]. This information should be interpreted as follows: William Lloyd Garrison was born in 1805, in the city of Newburyport, in the state of Massachusetts, in the country of the United States of America. He died in 1879, in the city of New York, in the state of New York, in the country of the United States of America. When the names of places are not provided as part of the death information, this usually indicates that they are identical to the places of birth.

The beginning and end of events, eras, organizations, etc. are often marked by dates as well. For example: The newspaper *The Liberator* (1831-65). This information should be understood as follows: *The Liberator* was first published in 1831 and stopped publishing in 1865.

The author has conscientiously chosen to employ capital letters, Italics, and punctuation marks to better present, organize, or emphasize certain passages of this book. Although the standard rules of spelling and grammar are not always voluntarily followed, one hopes this good faith explanation will merit a benevolent acceptance and appreciation from you the reader.

The author's goal was to make this book enjoyable to write and read, or in other words – a book written to be read. To paraphrase Thorton Wilder…an author should write the book he would like to read. History should be savored and enjoyed by all, not only historians. Small print and sometimes distracting footnotes have been avoided in order to make this book "reader friendly". Although this work is presented without footnotes, it is based on documentation. Any general reader interested in discovering primary and secondary background materials and sources should locate, without difficulty, the references in the Bibliography. These references should also provide any knowledgeable scholar with the sources that substantiate the context.

The Bibliography lists the references drawn upon for the subject of this book but not its general background. The Bibliography therefore does not list every publication (book, pamphlet, essay, article, diary, letter etc.) that was read by the author relating to the subject's general historical period.

Finally, it should be noted that as part of the book cover, the contemporary flag of Canada is included along side Civil War era Union and Confederate flags. Although this Canadian flag was not in use during the War, it has nevertheless been included on the cover as a symbol for all the Civil War era territory and people under British jurisdiction in North America. The author has chosen to use this flag as well as the term "Canada" for familiarity and simplicity purposes.

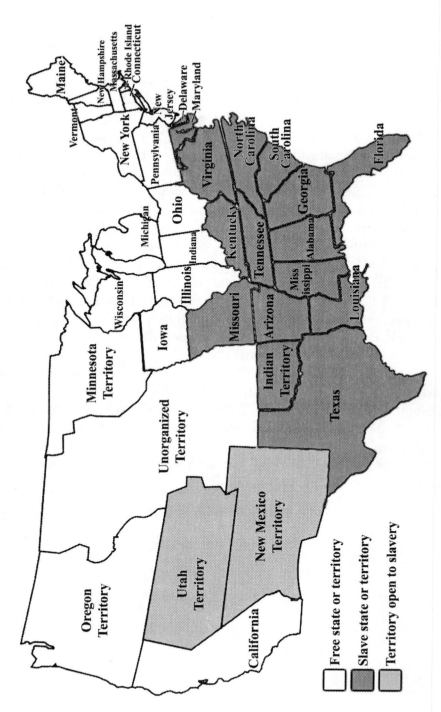

1850 Map of USA

PROLOGUE

History is not black and white, nothing is. Rainbow colors mixed with subtle shades of gray permeate within and around most events, occurrences, eras and personal lives so that in order to fully understand history, one must piece together a delicate puzzle of facts and impressions into a multicolored mosaic that is at best in focus. The degree of focus depends on the ability of the generation looking back to properly digest an enormous amount of information covering a wide span of time. This premise surely applies to the American Civil War. This historical period should not be put into a vacuum and understood only via its four years of painful military conflict. Instead, it should be analyzed and viewed on a more comprehensive scale and in the context of a generation of time. Objectivity remains any historian's ultimate but purely unattainable goal. No matter how hard one tries, life's many experiences and influences inevitably and most often unconsciously lead all spectators, reporters, and historians towards undeniable and universally natural, human subjective traits. With this in mind, I have nevertheless attempted in good faith to take it upon myself to explain events and attitudes as they were, and not as one might wish them to have been. Also, one should attempt to avoid the oversimplification of causes. Rarely is one event the direct cause of only, or simply, one other event. Situations and occurrences usually arise due to a variety and multitude of reasons that uncover and give the best and fullest understanding of what happened. It is thus with this open-minded prism-like attitude that one should look and search for the multiple causes that led to the American Civil War.

I have chosen to present the history of Canada and the American Civil War in a series of detailed books. The journey begins with this tome entitled Prelude to War that reviews the early pivotal causes that eventually led to War between the States. This work paints a canvass that illuminates the political, economic, and social landscapes of both countries up to the beginning of the tumultuous decade before the Civil War. Canadian influence and participation in important events, including the abolitionist movement, the slave trade, the institution of slavery, and the Underground Railroad are explored and in turn set the scene for a look at Canada on the eve of the great

American struggle. In order to understand both Canada and the United States in 1850, I attempt to voyage back to earlier times and incidents that set in motion a series of events that help explain the Canadian and American relationship as neighbors prior to the Civil War. This fascinating historical journey follows an unavoidable path of exciting episodes led by people who at times reached beyond their grasp to touch a key moment in time. The work sweeps across the grand issues of the day and concludes on the eve of the Compromise of 1850, and the Border War in Kansas – an ominous sign of things to come and the Civil War's bloody preview.

Enjoy the read,
Mark Vinet

Louis Hippolyte LaFontaine

Robert Baldwin

1. NEIGHBORS

The United States and Canada have many important geographic features and attributes in common. They share the coastlines of two oceans, the Appalachian Highlands, four of the Great Lakes, the Interior Plains, the Rocky Mountains, and many rivers. It is not surprising therefore that the history of the exploration and subsequent settlement of both of these countries are closely interrelated.

The complete history of the United States or Canada cannot be properly analyzed and understood without reference to the history of the other. Both nations realized its independence from Great Britain by two completely different paths. The United States became a free and independent country by a single great revolution and war of independence. Canada, on the other hand, achieved its autonomy in large part by gradual constitutional change and political evolution over many years.

In 1850, on the eve of the tumultuous decade leading up to the American Civil War, Canada and the United States were neighbors in more ways than one. Ever since the settling of each nation's respective territory, their common borders had been argued and fiercely fought over. The original founding European nations that colonized these lands were long standing enemies. The battle for North American lands was a prolonged and bitter struggle that immediately engulfed the native indigenous population and subsequently divided it mainly into two opposite camps, allies of Britain or France. By the mid-nineteenth century, the eastern part of the continent had been invaded, conquered, and settled by both the British and the French. This forced most of the vanquished Aboriginals to migrate westward to lands not yet occupied by the Europeans.

Throughout the first one hundred and fifty years of European settlement in North America, basic economic factors greatly influenced the development of the colonies. In 1704, the French Crown declared that its colonies existed solely to serve the mother country and should not compete for commerce, industry, or population. New France's economy was structured primarily around the fur trade. It controlled a large amount of land for the operation of its continental fur trading system. An elaborate network of military fortifications secured the system. This activity required a relatively small European work force due to the Aboriginal participation in the trade.

The English colonies to the south of New France, although active in the fur trade, successfully exploited the land with a labor-intensive agricultural economy. The agriculture based English economy was thus conducive to attracting a much larger population than did the French fur trade economy. These divergent economic conditions, along with other important factors and policies including religion, climate, and geography, help explain the initial population growth of the English colonies as opposed to New France.

During the latter part of the eighteenth century, New France was conquered by the British and merged into Britain's North American Empire. The Empire, however, was soon thereafter split as a result of the American Revolution (1775-83). The remaining British colonies then began their long journey towards forging an eventual Canadian nation. This nation was created by various ethnic groups, including primarily English and French speaking European descendants.

By 1850, The United States had enjoyed elected responsible government since their successful revolution against the British in the late 1700s. It was not until the late 1840s, however, that the Canadian colonies began to shed the imperialistic control of the British Crown and its representatives in Canada, led by the Governor General.

Influenced by past and contemporary enlightened thinkers and political systems, the United States created its unique form of democratic government based on several distinct principles that are maintained to this day. The first principle is that of popular sovereignty, meaning that the people are the ultimate source of the government's power. Every government has a source of its sovereignty, power, or authority, and most of the political structures of the American government apply the principle of popular sovereignty. Prior to the American Revolution, the source of sovereignty in most nations was the monarchy with the divine right of kings to reign. The United States place the source of power in the people who, in a democratic society, ultimately rule and collectively represent the country's power. They then manifest that power individually by electing leaders to represent them in government. This was a radically new and experimental notion in the late eighteenth century.

The second principle of American democracy is representative government. In a representative government, the citizens delegate their authority to elected representatives. In the United States, candidates vie for the Presidency, the Senate, and the House of Representatives, as well as for many regional offices. In turn, these elected officials represent the wishes of the citizens and guarantee that the government is answerable to its people. In a democracy, the people exercise authority through elections, which permit all adult citizens of the United States the opportunity to have their say and to influence government. With their vote, they can remove representatives who neglect their wishes or who betray and abuse their trust. Political officials are thus accountable as agents of the people. This accountability is a key element of the American system of representative government. Representative government, however, must represent all citizens in order to function properly. Before the Civil War, the only Americans permitted to vote were White adult males.

The third principle of democracy in the United States is the system of checks and balances. The three branches of government are the legislative, the executive, and the judicial. Each restrains and stabilizes one another through their disassociated roles. The legislative branch, represented by Congress, must pass bills before they can be enacted into law. The executive branch, namely the President, can veto bills passed by Congress, thus preventing them from becoming law. In turn, by a two-thirds vote, Congress can override the President's veto. The Supreme Court may nullify acts of Congress by proclaiming them contradictory to the Constitution of the United States. Congress can, however, modify the Constitution by way of the amendment process.

The final principle of American democracy is federalism, an arrangement where different levels of government share authority. In the American federal system, the states and the national government divide power. This division of authority helps prevent misuse by either the national or the state governments.

As of 1791, Canada did enjoy limited representative government through elected assemblies. Britain recognized that its colonists were entitled to representative institutions, but it did not want to risk or encourage a recurrence of the American Revolution. Generally, the British believed that the Revolution had resulted from allowing too much independence in the thirteen American colonies. Britain therefore wanted to tie the Canadians more closely to the

British Empire. To that end, Britain balanced the authority of elected assemblies with the power of the Governor General and Lieutenant Governors from Britain, who were assisted by an appointed legislative council for each colony. The council members were chosen from the elite leaders in Canadian society, loyal to the Crown.

The Canadian colonies had long demanded to govern themselves, but it was only after the unsuccessful armed Rebellions of 1837-38 that the British government took the pleas seriously. In the 1840s, French and English Canadian political reformers joined forces in a coalition that overrode ethnic divisions and eventually demonstrated that success in Canadian politics depended on bicultural cooperation and support. These reformers repeatedly insisted that the Governor General accept the assembly's recommendations in making official appointments. To these colonials, responsible government or popular rule meant a government accountable to the elected officials of the people. Accountability would be ensured by an executive council collectively dependent on the votes of a majority in the elected legislature. This essential principle of responsibility, whereby a government needed the support of Parliament, originated in established British tradition and practice. Its transfer to Canada would give the colonists control of their domestic affairs, since the Governor General would simply accept the recommendations and policies of responsible colonial ministers, except in imperial affairs. Furthermore, it was felt that this authority would slowly and naturally expand, permitting Canadians, through governments based on elected parliaments, to gradually acquire control of their own political destinies, thereby achieving national autonomy without violent revolution.

The Reform Party was a political reform movement in Ontario and the Maritime Provinces that came into prominence shortly before the Rebellions. Similar reformers in Quebec were known as Patriots. The Reformers demanded that the provincial legislative councils, and by implication even the governors and other officials, be made elective. They also proposed that the officials and advisers, or executive council, of the governors be made accountable or responsible to such elective legislative assemblies.

Many Reformers were active in the failed Rebellions against the existing systems of government, while other Reformers did not support the Rebellions at all. Controversial newspaper editor and politician William Lyon Mackenzie [1795, Dundee, Scotland, UK;

1861, Toronto, Ontario, Canada] became the principal organizer and leader of the Rebellion in Ontario. In Quebec, respected lawyer and politician Louis Joseph Papineau [1786, Montreal, Quebec, Canada; 1871, Montebello] led his Patriot Party on a course that resulted in armed conflict with the government.

In 1842-43 and 1848-54, Reform premiers were in power in what was then the unified province of Canada. This union occurred when the Act of Union merged Upper and Lower Canada into Canada West and Canada East, later called Ontario and Quebec. In the late 1840s, the Reform party was divided by a growing tide of radicalism. By the 1850s, the Reformers had split into a moderate wing and a more radical wing, the latter known as the Clear Grits. Eventually, Canada's future Prime Minister Sir John A. (Alexander) Macdonald [1815, Glasgow, Scotland, UK; 1891, Ottawa, Ontario, Canada] won many moderate Reformers over to the Conservative Party, while the Clear Grits provided the core of what evolved into Canada's Liberal Party.

Loyal admirers of the British model of government initially and principally took up the idea of responsible government in Canada in the 1830s. They sought it both to remedy dissatisfaction with inflexible local oligarchies and to keep the provinces securely, though freely, within the British Empire. Radicals such as Mackenzie and Papineau preferred the American elective system, but their successors realized that an organized British style party system was preferable. They built up strong, moderate Reform parties to achieve responsible government, and by the late 1840s saw it fully operating, with the blessing of a more liberal, yet steadfastly imperial, Britain.

Sir Louis Hippolyte LaFontaine [1807, Boucherville, Quebec, Canada; 1864, Montreal], a French Canadian lawyer and politician from Quebec, was among those mainly responsible for leading Canadians towards responsible government. A tall, portly man, resembling Napoleon Bonaparte, LaFontaine was a proficient politician who commanded respect and inspired many others with his vision, high ideals, logic, even temper, and patriotism. He was an orator of average eloquence and spoke English correctly but with a French accent. Educated at the College de Montreal, LaFontaine was called to the Quebec bar in 1828, and a year later he commenced his political career when elected to the Quebec Assembly for Terrebonne. His immediate success as a lawyer gave him the financial independence to devote time to public service. Although a radical follower of Papineau and supporter of the French Canadian grievances, he opposed the Rebellion in 1837, and instead traveled to London to request the British government to implement constitutional reform. With a second outbreak of armed rebellion in 1838, LaFontaine was arrested and imprisoned in Canada by British authorities and charged with treason. The charges were groundless and he was released without trial.

In 1840, LaFontaine took over the leadership of the French Canadian moderate Reformers from Papineau, now an exiled rebel leader. Following the creation of the province of Canada in 1841, he helped create a new political party of united Ontario and Quebec reformers. The leaders of the Ontario Reformers Robert Baldwin and Sir Francis Hincks joined LaFontaine in this task. A strong French Canadian nationalist, LaFontaine insisted on speaking French in the Assembly, and because of this, the British government later repealed the Act of Union clause prohibiting official use of the French language in the legislature.

In 1842, LaFontaine became, in the modern sense, the first Prime Minister of Canada when he formed a coalition government with Baldwin, known as the Liberal ministry, to govern the newly created province of Canada. Their government was active and successful, but conflicts with the Governor General's undemocratic political actions, including his refusal to consult them on political appointments, led to their protest resignations in late 1843. In 1847, Britain finally decided to resolve the political impasse. It installed a new Governor General with firm instructions to appoint a Canadian government supported by the majority party in the assembly. The Governor General was also instructed to sanction the Canadian government's policies whether he agreed with them or not.

After four years in opposition, LaFontaine and Baldwin won an overwhelming victory in the 1847 election. In 1848 under the newly appointed British Governor General of Canada Lord Elgin, LaFontaine and Baldwin formed their second Liberal administration, this time called the Great Ministry. This constituted the first government in the province of Canada accountable to the local legislature instead of the British government. Upon establishing responsible government, LaFontaine and Baldwin enacted other important reforms that greatly hastened the growth of democracy in Canada. Their achievements set the pattern for responsible government throughout the Canadian colonies and the British Empire.

Within a few years, responsible government spread across Canada's British colonies. Nova Scotia's reform party had already won the same victory as the province of Canada a few months earlier. Responsible government soon followed in New Brunswick in 1848, Prince Edward Island in 1851, and in Newfoundland in 1855. Britain preserved authority for foreign affairs, defense, and other matters including appointing the governors. The Canadian colonies, however, gained full local self-government with one of the broadest electoral franchises in the world.

Responsible government meant for Canada, not independence, but a growing democracy and freedom within the British Empire. The United States was slowly edging towards a great Civil War that would ultimately test its unique form of democracy, while Canada was only beginning to stretch its democratic wings.

The Great Ministry first demonstrated the formal attainment of responsible government with the passage of the controversial Rebellion Loses Bill that compensated victims of the insurrections, and the Amnesty Act that pardoned certain rebels. In addition, it secularized King's College into the University of Toronto, incorporated many French Canadian colleges, established Laval University, enacted significant railroad legislation, and, reformed judicial and municipal institutions.

In 1851, LaFontaine no longer felt in harmony with the more radical elements of his party and decided to retired to private life. He was appointed chief justice of Quebec and president of the seigniorial court in 1853. In 1854, he was created a baronet by Queen Victoria, and a papal knight by Pope Pius IX. His two sons and heirs died in infancy, and the baronetcy became extinct upon his death. LaFontaine was buried in Montreal's Cote des Neiges Cemetery as a revered French Canadian Catholic nationalist and crusader.

Robert Baldwin [1804, York (now Toronto), Ontario, Canada; 1858, Toronto] led a much less understood and appreciated existence. He was the eldest son of doctor, lawyer, and prominent politician William Warren Baldwin [1775, Knockmore, Ireland; 1844, Toronto, Ontario, Canada]. William Baldwin had arrived in Ontario in 1799, eventually settling at York. Sophisticated, ingenious, and eventually wealthy, he established a successful and distinguished law practice.

Although he served only two terms as a legislator, he made an important contribution to the cause of Canadian political reform and organization. He was an Irish, liberal gentleman who supported aristocracy, ministerial responsibility, and the religious and civil liberties of the British constitution. His great objective was responsible government for Canada. His son, Robert, later successfully carried on the mission.

During the political conflict that beset the Canadian colonial government following the War of 1812, Robert and his father led the new political group known as the Reformers. They battled against the Conservatives, who controlled the government's executive assembly. The Reformers wanted to prevent Conservative supremacy by making the government's executive branch responsible to the elected assembly. Robert believed that self-government obtained by such constitutional reform would reduce the discord between the colonial and British imperial authorities, and strengthen bonds of loyalty and endearment to Canada. Both Robert and his father opposed the more drastically anti-British plans of the Radicals and condemned the violent Rebellion of 1837.

Intellectually and temperamentally different from his talented father, the shy, withdrawn Robert was called to the bar in 1825. He then entered politics in 1829 as a Reformer, winning a seat in the Assembly in a by-election. He thus began his political career as a member of the Legislative Assembly of Ontario for York but was defeated the following year and retired to private life. His life and happiness revolved around his family despite his melancholic moods. He was especially close to his wife, whom he had married in 1827. Her death in 1836 crushed him emotionally and led to the severe depressive illness that haunted him in later years. Despite his grief and a deep dislike for public life, his Christian sense of duty impelled him, again, to accept political office the following month. He thus served briefly on the Executive Council of Upper Canada and supported the union of both Upper and Lower Canada.

Baldwin and the other councilors resigned in 1836 over the Lieutenant Governor's refusal to consult them. This spun the colony into a deep political and constitutional crisis that, in part, led to the Rebellion of 1837. Baldwin remained neutral during the revolt. In its aftermath, he and his father met briefly with the Governor General of Canada John George Lambton, 1st earl of Durham, known as Lord

Durham [1792, London, England; 1840, Cowes]. During Durham's visit to Toronto in July 1838, Baldwin submitted to him a detailed memorandum on the principle of responsible government for Canada. His suggestions most likely influenced Durham's adoption of the principle in his influential report offering remedies for political dissatisfaction in Canada. Baldwin then became the key figure in rebuilding the post-Rebellion Reform opposition, and cementing an alliance with LaFontaine's Quebec Liberals.

Although not a naturally gifted politician or an outstanding intellect, Baldwin commanded respect and exercised moral leadership because of his character. In a pre-industrial age that revered the code of gentlemen, he embodied the treasured virtues of adherence to honor, principle, and duty. Each time he gained office he chose to resign rather than compromise his principles.

In the Assembly, Baldwin and LaFontaine gradually attracted members to the cause of responsible government until they twice attained office in 1840s. During their two ministries, Baldwin served as co-prime minister of Canada and attorney general in Ontario. In order to confirm the realization of responsible government, he reluctantly supported the Rebellion Loses Bill, despite his dislike for the measure and harsh opposition and violent demonstrations from certain segments of the population.

By 1851, however, Baldwin's control on power was lessened by various factors, including, differences over economic policy with Francis Hincks, a left-wing uprising in his party by the new faction known as the Clear Grits, and his deteriorating health. He felt increasingly out of favor with the progressive reformers in his party, and was antagonized by an attempt to abolish the Court of Chancery in Ontario that he had helped to establish. These conditions prompted him to resign. Later that year he sought re-election to Parliament in Toronto but was defeated.

In 1858, the coalition Liberal-Conservative Party invited him to accept a seat in the upper house, but, dissociated from the radicals, he could not identify with the conservative element of the Liberal Party either. Discouraged and tormented by depression, Baldwin withdrew to his home, still grieving for his dead wife. In retirement, he devoted himself to the improvement of English and French relations in Canada remaining little understood, loved, or appreciated by his contemporaries. His reputation was forever secured, however, as a key instigator of responsible government and one of the first advocates of a bicultural Canada.

The third founder of the united party of Ontario and Quebec reformers was Canadian politician and colonial administrator Sir Francis Hincks [1807, Cork, County Cork, Ireland; 1885, Montreal, Quebec, Canada]. As a newspaper publisher, Hincks established the *Toronto Examiner* in 1838 and the *Montreal Pilot* in 1844. Convinced of the need for a bicultural English-French partnership in the United Province of Canada, Hincks joined Baldwin and LaFontaine in 1841 to create the Reform Party. He entered the executive council in 1842, but resigned in protest with Baldwin and LaFontaine in 1843. Throughout this period, Hincks acted as a brilliant strategist and strong proponent of colonial self-government. His efforts welded the followers of Baldwin and LaFontaine into an effective political party.

Hincks became inspector general in the Great Ministry, encouraging the building of railroads and restoring provincial finances. He replaced Baldwin as leader and co-prime minister in 1851. Unable to deal with growing sectional feeling and tainted by railway corruption, Hincks' ministry was defeated in 1854. He went on to become governor of two Caribbean colonies from 1856 to 1869. In 1869 he returned to Canada and became federal finance minister in Sir John A. Macdonald's government, focusing on banking and currency regulation. He quit politics for business in 1874 and later published his writings, including his *Reminiscences* in 1884.

In addition to Hincks, Baldwin, and LaFontaine, the other important leader in Canada during the mid-eighteenth century was James Bruce, 8th Earl of Elgin and 12th Earl Of Kincardine [1811, London, England; 1863, Dharmsala, India], known as Lord Elgin. As Governor General of Canada from 1847-54, Lord Elgin's conduct in office defined the role for his successors. As a student at Eton and Oxford, Elgin displayed the brilliance that ignited his later reputation as an inspired speaker, cultured humanist, and judicious administrator. Elgin was elected to the British House of Commons for Southampton as a liberal Tory in 1841, but later that year he inherited his father's Scottish peerage title and left the Commons. In 1842, he was appointed governor of Jamaica. In 1847, he arrived in Montreal as the newly named Governor General of Canada. He was immediately delegated the task of implementing the policy of responsible government recommended by his father-in-law and former Governor General, Lord

Durham. Britain's Colonial Office had previously resisted the concession of responsible government as demanded by Canadian Reformers, but Elgin and the new Colonial Secretary, Earl Grey, felt it offered the best opportunity to solve Canadian political discord. Following the Reform party's election victory in 1847, Elgin commissioned LaFontaine in 1848 to form the first truly responsible government in the province of Canada.

In 1849 he was created Baron Elgin, United Kingdom peerage, and was made a privy councilor. He negotiated the 1854 Reciprocity Treaty between the Canadian colonies and the United States. With much diplomatic finesse, he secured ratification by the American Senate of the Treaty, a measure much desired by Canadians at the time as a remedy to economic recession. He also worked on the Canadian educational system and abolished seigniorial tenure in Quebec.

After leaving Canada in 1854, Elgin was special commissioner to China in 1857-59 and 1860-61, and in 1858, he made an official visit to Japan. In between these appointments, he served in England as postmaster general. In 1862 he was appointed viceroy and Governor General of India. Yet, it was his earlier Canadian experience that molded his political and diplomatic skills.

In 1849, Elgin witnessed events that severely tested Canada's legislative independence and briefly brought the issue of Canada's annexation to the United States to the political forefront. In 1848, the LaFontaine Baldwin government's introduction of the Rebellion Loses Bill brought on a crisis. This bill intended to compensate those who suffered material damages at the hands of British Troops during the 1837-38 Rebellion in Quebec. Compensation for property had already been given in Ontario, and Quebec was now to have similar treatment. Although the bill refused compensation to anyone who had actually aided the Rebellion, opponents decided not to allow any compensation. Riots spread throughout the province of Canada and opposition Tories insisted that Elgin not sign the bill if passed by the legislature. Although Elgin did not personally support all the details of the proposed law, he was nevertheless determined to support the principle of responsible government. On April 25, 1849, Elgin signed the bill into law and upon leaving the Montreal Parliament buildings, home of Canada's legislature, a raucous crowd pelted him with insults and projectiles. That night a riotous mob rushed into the Parliament buildings and chased the members out onto the streets. The mob then burned the Parliament buildings and it's library to the ground, destroying all but two hundred of its twelve thousand books. Montreal had become the first capital of Canada in 1844 but forever lost this position following the riots.

For three days, Montreal streets were filled with disorder and the city was engulfed in revolutionary zeal and terror. English Montrealers targeted French Canadians and their institutions while Elgin, Baldwin, and LaFontaine's lives and property were threatened. The mob attacked LaFontaine's home and sacked Baldwin's rooming house while Lord Elgin was stoned by the mob. Though Elgin escaped, enough stones were thrown at his carriage to drive in all the panels. Through the whole crises, LaFontaine remained steadfast and Elgin upheld the practice and spirit of responsible government. Despite vehement Tory opposition, Elgin weathered this crisis without compromise, ensuring that responsible government would prevail.

A bitter consequence of this violent protest was the creation of the Annexation Association, founded in 1849 to promote Canadian-American political union. In October and December of 1849, it published two versions of an "Annexation Manifesto". This lengthy document was published in newspapers across Canada. The Annexation Manifesto published in the *Montreal Gazette* newspaper on October 11, 1849 began as follows: "MONTREAL ANNEXATION MANIFESTO – To the People of Canada. The number and magnitude of the evils that afflict our country, and the universal and increasing depression of its material interests, call upon all persons animated by a sincere desire for its welfare to combine for the purposes of inquiry and preparation with a view to the adoption of such remedies as a mature and dispassionate investigation may suggest."

It went on to detail the Association's grievances against the British Government and proposed the solution of annexing Canada to the United States. Most of those who signed it were from the powerful English-speaking business communities in Quebec City and Montreal, and the French Canadian radical nationalist movement led by Louis Joseph Papineau.

In addition to Papineau, the Manifesto was signed by three hundred and twenty-four other prominent Canadians including: future Canadian Prime Minister Sir John Abbott [1821, St Andrews East (St-André-Est), Lower Canada; 1893, Montreal, Quebec, Canada]; future father of Canadian Confederation Sir Alexander Tilloch Galt [1817,

London, England; 1893, Montreal, Quebec, Canada]; brewer, banker, and steamship builder John Molson [1763, Spalding, England; 1836, Ile Ste-Marguerite, Quebec, Canada]; politician and businessman Sir David Lewis Macpherson [1818, Castle Leathers, near Inverness, Scotland; 1896, at sea]; politician, banker, and diplomat Sir John Rose [1820, Turriff, Scotland; 1888, Langwell Forest]; philanthropist Peter Redpath and self-made construction magnate John Redpath; John, James, David and J.W. Torrence; Jacob De Witt; William and Benjamin Workman; L.H. Holton; Benjamin Holmes; Q.C. Edward Goff Penny; William Molson; and D. Lorn Macdougall. Many of these men in later years subsequently recanted their endorsement with considerable embarrassment.

The true motives behind this dramatic gesture varied. Some proponents believed that the threat of annexation on the part of the Canadians was used more for the purpose of extracting concessions from Britain than for seriously proposing to merge with the United States. In any event, it was clear that Tory loyalty to the British Empire was no longer to be taken for granted. Economic and political self-interest was the ultimate priority and motivation, whatever the consequences.

Ironically, Canadian Tories had suddenly turned against the British Crown after having persecuted its opponents, the Reformers, only a decade earlier during the Rebellions. Prevalent nationalist racist attitudes prompted some Montrealers to favor annexation by the United States in order to achieve English Protestant ascendancy over the French Roman Catholic majority in Quebec. Also, many nationalists were republicans who favored American political institutions. Others believed the real cause of discontent was economic, not political. They felt the Manifesto was prompted by recent economic stagnation. Britain's removal of tariffs and abolition of preferential duties on Canadian lumber, wheat, flour products, and other colonial products, discontented many businessmen. It was felt that Canada's growth, as compared to the United States, had been stunted by its colonial status. Finally, many were simply outraged by the government's decision to consent to the Rebellion Loses Bill.

Together these groups of malcontents called for the Canadian colonies to relinquish their ties with Britain and join the United States. The movement made sure to underline the economic and territorial advantages annexation would bring to the United States.

Because of the Manifesto, Governor Elgin put troops on alert in anticipation of an American invasion that never came. The United States did not openly support the Manifesto or the Canadian annexation movement. A *New York Herald* editorial responded in 1849 as follows: "It is very certain that the United States will never solicit the Canadians to annex themselves to this Republic, under any circumstances whatever. But while we assert this, we are willing, on the other hand, to say that, if the Canadians will at some future time procure the consent of Great Britain to be annexed to the United States, we will, when that consent shall have been obtained, and on their solicitation and earnest request, take the question into consideration; and, if we can adjust some preliminary arrangements concerning our domestic relations, satisfactorily to the varied interests of this country, we will allow them to come in and partake of the great political blessings which we in the United States enjoy. The first thing for the people of Canada to do, however, is to obtain England's consent to dispose of themselves as they think proper."

The annexation movement failed to capture popular Canadian support and thus ended abruptly. Strongly opposed by various interest groups and prominent individuals, including Louis Hippolyte LaFontaine and his followers, the movement died out after the 1854 Reciprocity Treaty on trade was signed between the two neighboring countries. The question of Canadian annexation to the United States nevertheless continued to be an issue leading up to the Civil War. The physical proximity and common border of the two nations precluded otherwise.

Ever since the early arrival and colonization of North America by the Europeans, the international boundary between Canada and the United States shifted and fluctuated for over two centuries. Several diplomatic and military conflicts, wars and threats of war, political maneuvers and compromises, treaties, and colonization settlements, gradually established a recognized border between the two nations. The international boundary that slowly and sometimes painfully emerged took the general form, by 1850, of the present day border Canadians and Americans recognize today.

Canada occupied almost all of North America north of latitude forty-nine degrees north and east of longitude one hundred and forty-one degrees west. Long distances and a challenging physical environment made communication and transportation across the country extremely difficult. The international border, on the other hand, was proximate, accessible, mostly unguarded, undefended, and freely crossed by citizens of both countries. The daily business activities of Canadians brought them into close contact with the United States. When the St. Lawrence river ports of Quebec and Montreal were frozen in, news and even passengers traveled on the new American railroads across the Eastern states to the Canadian border from New York and Portland, Maine. New technology also improved communications, for example, the newly invented magnetic telegraph, installed in Toronto in 1846, soon connected that city not only with Quebec but also with New York City and New Orleans in the United States.

The population of the United States in 1851 was more than 23 million, while about 2.4 million people inhabited Canada. This ten to one ratio, in favor of the Americans, has generally been maintained throughout the history of both nations. In the United States, the population was spread throughout thirty-one states and several Western territories. In Canada, its people populated the British colonies of Canada East & West, Nova Scotia, Newfoundland, Prince Edward Island, New Brunswick, the North Western Territories, Rupert's Land (Hudson's Bay Company), New Caledonia (the northern portion of the Oregon Territory), and Vancouver's Island.

The more populous United States, always seeking new frontier lands to settle, posed a constant threat to Canada's sovereignty over its sparsely populated territory. Canada's lengthy and poorly defended international border only made things more tempting for American expansionists. As a result, and beginning with the American Revolution, various unsuccessful diplomatic and military attempts were made by the United States to persuade Canada to join the republic or to forcibly annex its territories. These failed invasions and threats of annexation were omnipresent in the minds of Canadians as tensions rose between both countries throughout the decades before the commencement of the Civil War. During this period, both nations dealt with an unfolding series of crucial events and unavoidable issues that eventually led to the American crisis. The magnitude and tensions brought about by these affairs provided inevitable and incalculable influence on Canada's development. These events and issues would also greatly and dramatically affect the nature of Canada and the United States' short and long term relationship as neighbors.

Lord Elgin

Houses of Assembly fire, Montreal, 1849

2. SECTIONALISM

Prior to the American Civil War, both the United States and Canada experienced decades of nearly nonstop political crisis. For the United States, the basic problem was the fact that America in the early nineteenth century had been a federation, not a country. The important functions of government, those relating to health, education, public security, commerce, and transportation, were carried out on the local or state level. The nation was bound together by little more than a loose allegiance to the federal government in Washington, D.C. (District of Columbia), a few national organizations and institutions such as political parties and churches, and a common knowledge of the republic's late eighteenth century struggle for independence against the British. White Americans experienced divided loyalties in the republic's early years, unsure whether their identity derived from the new nation or from their European roots.

Loyalty to one's state often took precedence over loyalty to one's nation. A Pennsylvanian or a Georgian would refer to his state as his country. The Union was considered by many as a federation voluntarily entered into by sovereign, independent states for as long as it served their needs to be so joined. In the republic's early years, both North and South lacked any strong sense of the permanence of the Union. The New England states, for example, once thought of leaving the Union, because the War of 1812 (1812-15) prevented commerce with Britain.

Within this loosely structured society every section, state, region, locality, and group could mostly go its own way and chart its own course. Gradually, however, important rapid changes and dynamic developments in the economy and technology were bringing all the elements of the nation into proximity. Private and publicly funded improvements in transportation, first canals and the steamship, then all-weather stone paved toll roads, and especially railroads, broke down isolation. This transportation revolution encouraged young men to leave the family farm and migrate to either the growing eastern cities or unclaimed farmland to the West. The economy was transformed from one of self-sufficient pre-industrialized farming and cottage hand made products, to an economy with more specialized and industrialized farming and standardized production of a variety of goods and products. A new large and thriving middle class of entrepreneurs emerged as capitalists leading a new American economy. Based on the concept of mass consumption and production, their new methods improved efficiency by lowering costs and creating a specialized work force. By the mid-1800s, the United States had achieved one of the world's highest standard of living and industrial output. Each region within the United States developed and benefited from these improvements in different ways and at varying levels.

Improvements in the printing press, which permitted the publication of inexpensive newspapers delivered quickly nationwide, and the development of the magnetic telegraph system broke through the communication barriers caused by distance. This communication revolution permitted everyone the opportunity to be instantly made aware of what was going on throughout the nation. As railroad networks expanded, the fledgling Union had to have some sort of central direction and control. Several interest groups called for the federal government to assume that role.

Many Americans resisted the abrupt and painful move from a largely rural, slow paced, fragmented society in the early nineteenth century to a bustling, and integrated national social order in the mid-1800s. Occasionally, resentment against change expressed itself in severe attacks upon those who appeared to be responsible, especially immigrants. Up until 1830, the American population was predominately of British Protestant heritage. During the next decade, a flood of immigrants arrived. They seemed to represent the currents that were altering the older and more traditional America. As a direct result of these sentiments, determined nationalist movements appeared in most American cities during the 1840s. The anti-foreign feelings reached their apex in the 1850s when the many German and Irish newcomers of the prior decade became eligible to vote. An ever-growing number of harsh criticisms were directed both against immigrants and the Roman Catholic Church, to which so many of them belonged.

A more lasting demonstration of animosity toward the nationalizing inclinations in American life was the reassertion of strong sectional loyalty. New Englanders felt threatened by the Western states and territories believing it drained off the best and most energetic workers of the Northeastern labor force. In addition, once the railroad network was complete, The vibrant West used the recently completed railroad system to successfully produce grain and wool that undersold the products of the impoverished New England countryside. The Western region also quickly developed a strong positive sense of uniqueness and sectional feeling. This, despite its feeling of being looked down upon as unsophisticated and raw, and its awareness that it was being taken advantage of by Eastern businessmen.

The most noticeable and distinctive section, however, was the South. This region of the country was set apart by climate, social customs, economics, and the continued institution of Black slavery. The Southern economy relied mainly on a slave labor based plantation system designed for the production of profitable staple crops such as cotton, tobacco, rice, indigo, corn, sugar, hemp, and wheat.

By 1850, the South and the North had developed into two very distinctive regions. The boundary between the two regions came to be known as the Mason-Dixon Line, named for the men who originally surveyed the Maryland-Pennsylvania border. Different economic, political, and social viewpoints, stemming as far back as colonial times, progressively drove both regions farther apart. Each section attempted to impose its opinions and convictions on the country as a whole. Although compromises had kept the Union together for many years, throughout the 1850s the tensions rose sharply.

During the first half of the 1800s, economic contrasts and needs sharpened sectional differences, increasing interregional hostility and causing serious problems. The North had developed into a labor-intensive industrial society. In order to satisfy its labor needs, the North chose not to rely on slave labor, but instead encouraged European immigration. Immigrants worked in factories, built the Northern railroads, and settled the Western lands. Only a few immigrants chose to settle in the South. The South resisted industrialization and therefore manufactured little. Nearly all manufactured goods had to be imported into the South. Southerners therefore opposed high tariffs and taxes imposed on imported wares that increased the price of manufactured articles. On the other hand, the manufacturing economy of the North called for high tariffs to protect its own goods from inexpensive foreign competition.

Prior to the Civil War, the federal government's main source of revenue was the tariff. This duty tax was levied on imports and exports as the goods crossed the international border to and from other countries. There were few other sources of revenue in the central government's arsenal. At that time, neither personal nor corporate income taxes existed. The tariff paid for many of the internal transportation improvements made by the federal government, such as roads, bridges, turnpikes, and canals. To keep tariffs low, the South generally preferred to do without these improvements.

The expanding Northwest Territory, made up of the present day states of Indiana, Illinois, Michigan, Ohio, Wisconsin, and part of Minnesota, supported the Northeast's demands for high tariffs. The Northwest was far from the Northeastern markets, making delivery of its produce and livestock a challenge. It needed internal improvements for short-term survival and long term growth. In return, the Northeast supported many of the federally financed improvements undertaken in the Northwest Territory. Consequently, although both the South and the West were agricultural societies, the West generally supported the Northern viewpoint, rather than the Southern.

As Northern and Southern ways of living diverged, their political philosophies also developed striking differences. The North wanted a strong central government capable of building an infrastructure of roads, bridges, canals, and railways, protecting its intricate financial and trading interests, and managing the national currency. The South depended much less on the central government than did other regions, and Southerners therefore felt no necessity to strengthen it. In addition, Southern patriots were concerned that a strong federal government might interfere with slavery.

Since the founding of the first European settlements along the Southern coast of North America, slavery had progressively become an important Southern institution. Abolition of slavery in the North, initiated in the revolutionary era and largely accomplished by the 1830s, divided the United States into regions known as the "free North" and the "slave South". Slavery thus came to define the very essence of the South. To support slavery was to be pro-South, whereas opposition to slavery was considered anti-South. In reality, most Southern Whites did not own slaves. In fact, the proportion of White families that owned slaves declined from thirty-five to twenty-six percent between 1830 and 1860. Slavery nevertheless in many ways estranged the South from the rest of the United States, Canada, and Western Europe. Although slavery had once been common in much of the Americas, by the mid-nineteenth century it survived only in Cuba,

Puerto Rico, and the Southern United States. In an enlightened era that celebrated equality and liberty, many outsiders viewed the slaveholding Southern states as repressive and archaic.

Despite this negative perception, the Southern slave economy grew rapidly. The South prospered as a result of the dramatic increase in cotton cultivation sparked by the growing demand of Northern and European textile manufacturers. In an age when progress was measured by the amount of railway tracks laid out, the cotton trade that in turn propagated slavery mainly financed Southern railroads. Continued Southern economic growth was based largely on the cultivation of additional land. Slavery's expansion to new unsettled lands therefore became essential to the South's economic future.

The Southern states did not undergo the industrial revolution that was beginning to transform the North. The South remained almost completely rural. In 1860, there were only five Southern cities with more than fifty thousand people. Only one, New Orleans, was in the lower or Deep South. Less than ten percent of Southerners lived in towns of at least two thousand five hundred inhabitants, compared to more than twenty-five percent of Northerners. The South also increasingly trailed in other signs of modernization, from railroad development to public education and literacy. The biggest difference between South and North, however, was ideological. In the North, slavery was abolished and a small but vocal group of abolitionists developed. In the South, White spokespersons, including authors, politicians, newspaper editors, and ministers, defended slavery as the foundation of Southern society. Advocates of slavery perfected various theories to support their position. Their arguments were most often based on race, economic necessity, and religion. They made heavy use of religious themes when portraying slavery as part of God's divine plan and vision for civilizing a non-Christian, primitive race of people.

Southern leaders furthermore used social arguments to defend their institution of slavery. They compared the orderly, stable, and religiously conservative society that they claimed existed in the South with the turbulent, heretical, and mercenary ways of the North. They contended that the Northern states were divided and plagued by individualism, class and social conflict, radical reform, and, worst yet, Abolitionism.

The argument increasingly popular in the North was based on the fundamental concept of free soil and free labor, as opposed to the trappings of the institution of slavery. This Northern view charged that slavery kept the South poor, debased, backward, and inefficient. Pro-slavery defenders responded that only slavery could save the South from the evils of Northern industrial modernity. Southerners also pointed to the Northern industrialist's slave-like exploitation of immigrant factory workers, arguing that Black slaves in the South were treated better and lived a more comfortable existence, thus making slavery a "postive good".

So-called Free Soil Northerners were committed to the notion that unsettled Western territories should be put aside exclusively for non-slave-owning White settlers. They quarreled endlessly with Southerners who insisted that any limitation on slavery's expansion was unconstitutional interference with the Southern order and a serious insult to Southern honor. From the mid-1840s, the struggle over slavery became pivotal to American politics. In 1860, the election of Abraham Lincoln [1809, Hardin (now Larue) County, Kentucky, USA; Washington, 1865] as President on a Free Soil platform, ignited a major constitutional and political crisis. This crisis led directly to a war between the North and South that finally decided conclusively the fate of slavery in the United States.

Throughout the early and mid-nineteenth century, Canada too was plagued in its own way with problems caused by sectionalism. The nation's historical foundations were laid in French settlements mainly along the St.-Lawrence river, and British maritime settlements along the Atlantic coast. For over a century and a half the French colony of New France dominated the Canadian territory. A sudden change occurred in 1763 at the end of the Seven Years' War (1756-63), also called the French and Indian War or Nine Years' War (1754-63). Because of this world war between the great European powers, the colony of New France fell under the control of Great Britain. France thus ceded the whole of her mainland North American Empire east of the Mississippi to the English. In 1763, New France was renamed the colony or province of Quebec and became part of the British North American colonies.

Although Quebec's population remained primarily French speaking and Catholic, its commerce and government were now controlled by a small group of newly arrived British Protestant officials, bureaucrats, and businessmen. Though various English attempts to assimilate the French Canadians were unsuccessful, loyal British subjects nevertheless gradually settled in the territory. The first important wave of these British immigrants was American Loyalists fleeing the United States after the revolution. A subsequent flow of Loyalist settlers, primarily land seekers, arrived from the Northern American states as late as 1812. These newly arrived United Empire Loyalists increased the population and profoundly changed the make-up of the French speaking colony of Quebec.

The Loyalist element also added to the increasing diversity of the population of the other British North American colonies. In Nova Scotia there were, in addition to Loyalists and New Englanders, the Germans of Lunenburg, Yorkshiremen, and the Highland Scots of Pictou County and of Cape Breton Island. New Brunswick had a population of mostly Loyalists and Southern Irish, while the inhabitants of Prince Edward Island were a diverse mixture of Acadians, Loyalists, English, Irish, and Scots. In Newfoundland, the population included the west country English and a growing number of Irish.

By the start of the nineteenth century, the foundations of the Canadian ethnic and cultural tapestry had taken form. For almost a century, a population of French, British, and German peoples dominated the Canadian landscape. Immigrants arriving from Northern England via Liverpool, Southern and Northern Ireland, and the Scottish Highlands and Lowlands regularly reinforced the British factor. For example, early in the eighteenth century Nova Scotia's Cape Breton Island witnessed an influx of Gaelic-speaking farmers from the Scottish Highlands. These newcomers joined Acadians and other French settlers and United Empire Loyalists already established on the island. The immediate effect of this ethnic diversity was the formation of a unique nation in which religious freedom and a remarkable amount of social parity were needed for political, social, and economic union.

In reality, the actual number of immigrants to Canada was modest up until 1815, but they increased dramatically during the next four decades. A flood of newcomers began to arrive after the War of 1812, mostly from the British Isles. It was during the 1830s that the English, Irish, and Scottish came to Canada in great numbers. Approximately eight hundred thousand immigrants arrived between 1815 and 1850. This vibrant era came to be known as Canada's Great

Migration. By the 1850s, Canada was swelling with settlers. In addition, the foundations of a British colony on the Pacific west coast were being established.

The challenges and difficulties faced by the new settlers were numerous. The hardships often began in the crowded cholera infested and poorly provisioned sailing vessels that brought immigrants in large groups across the Atlantic. The founding and building of new communities across Canada proceeded at a quick pace, especially in Ontario, where the largest tracts of land were available for settlement. The opening of new subdivisions in the dense forests was an almost continuous process throughout this whole period. These newcomers quickly changed the face of Canada in many ways. Except in Quebec, their presence gradually gave the nation a predominately British heritage and attitude. This important transformation was to set the course of Canadian history for the next century.

The decades leading to the Civil War witnessed important changes in Canada. Canadian laws and institutions were remodeled to fit the individual needs of each region, and western expansion was part of the nation's agenda. During this vibrant period, population growth continued throughout the country, while industry and commerce instigated urban development. The cities came to be ruled and characterized by a new vigorous and affluent middle class.

In many ways, pioneer life was very similar in Canada and the United States. Before the arrival of the railway, the principal method of transporting heavy freight over long distances was by water. Canals throughout Canada were therefore improved, and new ones were dug. Roads were cut through the forests to connect the isolated centers of settlement with rivers, lakes, and ocean ports. On the backwoods farms, great branding fires burned steadily as the pioneers slowly cleared their lands. The tree stumps were usually left in the ground to rot, which required from four to six years for most woods. Cedar and pine roots sometimes hampered the use of horse-drawn plows for as long as twenty years.

The first Canadian passenger railroad was constructed near the city of Montreal in 1836, and during the 1850s, thousands of miles of track and telegraph lines were built. This period was also Atlantic Canada's golden age. It prospered from building wooden ships and delivering them into the service of the overseas trade. Only those of the United States and Britain exceeded Canada's shipping fleet. Shipyards throughout the Maritimes produced a quarter of the British Empire's merchant fleet. The region's prosperous businessmen, with close connections to the other important sea port cities of London, New York, and Boston, became powerful, wealthy, and philanthropic. Maritime community schools and universities benefited while Nova Scotia began to view itself as the cultural capital of Canada.

Nostalgia and sentiment bound the individual Canadian colonies more closely to England than to each other. There were different standards of currency in use in the several colonies, and customs barriers hampered trade between them. Geographical distances and obstacles also made communications and transportation extremely difficult. This reality made it a challenge and a formidable task for Canadians to create and maintain a sense of nationhood. Most of Canada's English speaking population was proud of its attachment to the British Empire and desired to preserve it. The symbol of the era was Britain's monarch, Queen Victoria [1819, London, UK; 1901, Isle of Wight (reigned 1837-1901)], whose personal stability and high moral stature seemed to personify the best in British virtues. Despite this attachment, Canada continuously yearned for increased autonomy that would allow it to evolve from colonial status to greater self-rule.

Canada faced other serious divisions because of its religious diversity. Protestant churches were important in English speaking Canadian society, with most people belonging to the Church of England, the Presbyterians, or the Methodists. The churches provided spiritual and social services for community residents. Many middle class citizens launched moral campaigns to preserve the sanctity of the Sabbath, eliminate gambling and prostitution, ban obscene literature, stop the traffic of alcohol, and better the moral education of the impoverished populace and school children.

Women of English speaking society in that era were expected to limit themselves to domestic affairs. They were largely excluded from the fields of business, higher education, and politics. Men and women were expected to function in separate circles. This meant, however, that women had great authority in the home and over the children. Women gradually came to control elementary teaching and many areas of charitable and social work. They also defined public morals and social standards and became important leaders and supporters of religious and temperance campaigns.

In Quebec, French Canadians possessed the voting power to preserve their French speaking society. This meant ensuring the status of the French language and continuing the Catholic Church's control of social programs and education. These political tools enabled Quebec to protect its individuality and thus resist Britain's assimilation policy. Quebec society modernized as more municipal and local governments were formed. These governments invested to expand transportation, public education, and other public services. The old French land holding seigniorial system was abolished, the antiquated French civil law updated, and the farm communities became better connected to markets. Rural population pressure was relieved by widespread migration to the cities, to Western frontier areas, and to the New England states.

During the first half on the 1800s, the Catholic Church greatly expanded its social activities and its political influence. For the first time, the Church was well provided with French Canadian clergy. They developed hospitals, schools, and other social services that were elsewhere operated by the state. Education and literacy became widely accessible to rural French Canada. The Church, however, was very slow and sometimes reluctant to accept social change. It fought hard to control French Canada's cultural life and to discredit many secular ideas popular at the time, such as separation of church and state.

In 1850, historical tensions and mistrust persisted in Central Canada between English Protestant Ontario and French Catholic Quebec. The Maritime colonies developed a distinctive cultural and economic society much different to Central and Western Canada. As for the new colonies of Western Canada, they developed isolated by geography from the other regions. To many, it seemed the differences between Canada's diverse regions outweighed the similarities. Any realistic hope of an eventual political and territorial Canadian union seemed highly improbable.

Five generations of one slave family

3. THE "PECULIAR INSTITUTION" OF SLAVERY

Slavery began in prehistoric times and has since appeared throughout history in many forms and many places. The slavery of ancient times reached its peak throughout the empires of Greece and Rome. After the institution of Greek and Roman slavery declined and slowly evolved into that of medieval serfdom, slavery was virtually unknown in Western Europe until 1442. In that year, Portuguese explorers and traders brought Black slaves back to Europe from the sub-Saharan West Coast of the African continent. The first cargo of African slaves arrived in the West Indies in 1518. Shortly after, the need for plantation labor in the colonies of North America, South America, and the Caribbean created a huge market for slaves, also known as bondpeople. Black West Africans were thus traded and brought to the Americas while the Arab and Persian nations did the same along the eastern coast of Africa. This Black holocaust would last for the next four hundred years. Europeans justified this brutality on grounds of economic necessity, race superiority, and their self-imposed Christian duty to Christianize and civilize inferior races. Slavery in the Americas was historically unique for its racial exclusivity.

During the first half of the seventeenth century, Portugal and the Netherlands dominated the transatlantic African slave trade. The number of Africans available to English colonists was limited because both the Portuguese and the Dutch used slave labor to produce crops in their own New World colonies. From the mid-1700s onwards, English naval superiority gave England a dominant position in the slave trade. This allowed English traders to transport millions of Africans across the Atlantic Ocean for profit, and satisfy its colonial labor needs.

Between the fifteenth and nineteenth centuries, an estimated eleven million Africans were forcibly transported to the Americas. By far the largest importers of African slaves were the West Indies colonies and South America. Together, they received more than seventy-five percent of all Africans brought to the Americas. Brazil's giant and lucrative coffee trade made it the largest importer of slaves and the last country in the western hemisphere to end slavery in 1888. Approximately six hundred thousand men, women, and children were brought to the North American mainland to what is now the United States. Seventy percent of them entered at the seaport of Charleston, South Carolina.

Ironically, indigenous Black Africans were principally responsible for the capture and sale into slavery of fellow Black Africans. Tribal wars and profitable trade with the Europeans fueled these activities. The Europeans were initially drawn to Africa by the search for gold and other precious metals. When they first arrived along the West African coast, they found Black kingdoms with well-established political and economic systems that already included slavery. The Europeans obtained slaves directly from Black Africans who sold their captives, criminals, and war prisoners, or traded them for cloth, rum, and other items, especially guns and ammunition. The Africans needed the guns for use in their continual warfare with neighboring tribes. The slave trade also allowed them to accumulated great wealth and developed powerful Black African kingdoms. In short, this lucrative trade of human beings was initially fueled by the widespread practice of Blacks capturing and trading Blacks. However, it was the European's insatiable appetite for slaves that gradually transformed the area from a gold coast to a slave coast.

After being kidnapped deep inland, the chained captives were sometimes forced to march several hundred miles for months towards the coast. Taken from their homes, these men, women, and children were delivered to the Europeans and warehoused at inhumane slave prisons along the African coastline. These prisons, sometimes called warehouses and factories, also housed the European government officials and traders. The mortality rate of Whites living in this foreign African land and environment was high. Life expectancy of only a few years made it imperative for them to quickly make their fortune as traders.

Many powerful Black kings and rulers forged partnerships with European slave traders. Europeans obtained permission from the former to build infamous slave castles and forts into the coastal cliffs of places such as the Ivory Coast, Ghana, Togo, Benin, Nigeria, and Gambia. Over fifty fortress prisons were built and financed by European government-approved slave trading companies like the British Royal African Company, the Danish West India Company, and the Bank of Amsterdam. These companies often paid rent to the local African rulers.

The crowded prison dungeons were known as "points of no return" for the estimated fifteen million Africans who suffered in the cold, damp darkness, and wretched smell. Under these harsh conditions many died. The survivors, still in chains, were branded for identification and herded onto ships, where they were sometimes packed so tightly that they could hardly move. These involuntary passengers then departed on long and miserable journeys to strange destinations. The Atlantic crossing could last from six weeks to six months. Disease and violent storms made the conditions on board disheartening. On overlong voyages, food shortages caused captives to be forcibly thrown overboard as a rationing measure. Others, if given a chance to escape their fate, would commit suicide by leaping overboard. The constant threat of revolt by the captives prompted the crews to impose strict control. Onboard terror and fear was accomplished with violent displays of discipline. Beatings, torture, and rape were commonplace. To avoid uprisings, ships usually carried slaves from various parts of Africa who did not share the same languages, making it difficult for them to communicate and plot as a group. It was evident that the common humanity of slave traders was suppressed indefinitely in the name of profit.

Europeans made over fifty-four thousand voyages of this type. It is estimated that over twenty percent of the human cargo never reached the Americas, dying during what came to be known as the Middle Passage. The grotesque abominations and obscenities suffered during these journeys constituted but one side of the systematized traffic in slaves called the Triangular Trade. The British slave trade ships started in England and made an initial passage to Africa with goods to trade for slaves. These slaves were then transported on the same ships continuing on the Middle Passage to the Americas where the slaves were traded for goods or money. The ships would then complete the triangle by making the return passage back to England with the profits, and then often start the whole process again shortly thereafter. The last slave ship to leave the African West Coast headed for Brazil in 1888.

Throughout history, slaves have served in capacities as diverse as servants, skilled workers, tutors, warriors, and concubines. On the American continents, however, slavery emerged as a system of forced labor designed for the cultivation of staple crops. Depending on location, these crops included cotton, tobacco, sugar, rice, indigo, and coffee. In the Southern United States, the most important staples were cotton and tobacco. Unlike the slavery that existed in many other times and places, this modern type of slavery distinguished itself based on race. The large majority of slaves and their descendants were Black and of African origin, while most of the owners and their descendants were White and of Europeans origin.

Slavery in the United States was not a Southern institution; it was an American institution. Black slaves arrived in the United States almost at the same time as the first White European settlers in the sixteenth century. In 1526, Spaniards brought the first Blacks to mainland North America near present day Sapelo Sound, Georgia. African slaves were brought to Jamestown, Virginia as early as 1619. These particular Blacks had been earlier Christianized by the Spanish. Since English law at the time prohibited the lifetime servitude of a Christian, the Africans were sold as indentured servants to American owners with limitations on the length of their service. Throughout most of the 1600s the number of Africans in the English mainland colonies increased slowly. During this time, colonists also experimented with two other sources of forced labor. Native American slaves and White European indentured servants helped fill early America's labor needs, but their numbers were not sufficient. The number of Native American slaves was limited in part because the Native Americans were in their homeland. They knew the surrounding terrain and could flee quite easily. Although some Native American slaves could be found in every colony, the number was limited. The White settlers found it easier to sell Native Americans captured in war to planters in the West Indies, rather than turn them into slaves on their own land.

More significant as a form of labor was indentured servitude. Although some were Black, most indentured servants were poor White Europeans who wanted to leave difficult living conditions and take advantage of fresh opportunities in the United States. They traded three to seven years of their labor in exchange for the transatlantic passage. They signed a contract that set out the length and conditions of their servitude, and, guaranteed them land upon completion. At first, indentured servants came mainly from England, but later they came increasingly from Germany, Ireland, and Wales. They were mostly, although not exclusively, young males. Once in the colonies, they were usually considered and treated like temporary slaves. Most served as farm laborers, while some, especially in the North, were taught skilled trades. Throughout the seventeenth century, they performed most of the heavy manual labor in the Southern colonies and provided the majority of immigrants to those areas.

Toward the latter part of the 1600s, the number of people willing to sell themselves into indentured servitude fell sharply. Word of the harsh conditions in America, improved living and working conditions in Europe, and a variety of other reasons caused a sharp decline in servant migration. Because the labor needs of the rapidly growing colonies were increasing, a labor crisis arose. To solve it, landowners turned to African slaves, who from the 1680s began to replace indentured servants and provide a stable labor force. It became apparent that Black slavery was the most profitable type of labor. It was calculated that one Black person enslaved for life was worth four or five White indentured servants, who were usually bound for a limited period of less than ten years. Aware that enormous profits could be generated from this particular type of racial bondage, the colonies collectively laid the groundwork for its institutionalization, thus ensuring their growth and survival.

Slavery spread rapidly throughout the American colonies. In Virginia, for example, Blacks, the great majority of whom were bondpeople, increased from about seven percent of the population in 1680 to more than forty percent by the mid-1800s. In 1750, Georgia became the last of the original thirteen American colonies to legalize slavery. By the 1770s, slaves constituted about forty percent of the people living in the Southern colonies, with the highest concentration in South Carolina, where more than fifty percent of the population were slaves.

At first, the legal status of Africans in America was poorly defined. Some Blacks, like European indentured servants, were able to become free after several years of service. Beginning in the 1640s, however, a transformation occurred when the colonies began enacting laws that regulated and defined slave status and conditions. The key feature to these laws was the provision that Black slaves, and the children of slave women, would serve for life. In 1641, Massachusetts became the first British colony in North America to legally recognize slavery; the other colonies quickly followed suit. At this point in America's early development, slavery was no longer being limited to a number of years but instead meant lifetime servitude. The definition of who could be a slave also shifted from non-Christian to non-White. The legal net supporting lifetime indenture thus tightened and few Africans could claim a right to freedom by the end of the seventeenth century. It was not until the 1720s, however, that British law fully confirmed that the slave was a chattel or personal property. It was now becoming increasingly clear that slavery would be defined by race and perpetuated through heredity. Consequently, many free Blacks, or freedmen, were forcibly sold back into slavery.

Slaves were used by their masters to perform numerous tasks, including clearing forests, serving as trappers, guides, craftsmen, house servants, and nurses. For the most part, however, they were utilized as farm workers. The Americas benefited from the advanced agricultural skills many Blacks brought with them from their African homeland. Slaves were most numerous where landowners grew staple crops for market; such as tobacco in the upper Southern states of Maryland, Virginia, and North Carolina, and rice in the lower Southern states of South Carolina and Georgia. Some owners sent their slaves to the large cities as self-hired bondpeople. The slaves hired out their time and labor for wages that were sent back to their owners.

Slavery never became as economically important to the North as it did in the South, although slaves did labor on horse breeding farms in Rhode Island and big wheat producing estates in New York. The North's economic activity centered on small farms and industries. Soil quality and climate generally restricted the development of commercial agriculture. Slaves in the North were usually kept in small numbers, and most served as domestic servants. Only in New York, the largest slave trade ocean port in the North, did they make up more than ten percent of the population. In the Northern states as a whole, less than five percent of the population were slaves.

By the mid-seventeenth century, American slavery had taken on a number of distinct features. More than ninety percent of American slaves lived in the South where conditions differed sharply with those in the North. In most West Indies colonies, including Jamaica and Saint-Domingue, Blacks outnumbered Whites by more than ten to one. On these islands, slaves often lived on large land holdings with hundreds of other bondpeople. In America's Northern colonies, Blacks were few in numbers and slaves were typically held in small groups of six or less. The American South, by contrast, was neither predominately White or Black. Slaves formed a large minority of the population. Most slaves lived on small and medium sized estates containing between six and fifty slaves. Some slaves, however, lived on large estates owned by the wealthiest of Southern families. The Hairstons, of Scottish decent, were one such family. They owned a vast plantation empire stretching across three states and including forty-five plantations and farms in Virginia, North Carolina, and Mississippi. They owned more than ten thousand slaves.

The other distinct feature of American slavery was in many ways the most important. In contrast to slaves in most other regions of the Americas, those in the United States experienced natural population growth. American slaves were often bred like cattle. Elsewhere, in areas as diverse as Cuba, Saint-Domingue, Jamaica, and Brazil, slave death rates greatly surpassed birth rates. Generally, slave-owners in these territories mistreated slaves and found it economically advantageous to work slaves to death and simply replace them. Thus in these regions, increase of the slave population depended on the importation of new slaves from Africa. As soon as the slave trade was outlawed and importation ended, the slave population began to decrease. In the American colonies, mortality among slaves at first also exceeded births. During the 1700s, however, the birth rates rose while the death rates declined, and the slave population became self-reproducing. This phenomenon transpired earlier in the upper than in the Deep South. Even after slave imports were outlawed in the United States in 1808, the number of slaves continued to increase rapidly. During the next fifty years, the slave population of the United States increased from one million to almost four million in 1860. The natural population growth of slaves confirmed that slavery could survive and even flourish in the United States without new slave imports from Africa.

The increase in natural population also accelerated the transition from an African to a Black American slave population. By the 1770s, only about twenty percent of slaves in the colonies were African born, although the concentration of Africans remained higher in Georgia and South Carolina. After 1808 the proportion of African born slaves declined rapidly. The emergence of a native-born slave population had many important results. For example, among African born slaves who were imported for their ability to perform physical labor, there were few children, and men outnumbered women by about two to one. In contrast, American born slaves began their slave careers as children and included approximately even numbers of males and females. Owners went through a similar process of Americanization. Those born in the United States usually felt at home on their estates. West Indies planters often sought to make their fortunes rapidly and then retire to a life of comfort and leisure in Europe. By contrast, American slave-owners usually assumed an active role in running their estates, and were thus less likely to become absentee masters.

Throughout most of the colonial period, opposition to enslavement among White Americans was practically nonexistent. Settlers in the seventeenth and early eighteenth centuries came from distinctly stratified European societies in which the rich often ruthlessly exploited people of the lower classes. Not yet influenced by the later generation's enlightened belief in natural human equality, they saw little reason to question the enslavement of Africans. As planters sought to create a submissive labor force, they freely resorted to harsh, violent, repressive measures that included frequent use of branding, the lash, and loaded handle whips that doubled as clubs.

Gradually, changes occurred in the way owners viewed both their bondpeople and themselves. Many second-generation owners, unlike their parents, had grown up with slaves. They came to consider them inferior members of their extended families. These slave masters looked upon themselves as benevolent patriarchs who, like altruistic despots, ruled their people firmly but fairly and looked after their wants and needs. Despite this change in attitude, slavery remained harshly repressive. Owners continued to rely heavily on the whip for discipline and few if any slaves saw their masters as the kindly guardians that they proclaimed themselves to be. Nevertheless, many slave masters adhered to the notion that they should treat their slaves humanely.

Slavery was at the core of the early development of the United States. Blacks constituted a large and productive group of involuntary immigrants. In many ways, the growth of slavery mirrored the growth of the nation. Encouraged by a growing international demand for cotton, the invention of the Cotton Gin in 1793 made cotton production economical, which lead to a dramatic expansion in the American cotton industry. This growth contributed to an increase of slave labor in the South. Its direct effects also instigated the rapid spreading of cotton cultivation and slavery onto uncultivated lands westward. By 1860, cotton was the principle crop of the South, and it represented fifty-seven percent of all American exports. The profitability of cotton, known as King Cotton, cemented the South's reliance on the plantation system and its indispensable element, slavery. Many in United States felt that slavery was the soul of American progress, without it there would be no future.

The arrival of the Cotton Gin and its effects on America should not be underestimated. Simple cotton engines, or gins, were first used in India during ancient times. A version of these gins, the roller gin, had reached the American Colonies by the 1740s. The invention of the Cotton Gin, however, revolutionized the process. This invention had a great impact on the development of the Southern states. With the Cotton Gin, cotton could be cleaned so efficiently that it became the most important crop in the South and the foundation of the region's lucrative agricultural economy.

The machine was used to separate the fibers of cotton from the seeds. Before the invention of the Cotton Gin, seeds had to be removed from cotton fibers by hand. This labor intensive and time consuming process made growing and harvesting cotton unprofitable. The Cotton Gin now allowed the seeds to be removed mechanically and rapidly from the cotton fibers. The Cotton Gin, sometimes called a saw gin, consisted of a cylinder to which a number of saw-like teeth were attached. As the crank on the gin turned, a cylinder covered with rows of wire teeth revolved. As the cylinder revolved, the teeth passed through the closely spaced ribs of a fixed comb. When cotton was fed into the gin, the teeth caught the cotton fibers and pulled them through the comb. The teeth drew the cotton through slots so tightly spaced that the seeds could not enter. A roller with brushes removed the cotton fibers from the teeth and deposited them in a hopper. The larger gins could process fifty times as much cotton in a day as could fifty people working by hand. Short-staple cotton thus rapidly became a cash crop.

This principle, with virtually no modifications, is still employed in modern automatic saw gins used to process the bulk of the American cotton crop. One disadvantage of the saw gin was its tendency to damage the fiber, particularly in the case of long-staple cottons. For ginning such cottons, which included the Sea Island, Egyptian, and Pima varieties, the roller gin was used. Roller gins consisted of a pair of grooved wooden rollers that pressed the seeds from the cotton. The cotton was then carried on the surface of a leather-covered roller that had a blade fixed parallel to the axis of the roller and almost touching its surface. The cotton fiber passed under the blade on the roller, but the seeds could not pass the blade and were forced out of the fiber. The roller gin was slow, so it was used only for premium grades of cotton.

The American inventor Eli Whitney [1765, Westborough, Massachusetts, USA; 1825, New Haven, Connecticut] is generally credited with inventing the Cotton Gin. Early in life, Whitney had developed natural mechanical skills. He made a violin when he was only twelve and started a nail-making business when he was still a teenager. From 1783 to 1789, Whitney taught at a grammar school. He entered Yale College, now Yale University, in 1789 and graduated three years later.

In 1792, Whitney went to Savannah, Georgia, to teach and study law. Upon his arrival, he found that someone had taken the teaching job he expected to get. He then met plantation owner Catherine Littlefield Greene, widow of the American Revolutionary War hero, General Nathanael Greene. She invited Whitney to be her guest while he studied law. In appreciation, Whitney began fixing things around the house. His mechanical skill impressed her. One night, guests discussing green-seed cotton said they could not grow it economically because of the time and labor it took to clean. Mrs. Greene encouraged Whitney to solve the problem. Whitney designed and constructed a model for a machine that would separate the seeds from the fibers of the short staple cotton plant. Until that time, this type of work had been done manually by hand. His machine could clean as much cotton in a day as fifty people working by hand. He finished the first Cotton Gin in 1793.

Whitney obtained financial backing to exploit his invention by creating a partnership with Mrs. Greene's plantation manager, Phineas Miller. Together they manufactured Cotton Gins in New Haven, Connecticut. Soon, however, the business experienced problems, including the death of Miller and a disastrous factory fire that prevented Whitney from making enough gins to meet the surging demand. In addition, other manufacturers throughout the South had been producing imitations of Whitney's invention. These rivals claimed that a similar machine had earlier been constructed in Switzerland. Whitney sued them and won after years of court trials. Although Whitney received a patent on the gin in 1794, a decision protecting the patent was not rendered until 1807. By this time, the life of the patent had almost expired, and in 1812, the Congress of the United States denied Whitney's petition for renewal of the patent. In all, he profited little from his invention.

During the years he fought for his patent, Whitney also became a manufacturer of muskets and other weapons for the American government. In 1798, after the Department of the Treasury gave him a contract to produce ten thousand muskets, he built a factory near New Haven, at present day Hamden. There he experimented with a new system of manufacturing standardized, interchangeable parts. Up until then, guns had been handmade with no two made alike. Whitney most likely was aware of existing French and American techniques for the mass production of muskets. Consequently, Whitney designed a new gun and the machinery to make it. His milling machine manufactured parts exactly alike. Each part would fit any of the guns he made. Whitney also created division of labor, in which each person specialized in making one part of the gun. The final step simply involved the assembly of the interchangeable parts. For these achievements, he is generally credited as a prominent promoter and pioneer of mass production and the assembly line.

By the 1830s, Georgia, Louisiana, Mississippi, and Alabama formed the center, known as the Black Belt, of a new cotton kingdom. This area produced more than eighty percent of the nation's supply of the crop. The great bulk of this cotton was cultivated by bondpeople. In parts of the Black Belt, enslaved African Americans made up more than three-fourths of the total population. In order to produce enough cotton to meet the demands of England's newly invented spinning and weaving machines, planters began moving west towards uncultivated lands.

As slavery diminished in the Northeast, it flourished in the Southwest. Between 1790 and 1860, approximately one million slaves were moved west, almost double the number of Africans shipped to the United States during the whole period of the transatlantic slave trade. Some slaves moved with their owners while others moved as part of a new domestic slave trade. This new trade had owners from the coastal states selling surplus slaves to planters in the cotton growing states of the new Southwest. Between 1820 and 1860 more than sixty percent of the Upper South's enslaved population was sold to the Deep South. Covering almost thirty miles per day on foot, men, women, and children marched south in large groups called Coffles. Slave traders bound the women together with rope. They fastened the men first with chains around their necks and then handcuffed them in pairs. The traders removed the restraints only when the Coffle approached the slave market.

As the institution of slavery flourished, so too did its variations. Slavery varied according to location, crops, and the size of estates. On farms and small plantations most slaves came in frequent contact with their masters, but on very large plantations, where slave masters often employed managers or overseers, slaves might rarely see their owners. Some masters left their land entirely in the control of subordinates, White overseers, or occasionally trusted slaves. A few Southern slave masters were Aboriginals or even Black themselves. A small percentage of free Blacks owned slaves. In some cases, their motives included protecting family members, but more often, they too wished to profit from slave labor.

Most slaves on big plantations labored in groups, under the supervision of slave drivers and overseers. Others, especially in the coastal region of South Carolina and Georgia, worked under the task system. Under this system, slaves were required to complete a certain amount of work per day, received less supervision, and were free to use their time as they desired once they had completed their daily workload. In addition to performing fieldwork, slaves also served as carpenters, drivers, blacksmiths, preachers, handymen, gardeners, nurses, midwives, and house servants.

Despite such diversity, the institution developed certain recognizable and universal attributes. Slavery was overwhelmingly rural. In 1860 only about five percent of all slaves lived in towns of two thousand five hundred inhabitants or more. Although some slaves lived on huge plantations and others on small estates or farms, most were found on average sized holdings. In 1860, about fifty percent of all slaves lived on plantations, farms, establishments, or holdings of ten to forty-nine slaves. The remaining half of the slave population was evenly divided between larger and smaller holdings. Plantations tended to be larger in the Deep South than in the Upper South.

Most slaves lived with resident owners. Owner absenteeism was most prevalent in the Georgia and South Carolina low country, but in the South as a whole, it was less common than in the West Indies. Most healthy adult slaves labored in the field. Field hands worked harder and longer than any other kind of slave. Their workday generally lasted from sunrise to sunset, and they often lived under the worst conditions. Only the largest holdings could spare able-bodied adults for full-time exclusive assignment to specialized occupations. The main business of Southern farms, estates, and plantations, and of the slaves who supported them, was to grow staple crops.

During the nineteenth century, most of the plantation slaves were field hands that planted and picked cotton. Other plantation slaves became skilled craft workers such as carpenters, bricklayers, or cabinetmakers. Slaves also had a variety of occupations in Southern cities and towns. Many worked in factories or labored in mines. Others became dockworkers, riverboat pilots, lumberjacks, office clerks, or construction workers on canals and railroads.

Masters relied heavily on children, the elderly, and the infirm for nonproductive work such as house service, which included the various jobs of cook, seamstress, butler, nanny, and surrogate mother. Most house slaves lived in their master's home, sometimes referred to as the "the big house". They labored fewer hours and had more privileges than did field hands, but were more subject to the wishes of the master's family. This proximity occasionally created emotional bonds. Most of the slaves eventually freed by their masters had worked as house servants. Owners chose the weakest and least threatening slaves to live with them, partly because they constantly feared for their own personal safety. Slave-families were always aware that given the chance, their own bondpeople – viewed as the enemy within – might exact revenge against them for their enslavement.

Southern slaveholders assumed an active part in managing their property. They generally kept meticulous written records regarding their slaves, including birth and death dates, and names given them. Age was particularly important because some states considered slaves aged between twelve and fifty as taxable property. Slaveholders also provided for the essential material needs of their slaves. The amount and quality of these provisions varied widely. The purely material conditions – such as food, housing, clothing, and medical attention – were usually better in the pre-Civil War period than in the colonial period. Based on records of slave height and life expectancy, material conditions seemed better in the Southern states than in South America or the West Indies. Effective slave management – the science of caring for and working Negro slaves – was widely discussed in agricultural journals. Efficient management hierarchies were put into place on large plantations. Blacks occasionally assumed lower management positions, and consequently, were sometimes viewed as traitors by the other slaves.

Although children were often under fed, most working slaves were given steady rations of corn and pork, which provided sufficient energy to fuel their labor. Slaves often supplemented their rations with crops that they cultivated on garden plots apportioned to them. Clothing and housing were basic but adequate and functional. Slaves usually received a blanket at birth and long shirts during childhood. Men received four crude suits, pants, and shirts, while women were supplied with simple but functional dresses. Each family lived in small wooden cabins, one to a family. The collection of these slave cabins on large plantations were called slave quarters and usually resembled a miniature village. Wealthy slave masters often sent doctors to treat injured or sick slaves.

Owners intervened continually in the lives of their slaves, from determining their labor to allowing or disallowing marriages. Some owners made complex rules, and most engaged in constant directing, interference, threatening, and punishing. Many took advantage of their status to exploit slave women sexually and by doing so fathered countless mulatto slave children. What many slaves seem to have despised the most about their situation was the obvious lack of autonomy and control over their lives. Owners may have prided themselves on the care they provided, but the slaves resented the constant meddling in their lives and tried to achieve whatever freedom they could within their state of bondage. In the slave quarters, bondpeople developed their own way of life and struggled to increase their independence while their owners strove to contain it. Owners rarely controlled the lives of their slaves as much as they wished.

No Southern state gave slaves the legal rights to own property, testify in court, wed, or earn their freedom. State laws prohibited the education of slaves. Some slaves, nonetheless, managed to do all these things in one form or another. Gradually, slaves developed their own customs, traditions, language, dialect, mannerisms, music, and other means of communication. Owners had no guarantee of receiving willing obedience or even loyal service from their bondpeople. To encourage faithful service, some slave-owners treated their slaves kindly and promised them such privileges as money and gifts. Other masters relied on punishment, such as whippings, withholding food, and threats to sell members of the slave's family. It was common for plantation owners to systematically dehumanized their slaves. A prominent tactic to maintain repression was through separation of husbands, wives, and children. Most owners refused to see the Black slaves as equals, both biologically and emotionally. A slave possessed no social standing and in servitude was rendered powerless. This induced a state of identity loss that made them obedient. The spirit and humanity of the slaves was broken down into submission in an attempt to insure that no revolt was to occur, and that only obedience was to be tolerated. Whatever the system of discipline, slavery resulted in a struggle of wills between masters and slaves. In this unequal struggle, the masters held all the power of reward and punishment. Slaves, nevertheless, used sabotage, flattery, and many other methods to outsmart them.

Away from the view of masters and overseers, slaves lived their own lives. They made friends, played, fell in love, sang, prayed, told stories, and participated in the necessary tasks of daily living, from cooking, cleaning house and sewing, to working on garden plots. Most important as corner stones of the slaves' lives were their families and their faith. Throughout the South, the family defined the actual living arrangements of slaves. Most slaves lived together in traditional families with a mother, father, and children. The stability and security of these families faced harsh challenges since no state law recognized marriage among slaves. To show commitment to each other, couples would jump over a broom as a symbol of their unity. Owners rather than parents had legal authority over slave children, and the possibility of forced separation, through sale, threatened every family. These separations were most frequent in the slave exporting states of the Upper South. Despite their unstable status, families nevertheless served as the slaves' most basic refuge, the center of private lives that masters could never fully control.

The religion of the slaves played an important role in helping them survive the harshness of slavery. This religion, a mixture of African and Christian creeds, made the slaves feel part of a community. It also provided them with hope of a better afterlife in heaven. During the colonial period, African slaves usually kept their native religions. Many slave masters were suspicious of outsiders who sought to convert their slaves to Christianity, in part because they feared that converted slaves would have to be freed in accordance to moral law and expectations. During the decades following the American Revolution, however, Christianity was increasingly central to the slaves' cultural life. Many slaves were converted during the religious revivals or Great Awakenings that swept the South in the late eighteenth and early nineteenth centuries. Slaves typically belonged to the same denominations as White Southerners, the largest of which were the Methodists and Baptists. Ministers calmed slaveholder fears by emphasizing the belief that good Christians always made good servants. Some owners actually encouraged their bondpeople to come to the White church, where they usually were forced to sit in a special slave balcony. There they were lectured and given advice about being obedient to their owners. In the slave quarters, however, there developed a secret parallel or invisible church controlled by the bondpeople. They listened to sermons delivered by their own Black pastors and responded with rapturous singing, chanting, and shouting. These clandestine worship services were often disguised as Sunday picnics, since it was illegal for slaves to conduct religious services without the presence of at least one White person.

Not all slaves had access to these ministers and not all adhered to their message, but for many, their faith served as a great comfort and a beacon of hope. The Bible's many stories, including the plight of the Jews from bondage in Egypt to their promised land, had relevance for American slaves. Sunday church services were often the only legal opportunity for slaves to congregate and exchange information. Sometimes they obtained news or letters received by the church from dispersed family members, free and slave.

By the mid-1800s the Southern slavocracy became extremely protective of their "peculiar institution", as it was then often politely called by some prominent Southerners. By "peculiar" they did not mean that the institution was odd or strange, instead, they meant that slavery was confined, distinctive, particular, or unique to certain areas of the country and not the affair of any outsiders. It should not be thought that all or even most White Southerners were directly involved in its activities. In 1850, there were only about three hundred and fifty thousand slave-owners in a total White population of about six million in the slave states. Fifty percent of these owned four slaves or less and could not be considered planters. In the entire South, fewer than one thousand eight hundred persons owned more than one hundred slaves.

Nevertheless, slavery did convey an indelible image of Southern life. Although the large planters were few in numbers, they were very prestigious, powerful, and wealthy. About forty-five thousand planters owned over fifty percent of the slaves, and these planters controlled the economy and government of the Southern states. Even the many Southerners who did not own slaves accepted the planters' prediction that the South's economy would crumble without slavery. Money invested in slavery was by far the largest concentration of capital in the country. The planters were the economic as well as the political leaders of the South. Their beliefs touched every level of Southern society. Instead of opposing slavery, small Southern farmers thought that they too might, with good fortune and hard work, someday join the ranks of the planter class.

At the root of this almost unanimous White Southern support of slavery, lay the universal creed, shared by many Whites in the North and West, that Blacks were an inherently inferior race. It was believed that Blacks had developed only to a state of primitive barbarism in their native Africa and could live in a civilized society only if reared and disciplined through institutionalized bondage. By 1860, there were about two hundred and fifty thousand free Blacks in the South, of which a few were themselves owners of Black slaves. Despite this fact, most Southern Whites refused to believe that the slaves, if freed, could ever coexist peacefully with their former owners. With fear and distrust, they referred to several uprisings of Black slaves as evidence that Blacks had to be kept under strict control.

Behind the "Cotton Curtain" of the Southern states was a slavocracy that, in spite of mounting domestic and international opposition, maintained its grip on America's Black population. To counter this growing universal opposition to slavery, Southerners and the slavocracy had developed by 1850, an elaborate proslavery argument, defending the institution on economic, sociological, religious and biblical grounds. Up until the Civil War, however, the high profits that resulted from slavery had far greater influence than did any moral arguments.

Blacks in Canada, slave or free, never constituted a large segment of the Canadian population, but their history is significant. From 1628 to 1834, only sixteen hundred African slaves were brought into Canada directly from Africa, Britain, and Europe. The vast majority of Canadian Blacks arrived from various parts of the Americas at different times and for different reasons. Before the Civil War, their entry can be identified and associated with seven distinctive periods in North American history. New France Slaves: (1600-1763) French colonial imports; Black Pioneers: members of a Black slave military regiment organized by the British during the American Revolution and who were subsequently given land in Canada after the War; Black Loyalists: Free and slave Blacks arriving alone or with Loyalist masters after 1783; Jamaican Maroons: Black Jamaican slave rebels captured and relocated by the British to Nova Scotia and New Brunswick in 1796; Refugee Negroes: (1813-1816) slaves fleeing to the British lines during the War of 1812 and subsequently given land in Nova Scotia and Ontario; California Free Blacks: (late 1850s) almost one thousand free African Americans migrated from California to Vancouver Island seeking to escape the racial discrimination that was imposed by law in their home state; Fugitive Slaves: (1815-1861) escaped slaves arriving via the Underground Railroad.

Before the arrival of Europeans, slavery in Canada was practiced by a number of Native Indian tribes, notably those on the Northwest coast. As practiced by Europeans, it probably originated with the Portuguese explorer and navigator Gaspar Corte-Real [circa 1450; circa 1501]. When exploring the coast of Labrador and Newfoundland in 1500, Corte-Real enslaved fifty Indian men and women. The French introduced Black slaves as early as their first permanent settlement at Quebec City in 1608. Olivier Le Jeune [circa 1621, Madagascar; 1654, Canada] is the first recorded bondman to have been transported directly from Africa to Canada. He was purchased at the approximate age of seven by the British Commander David Kirke during his 1628 invasion of New France. He was then sold to Olivier Le Tardiff in Quebec in 1628, head clerk of the French Colony. When Quebec was handed back to the French in 1632, Le Tardiff, who had often aided the British, was forced to flee. He sold his slave to a Quebec City resident. The boy was educated in a school founded by the Jesuit priest, Father Le Jeune. He was later baptized and named Olivier Le Jeune, adopting the first name of the French clerk and the surname of the Jesuit priest. By the time of his death, it appears that Olivier Le Jeune's official status was changed from domestic servant to freeman.

Although France's King Louis XIV [1638, Saint-Germain-en-Laye, France; 1715, Versailles (reigned 1643-1715)] in 1689 authorized the importation of slaves from the Caribbean, few were brought to Canada. The legality of slavery was recognized in New France between 1689 and 1709. Its recognition was based on various French governmental decrees and customary law, including the influential Code Noir of 1685 that regulated the presence of slaves in France's colonies. The French crown and its colonies seemed to disagree on the legal nature of slavery and its application and implementation. Although slaves did serve in France, the legality of the institution had never actually been recognized. Intendant (1705-10) Jacques Randot issued in 1709, an ordinance making slavery legal in French Canada. His proclamation also made it illegal to induce a slave to escape. In 1736, Intendant (1729-48) Gilles Hocquart [1694, Mortagne-au-Perche, France; 1783, Paris] issued a proclamation that provided for the uniform means of formal manumission. His ordinance stated that a registered notary's certificate was needed to free a slave by purchase or gift. In short, the legal regulation of slaves in New France only faintly mirrored the strict and harsh laws enacted during the same period in the Southern British American colonies.

By 1759, the year of the British conquest of New France, there were over three thousand six hundred recorded slaves in the colony. Approximately eleven hundred of these New France Slaves were of African origin. The others arrived mostly from New England or the Caribbean. Most of the slaves lived in or near Montreal and were owned by merchants, aristocrats, professionals, governors, military, and even members of the clergy. Slavery, which prospered in economies dependent upon one crop, mass production, and group labor, did not develop strongly among these colonists. The use and presence of slaves throughout New France nevertheless took hold in the manor homes, estate farms, ports, and on the frontier. The colony's slaves included Aboriginals, most of who were captured in wars. The French preferred to enslave Panis Indians, so called after the generally docile Pawnee tribe. Some Blacks were transplanted from Africa, but most arrived from the Southern American colonies or West Indies.

Before the American Revolution, almost all Black people in Canada were slaves. As the Seven Years' War ended and New France fell under British rule, slavery was granted specific protection by the terms of the 1763 treaty of capitulation between France and Britain.

Although Britain had no specific legislation legalizing slavery, convention ruled. Neither the French civil or English criminal law introduced in Quebec provided any noteworthy restrictions against enslavement. Indeed, 1763 brought no noticeable change in status for Quebec's Blacks. They continued to be non-persons under the law. They were chattels, to be used and transferred as their masters wished.

Slavery was an accepted part of eighteenth century life in Canada. Most slaves worked as domestic servants throughout the colonies. The evidence of slavery in Canada was plentiful, including slave auctions in Nova Scotia, newspapers advertising skilled Negroes for sale, wills detailing the inheritance of slaves, and bounties offered for the return of escapees. Europeans were unable to establish in Canada the plantation system of slave labor that flourished in the Southern United States or in the West Indies. Attempts to do so were frustrated by the nature of the fur trading economy and the relationships of feudal agriculture. With few businesses requiring a regular work force, such a system was not suitable to Canada. The ownership of domestic house slaves, however, was prevalent among the wealthier families. As was the case in the Northern United States, the institution of slavery in Canada did not flourish to the extent it did in the South. Although moral concerns and Christian benevolence did help discourage slavery in Canada, the main reason for its stunted growth and eventual demise was economic. Compared to the plantation economies of the American South and West Indies, its impact was minimal, to the extent that some later generations of Canadians would deny its very existence. Unlike the Southern states or the West Indies, slavery in Canada would not become an economic institution. Though there were recorded instances of harsh punishment and many advertisements for the return of runaway slaves, generally, slaves in Canada did not suffer the same degree of physical discipline or abuse common to the American South. Their low numbers eliminated the need for overseers, the devastating effects of slave breeding, and harsh controls arising from fears of armed Black rebellion.

The saga of Blacks arriving in Canada changed suddenly with the outbreak of the American Revolution. Some of the refugees or Loyalists fleeing to Canada during and after the war brought slaves north with them. Joseph Brant (born Thayendanegea) [circa 1742, Cayahoga, near Akron, Ohio, USA; 1807, Burlington Bay, Upper

Canada], the Loyalist Mohawk chief and statesman, owned several slaves, as did Laura Secord (born Ingersoll) [1775, Great Barrington, Massachusetts, USA; 1868, Chippawa, Niagara Falls, Ontario, Canada], who became famous in the War of 1812. A greater number of Blacks were runaways or arrived as free persons, many of them having won their freedom by supporting the British and serving with their military during the war. Amongst them were some of General George Washington's [1732, Wakefield, Pope's Creek Plantation, Westmoreland County, Virginia, USA; 1799, Mount Vernon] escaped slaves. One, named after his former owner, was Henry Washington. Henry later sailed from Nova Scotia to Africa. In 1800, he was part of an uprising in Sierra Leone that attempted to establish independence, but, unlike his former master's rebellion, it failed and he was banished from the colony.

Recognizing slavery to be a major weakness of the rebellious Southern colonies, British proclamations had encouraged slaves to desert rebel owners. The proclamations promised them their freedom upon seeking refuge behind British lines and making formal claim to British protection. In all, over one hundred thousand African Americans escaped bondage during the war. The victorious Americans requested the return of their property, including slaves, but the British denied the request and left the question of compensation for slaves unresolved. To make up for this loss, American slaveholders increased the importation of Africans.

Approximately two thousand African American slaves and four thousand free Blacks settled in Nova Scotia, New Brunswick, and Quebec's rich lands east of Montreal, known as the Eastern Townships. Encouraged by the British promise of free land – a promise that was often delayed or not kept – many Black Pioneers and free Blacks settled in Nova Scotia. The number of White and Black Loyalists arriving in Canada was far greater than the authorities had anticipated, and there were not enough qualified surveyors to divide out the land properly. Misunderstandings concerning the nature and size of the promised grants of land quickly became a cause for discontentment. Many of the new arrivals would soon die of starvation. The large influx of Loyalist refugees arriving in the Maritimes resulted, in 1784, in the creation of the new colony of New Brunswick. Although slavery expanded rapidly after 1783, the total number of slaves was never high. Slavery was generally unsuited to Canadian commerce or agriculture, and most of the Blacks who settled in the Maritimes immediately following the American Revolution were free. Within two decades, enslavement had virtually disappeared among the Loyalists.

In 1795, insurgent Blacks from Jamaica, known as Maroons, were deported by the British to Nova Scotia. They included descendants of Black slaves who had escaped from the Spanish and later the British rulers of Jamaica. The Jamaican Maroons were independent minded and fiercely rebellious. They had led numerous uprisings on the Jamaican Island and were feared and respected for their courage. The British chose Canada as an area to relocate these violent troublemakers. By this time, the British viewed Nova Scotia as a dumping ground for Blacks.

During the War of 1812, the British again issued proclamations targeting the slave population in the United States. The Cochrane Proclamation, issued by the commander of the British fleet on the Atlantic Coast, Vice-Admiral Sir Alexander Cochrane, encouraged slaves to desert their American owners and promised freedom and land upon seeking refuge behind British lines. It was also common for British troops to force slaves to leave against their wishes. The British government later established the Black settlement of Oro, Ontario for Black veterans who fought on the British side during the conflict. Oro was the only government-sponsored settlement in Ontario. In 1814, when British troops burned the American capital city of Washington during the War of 1812, they brought back to Halifax, Nova Scotia many slaves who had sought refuge with them. Again, the number of African American refugees arriving in Canada was far greater than the authorities had anticipated. Most of these several thousand Refugee Negroes were transported and resettled in the Maritimes, especially Nova Scotia. An inadequate and inefficient settlement organization made their arrival and adaptation more difficult than that experienced by earlier Black immigrants. Their recent state of bondage made them less equipped and skilled to deal with the harsh realities of a strange land and environment. Their successful integration into Canadian society was often slow and painful, with periods of harsh discrimination and prejudice from both White and previously settled Black Canadians. Animosity was prevalent within the established Black community concerning these recent arrivals. Some Blacks felt the newcomers were crude and ignorant, and would damage the progress they had made within Canadian society.

Many of the slaves owned by White Loyalists were taken to the Eastern Townships of Quebec. Most of the Black Loyalists, Maroons, and Refugees in the Maritimes were located by government policy in segregated communities on the outskirts of larger White towns. The communities of Halifax, Guysborough, Shelburne, and Digby in Nova Scotia, and Saint John and Fredericton in New Brunswick, had Black settlements in their immediate neighborhoods. The Black Loyalists, Maroons, and Refugees met with numerous barriers in trying to establish themselves in the Maritimes. The small land grants they received could not permit self-sufficiency through farming. Forced to find occasional manual work in neighboring White towns, the Black pioneers were susceptible to discrimination and exploitation in employment and salary. Throughout the Maritimes, Blacks received smaller parcels of farmland and lower salaries than Whites. Most Blacks worked in the low paying service jobs or as unskilled laborers. Poverty immediately entrenched itself as a harsh reality of the early African Canadian experience.

Partly due to the poor conditions faced in their new surroundings, a large number of these African Canadians left Nova Scotia and New Brunswick for Sierra Leone in West Africa. In 1792, almost one thousand two hundred Black Loyalists sailed from Halifax to establish the new African settlement of Freetown. Many of their direct descendants still live there today. In 1800, over five hundred Maroons followed the same route to Sierra Leone. Their arrival in Africa coincided with an uprising of the Black Loyalist settlers against their British governors. By siding with the colonial authorities, the Maroons ensured the failure of the revolt.

In 1820, approximately one hundred refugee Blacks left Halifax for Trinidad. Many African Canadians were encouraged to leave Canada by Caribbean and Nova Scotia officials, but most declined. Despite poor land, severe winters, and the competition of abundant White labor, the vast majority of Black immigrants were determined to remain and survive in Canada.

Another group of free American Blacks migrated from California to British Columbia in the late 1850s. Most settled on Vancouver Island (in the city of Victoria) and Saltspring Island, while some later moved inland. The British authorities, which needed settlers to populate and protect the fledgling colony, generally welcomed the California Free Blacks. They brought skills or savings that enabled them to establish small businesses. Many also worked on farms, wharves, or in shops.

The largest number of African Americans arrived in Canada independently, using the Underground Railroad. In 1834, slavery was outlawed in Canada when the British Parliament passed a law abolishing slavery in all British North American colonies. This meant that slaves became free upon entering Canadian territory. In addition, Canadian officials refused American requests for their return. To American slaves, escape to Canada meant freedom. Canada therefore quickly became a major destination of the Underground Railroad. The Railroad was actually a clandestine network of secret routes by which people who actively opposed slavery, spirited slaves out of the American South and assisted them in reaching Canada. The Underground Railroad's activities began a new chapter in Canada's long-standing relationship with Blacks. The Railroad transported thousands of fleeing Blacks into Canada, particularly to the Southern part of Ontario. Southern Ontario – Canada's southern most territory and easiest for runaway slaves to reach – quickly became an area where the Fugitive Slaves and free Blacks built homes and communities. These concentrated Black settlements were often the result of a need for mutual support and protection against White Canadian prejudice, discrimination, and American slave catchers. Most of Ontario's Black settlements were in and around places such as Windsor, Chatham, Sarnia, London, Saint Catharines, and Hamilton. Toronto had a Black district, and there were smaller concentrations of Blacks near Guelph, Barrie, and Owen Sound.

The fugitive Blacks who arrived in Ontario via the Underground Railroad usually arrived destitute. Without government land grants, they often earned wages by working the lands of others, although some managed to obtain and farm their own land successfully. Some even worked on railway construction.

Within their compact settlements, the early African Canadians had the opportunity to create a distinct community and retain their cultural characteristics. Unique styles of speech, music, worship, family structures and group traditions developed as a direct result of the realities of life in Canada. In slavery, Black women were traditionally forced to work to support themselves, and economic conditions perpetuated this trend in Canada. African Canadian women played a major economic role in family life and thus experienced considerable independence. Nurtured in a communal fashion by their grandparents or older neighbors, African Canadian children developed family-like relationships throughout the local community. A strong sense of mutual reliance and group identity, combined with the strong unity provided by the churches, produced a close-nit community life and a sanctuary against White discrimination.

The chief institutional support was the separate church, usually Methodist or Baptist, created when White congregations refused to admit Blacks as equal parishioners. The churches' spiritual sway influenced daily life and affected the vocabulary, thoughts, and ambitions of their parishioners. Inevitably, they assumed an important political and social role and the preachers became the natural community leaders. The many mutual-assistance organizations, fraternal bands, temperance societies, and anti-slavery groups formed by nineteenth century African Canadians were usually connected with one of the churches.

Schools for Blacks quickly flourished in Canada. Almost every African Canadian community had access to either a public or charity school. British charitable organizations sponsored schools in most of the Maritime African Canadian communities beginning in the 1780s. During the 1800s, British and American philanthropic societies established schools for African Canadians throughout Ontario. In addition, the governments of both Ontario and Nova Scotia created legally segregated public schools. Despite these efforts, however, funding was often inadequate and the quality of education tended to be substandard.

By the year 1850, African Canadians, in general, were considered equal under the law, although, in reality this was not always the case. Traditionally, Blacks were employed in low paying jobs and were thus always among the poorest and worst educated of Canada's inhabitants. Ontario and Nova Scotia still had legally segregated public schools, and the schools for Blacks were often poorly funded. Inferior schooling, combined with residential isolation and economic deprivation, helped to perpetuate a reality of limited opportunity and restricted mobility for Blacks. For example, in 1784, bad economic conditions led to rivalry between poor Whites and Blacks settled in

Nova Scotia. Race riots broke out in two villages that lasted for ten days, until the Governor sent the army and navy to restore order.

Many Blacks returned to the United States after the Civil War. Those who stayed showed a tradition of loyalty to Britain and Canada. Many African Canadians developed these sentiments from the beginning of their settlement in Canada. The Black Loyalists supported British rule in Canada, and their awareness that an American invasion could mean their re-enslavement incited them to join in Canada's military defense. African Canadian militiamen fought against American troops in the War of 1812 and were active in suppressing the Rebellions of 1837. Nearly one thousand Blacks joined the loyal militia that defeated the rebel army led by William Lyon Mackenzie. The British laws in Canada, with few major exceptions, asserted, in principle, the legal equality of African Canadians. African Canadian voters were thus inclined to support Conservative candidates committed to the preservation of British ties. African Canadians, however, never constituted a large enough group to exercise direct political influence.

Although African Canadians did suffer hardships, racism, and discrimination in Canada before the Civil War, these obstacles paled in comparison to the various difficulties experienced by Blacks in the United States. For many African Americans, especially those still held in bondage, Canada provided hope, opportunity, and a tangible example, albeit imperfect, of better days to come.

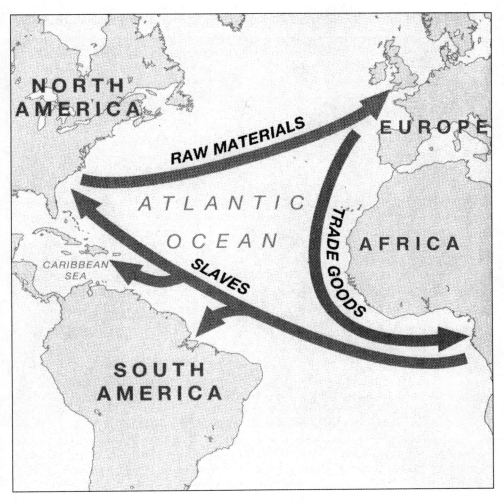

Map of The Triangle Trade

Nat Turner

4. SLAVE REBELLIONS

Throughout more than two hundred and fifty years of chattel slavery in the Americas, continuous rancor and dissatisfaction with the state of bondage led to several armed slave rebellions, mutinies and periodic episodes of violent resistance by Black slaves. Unfortunately for the slave population, these uprisings often resulted in more severe social control and repression in slaveholding areas. The ability of Black slaves to resist authority and protest against their condition was limited. A harsh ruling class that vehemently opposed any armed resistance confronted them. When it occurred, such resistance was always abruptly suppressed and followed by severe retribution designed to discourage future insurrections. In some cases, authorities stopped planned slave rebellions before any outbreak of violence.

Initial and immediate resistance to enslavement generally commenced when the Black Africans were captured in their villages or homeland. This resistance usually continued during the journey to the coastal prisons, on the transatlantic ships, and upon arrival in the New World. There were over three hundred documented slave ship uprisings and mutinies. Once in the Americas, the methods of resistance took on various forms.

Slave uprisings on Canadian soil were mostly few and small in comparison with other slaveholding nations. Canada nonetheless did experience its share of resistance as witnessed in the celebrated case of Marie Joseph Angelique. Angelique, the slave of a wealthy Montreal merchant, de Francheville, carried out one of Canada's most dramatic acts of slave resistance in 1734. Upon learning she was going to be sold, Marie-Joseph decided to leave. In order to facilitate her escape, she set fire to her master's home. The fire quickly spread and eventually engulfed half of Montreal, destroying forty-six buildings including the Hôtel Dieu hospital. Two months later she was apprehended, tortured, paraded through the streets of Montreal, then hanged and her body burned. The news of this event informed many White Canadians of the plight of Canadian slaves and the conditions they were made to endure.

In the United States, over two hundred and fifty revolts or attempted revolts involving ten or more slaves, fighting for their personal freedom, occurred during the two centuries preceding the Civil War. Yet, few of these were systematically planned and most were merely spontaneous and quite short-lived disturbances by small groups of slaves. Such insurrections were usually attempted by male slaves and were often betrayed by loyal house servants who identified more closely with their owners. Most ended violently with the death of both Whites and Blacks, and the implementation by authorities of exemplary punishment.

Aborted violent uprisings occurred in Virginia as early as the 1660s. Bacon's Rebellion in 1676 saw slaves take up arms against Native Americans and the Virginian colonial government. Other revolts occurred along the coast of South Carolina where rice plantations were so heavily populated by slaves that Blacks outnumbered the White population. Here, in what was known as Black Country, two major slave rebellions took place. The 1720 Primus Plot and the 1739 Stono Rebellion both unsuccessfully targeted the colonial center of Charleston. Following the revolts, South Carolina enacted stricter slave laws, including the denial of slaves to assemble, and encouraged an increase in European immigration to counterbalance the growing Black population.

Colonial America witnessed several other slave insurrections. Northern uprisings occurred in colonial New York City, which had a large slave population working the docks. In 1712, New York officials executed Black slaves and Native Americans for planning a rebellion. In 1741, four Whites were executed and seven exiled from the colony for taking part with slaves in a plot. Thirty-one slaves were executed with some burned at the stake. During the American Revolution and subsequent War of 1812, thousands of slaves escaped and joined the British army, which promised freedom to all slaves willing to fight with them.

A large and violent revolt by Black slaves in Saint-Domingue, on the West Indies Island of Hispaniola, alarmed American slaveholders. Known as the Haitian Slave Revolt, it began in 1791 as a rebellion against slavery and French plantation owners. The harshness and the cruelty of the cane fields of Haiti were surpassed only in their oppression by the cotton fields of the American South. The rebellion transformed itself into a political revolution that lasted for thirteen years and cost over one hundred thousand Black lives. It eventually resulted in Haiti's colonial independence from France in 1804. The Haitian leader, called the Black Napoleon, was a former slave named François Dominique Toussaint L'Ouverture [1743, near Cap-Français, Saint-Domingue (now Cap-Haïtien, Haiti); 1803, France]. Even though he was a bondman until he was almost fifty years old, Toussaint taught himself to read, write, and became well educated. In 1791, a slave revolt erupted in Saint Domingue and Toussaint became one of its leaders. He led a Black army against the French, helping to force France to abolish slavery in the colony in 1793. He then aided France by defeating British and Spanish troops that had invaded Saint Domingue. By 1796, he ruled the colony with the approval of its French governor. Saint Domingue prospered under Toussaint, but in 1801, France's ruler, the real Napoleon Bonaparte [1769, Ajaccio, Corsica, France; 1821, St. Helena, British Island], wished to return Saint-Domingue to French control. Bonaparte also intended to reinstate slavery as a means of bringing the colony back to its former prosperity. In 1802, Napoleon sent a large army to reestablish slavery in Saint Domingue and replace Toussaint with a trusted White general. Toussaint and others resisted and began a revolution to free the colony from French control. Later that year, Toussaint was tricked onto a ship, captured, taken to France, and imprisoned until his death in 1803.

Jean Jacques Dessalines [circa 1758, West Africa or Grande-Riviere-du-Nord, Saint-Domingue; 1806, Jacmel, Haiti] succeeded Toussaint as leader of the revolution. Born a slave, he served as an officer in the French army and in 1791 joined the slave revolt for freedom. During the next decade, he continued to fight under Toussaint as one of his Generals, until he became the revolution's leader. Dessalines, with the army that Toussaint had trained, then declared war on the French. After a bitter conflict, the former slaves defeated Napoleon's forces, massacred or drove all Whites off the island, and changed the name of the colony to the aboriginal name Haiti, meaning mountainous. On January 1, 1804, The republic of Haiti, created by former slaves, proudly declared its independence to the world. Upon declaring the colony independent, Dessalines became a national hero and became its first chief of state by assuming the title of Governor General for life. He soon proclaimed himself Emperor, but was assassinated by rivals in 1806.

Dessalines' successor was another Haitian revolutionary by the name of Henri Christophe [1767, Grenada or St. Christopher (now St.

Kitts), British West Indies; 1820, Cap Haitien, Haiti]. Born into slavery, he nevertheless learned to speak English, French, and Haitian Creole. In 1779, he and hundreds of other Haitians fought in America against the British during the American Revolution. Christophe then became a general in the French army in the colony of Saint Domingue and later served under Generals Toussaint L'Ouverture and Jean-Jacques Dessalines. Christophe fought in the Haitian Revolution, and was named Haiti's president in 1806 upon the death of Dessalines. Another general, Alexandre Petion soon challenged his authority. Consequently, Christophe became president in 1807 of Northern Haiti, and Petion became president of the southern region. In 1811, Christophe proclaimed himself king of Northern Haiti and set up his own kingdom with a capital at Cap Haitien. South of the city, he built a huge fortress, the Citadelle Laferriere. He ruled as King Henry I from his palace, Sans Souci, in Cap Haitien. He was a strong and capable leader who became best known as an industrious builder of forts and palaces. During his rule, however, laws were enacted that forced Haitian workers to continue to labor on plantations. The workers, hoping to work on their own private plots, rebelled in 1820. Paralyzed by a recent stroke making him unable to fight and in despair over his inability to bring peace to the country, Christophe committed suicide with a gun and a silver bullet.

The Haitian revolution had completely quashed the ruling White population, the plantation system, and the institution of slavery. The most prosperous colony of the Western Hemisphere transformed itself into the first independent Black republic in the world and the second independent nation in the Western Hemisphere, after the United States. The American government and President Thomas Jefferson (third President, 1800-08) [1743, Shadwell, Goochland (now Albermarle) County, Virginia, USA; July 4, 1826, Monticello] had not been sympathetic towards the rebels, and even gave tacit support to Napoleon's unsuccessful attempts to reinstall slavery on the island.

The immediate and important effects of the Haitian uprising spread far beyond the island. It contributed to the end of French colonial ambitions in the Americas, which ironically led France to sell its vast Louisiana territory in North America to the United States in 1803. Refugees from Haiti settled in Louisiana, helping to establish that area's distinct French Creole culture. The revolt also inspired fear of similar uprisings in other slaveholding areas of the West Indies and the United States. The slavocracy in these areas worked to isolate Haiti in order to keep the powerful idea of freedom from spreading.

The triumph of the Haitians was a source of pride to many free and slave African Americans in the United States. It served as an example to some in bondage who later attempted unsuccessful revolts in South Carolina and Virginia. Southern slaveholders, hearing of the massacres of Whites that preceded Haitian independence, were convinced that freeing slaves would result in a violent race war. This belief made them even less likely to end slavery peacefully.

Some fugitive American slaves later fled to Haiti in the hopes of tasting freedom and a better life. They reached their island destination by using various routes, including stops in the free Northern states or Canada. The harsh reality of Haitian conditions, however, often resulted in disappointment and disillusionment, thereby prompting many to return and settle in the Northern states and Canada.

The long-standing myth of the contented slave was key to the preservation of the American South's distinct institution. Distortion, censorship, and exaggeration often conveniently mired historical records of rebellions. American slaveholders often underscored with pride the relatively few uprisings on American soil. They claimed the lack of rebellion and escape attempts were due to masters' benevolence towards their slaves. In reality, Blacks often tolerated the system in order to preserve their family unity and safety. Many felt sabotage, escape, and resistance could only bring about reprisals and other hardships against themselves and other family members. Across the South, a large percentage of the slaves that did escape often did so to find separated family members. Slaves had little to value in their lives other than the emotional bonds of family.

Less organized and isolated resistance by slaves was more widespread and successful. Slaves would sometimes silently sabotage the system by destroying property or slowing down productivity by pretending to be ill, injured, unable to properly understand instructions, or unable to correctly use tools and livestock. Resistance also included individuals who retaliated physically, and often successfully, against what they perceived as cruel and unjust treatment.

Escape was the most popular form of resistance. During the sixteenth and seventeenth centuries, when slavery was legal throughout most of the Northern states and Canada, many Southern slaves escaped to the unsettled North American West, or south to Mexico or Latin America. In the Spanish colony of Florida, fugitive slaves were welcomed by the Spanish as potential Catholic converts and soldiers, or by the Seminole Indians as guides, interpreters, or warriors against the Europeans. Each year during the pre-Civil War decades, approximately one thousand slaves, mostly from the Upper South, escaped to the North. This number of escapees represented only a small percentage of those who tried to flee. Many fugitives stayed in the South, heading for cities, forests, or swamps. Some hid out near their plantations for days or weeks before either returning voluntarily or being tracked down, captured, and forcibly returned to their owners.

The first major slave insurrection on American soil was planned in the spring and summer of 1800 by Gabriel Prosser, a Black slave and blacksmith often known simply as Gabriel [circa 1775, near Richmond, Henrico County, Virginia, USA; 1800, Richmond]. A large man in stature and over six feet two inches tall, Gabriel was the son of an African woman who instilled in him the yearning and love of freedom. He grew up as the slave of Thomas H. Prosser. Under his mother's guidance he became devoutly religious and was strongly influenced by biblical text. Caught stealing a pig and maiming the White man who apprehended him, while in jail, Gabriel created a mission for himself. Inspired perhaps by the success of the Black revolutionaries of Haiti, upon his release, Gabriel and other bondsmen planned a slave uprising aimed at creating an independent Black state within Virginia, with Gabriel as ruler. He called for a three pronged assault on the city of Richmond (the state capitol) that would capture the city armories and kill all Whites except Quakers, Frenchmen, and Methodists, whom he considered friends of liberty. He also planned to capture other Virginia towns and free as many slaves as possible. Gabriel spent months recruiting and forging iron into weapons.

At midnight on the appointed Sunday night of August 30, 1800, as many as one thousand armed slaves assembled a few miles outside Richmond, ready to attack. They carried a flag with the motto "death or liberty". A torrential downpour and violent thunderstorm, however, inundated roads and washed away a bridge that was key to the groups' march. Prosser postponed the attack. That same night, two slaves informed their master about the conspiracy. The master then informed Virginia's Governor, James Monroe (future President of the United States) [1758, Westmoreland County, Virginia, USA; 1831, New

York, New York], who immediately ordered the state militia to act. Prosser and about thirty-five of his comrades were captured, tried, and hanged. The large-scale organization of his abortive revolt shocked many and greatly increased the Southern White population's fear of slaves.

Denmark Vesey [circa 1767, probably St. Thomas, Danish West Indies (now United States Virgin Islands); 1822, Charleston, South Carolina, USA] was a self-educated Black man who in 1822 planned the most extensive slave revolt in North American history in Charleston, South Carolina. Sold as a boy in 1781 to a Bermuda slaver captain named Joseph Vesey, young Denmark, who assumed his owner's surname, followed him on many trips and in 1783 settled with him in Charleston.

In 1800, Vesey won fifteen hundred dollars in a street lottery and used six hundred of it to purchase his freedom. He worked as a carpenter in Charleston and achieved local notoriety for his preaching against slavery, mostly to African American audiences. Charleston at the time had a sizable free African American population. He resented, however, the continued enslavement of his children who had all been born of a slave mother. He read anti-slavery literature and was familiar with the great Haitian slave uprising of the 1790s, having been in Haiti with his master helping French colonials flee the slave revolt. He was dissatisfied with his second class status as a free Black man and determined to help relieve the far more oppressive conditions of slaves he knew.

To this end, he began in 1821 to plan and organize a revolt of city and plantation Blacks. The plot called for the rebels to attack arsenals and guardhouses, seize their weapons, kill all Whites, burn and destroy the city, and free the slaves. Two to nine thousand Blacks may have been involved. The insurrection was precluded when a loyal Black house servant, alerted White authorities on the eve of the June 16, 1822 scheduled outbreak. Subsequent massive military preparations by the authorities doomed the planned insurrection. At first, only ten slaves were arrested. Their testimony, however, led to the arrest of Vesey and many others during the next few months. In all, approximately one hundred and thirty Blacks were captured and arrested. Vesey confessed nothing, saying that he had nothing to gain by freeing slaves. In the trials that followed, sixty-seven were convicted of trying to plot an uprising. Thirty-five of these, including

Vesey, were executed by hanging, and about thirty-five others were sold to West Indian plantation owners. In addition, four White men were fined and jailed for encouraging the conspiracy.

Less than ten years following Denmark Vesey's unsuccessful insurrection, a Black slave named Nat Turner [1800, Southampton County, Virginia, USA; 1831, Jerusalem, Virginia] instigated and led the most important American slave revolt ever. Turner, born the week before Gabriel was hanged, was the property of a prosperous small plantation owner in a remote area of Virginia. His mother was an African native who transmitted a passionate abhorrence of slavery to her son and encouraged him to become educated. The son of one of his owners taught him to read and write, and he enthusiastically embraced intensive religious training. In the early 1820s, he was sold to a neighboring farmer of modest means and learned carpentry. During the following decade, he became known as a forceful preacher whose religious zeal tended to approach fanaticism. He became convinced that he had been chosen by God to lead his people to freedom. He knew that God in the Old Testament often worked through acts of violence and protected his chosen people in the same way. Turner believed he was an avenging messiah and would justify his actions accordingly. He began to exert a powerful influence on many of the nearby slaves who called him "the Prophet".

In 1831, he was sold to an artisan named Joseph Travis. Shortly thereafter, a sign in the form of an eclipse of the Sun caused Turner to believe that the time had come to strike. His plan was to seize the arsenal at the county seat of Jerusalem, gather recruits, and continue on thirty miles to the east to the Great Dismal Swamp. The Swamp was a marshy region along the Coastal Plain of Southeastern Virginia and Northeastern North Carolina where Turner presupposed capture would be difficult. On the night of August 21, along with seven other slaves whom he trusted, Turner embarked on a violent campaign, murdering Travis and his family in their sleep and then setting forth on a bloody march of annihilation toward Jerusalem. In two days and nights, approximately sixty White people were mercilessly killed. Ill-fated from the start, Turner's uprising was handicapped by lack of discipline among his followers and by the fact that, in the end, only seventy-five African Americans joined his revolt. Armed resistance from the local Whites and the arrival of three thousand state militia ended the insurrection. Only a short distance from the county seat the rebels were dispersed and either slain or arrested. An unknown number of Blacks were lynched in revenge by White mobs and many other innocent slaves were slaughtered in the panic that followed. Turner eluded his pursuers for six weeks but was finally arrested, tried, hanged, and skinned.

Turner's rebellion quickly put an end to the White Southern myth that slaves were either contented with their situation or too submissive to organize an armed insurrection. Following the uprising, Turner's name became vilified by White Southerners but revered by slaves. Throughout Southampton County, Blacks came to remember the revolt as Old Nat's War or Nat's Fray. Henceforth, in African American churches throughout the country, the name Jerusalem referred not only to the Bible but also surreptitiously to the place where the brave rebel slave hero had met his death. In 1832, an account of the event, based on Turner's 1831 prison confessions, was published under the title: *Confessions of Nat Turner, Leader of the Late Insurrection in Southampton, Virginia, As Fully and Voluntarily Made to Thomas R. Grey*.

Turner's rebellion turned out to be the only effective sustained slave insurrection in American history. It spread terror throughout the White South, and brought about dire results for the general slave population. Following the insurrection, the Virginia legislature held a long session to debate the possible end of slavery. All proposed laws advocating the abolition of slavery, however, were defeated. Instead, Turner's actions launched a new wave of oppressive Southern legislation outlawing the education, movement, and assembly of slaves. Hardened pro-slavery, anti-abolitionist views persisted in that area until the Civil War. The movement to abolish slavery, which had previously enjoyed some support in the South, henceforth became a Northern phenomenon. Some Northern abolitionists viewed Turner's rebellion as the beginning of the end of slavery, while others believed it was a preview of the violence to come. (Nat Turner has been most widely popularized by William Styron in his 1967 novel *The Confessions of Nat Turner*, for which he won the Pulitzer Prize for literature.)

Multiple false rumors, usually exaggerated by the Southern newspapers of the 1840s and 50s, insisted that large-scale slave revolts led by White infiltrators and outside agitators were imminent.

Southerners feared that White blood would be spilled and Black kingdoms would be established throughout the South. Tensions rose and panic surfaced as paranoid Whites violently reacted against Blacks, accusing them of plotting these phantom conspiracies. This prevailing fear of possible slave insurrections did much to unsettle White Southerners and add to the growing tensions before the Civil War.

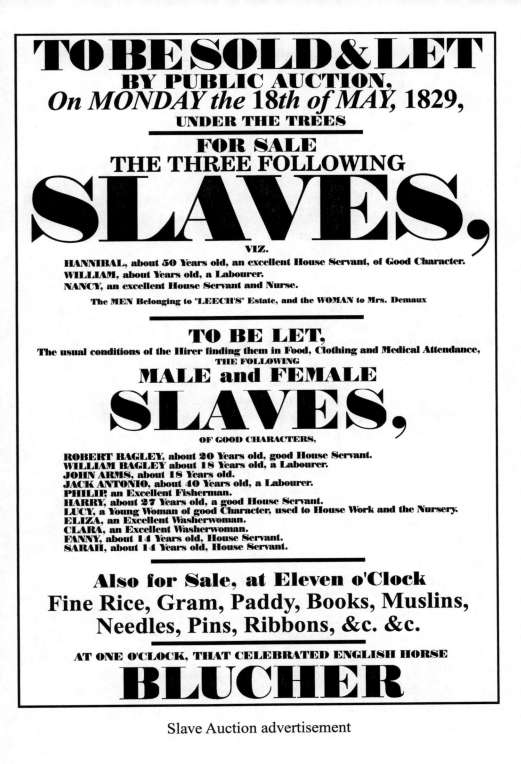

Slave Auction advertisement

5. ABOLITIONISM

During the eighteenth and nineteenth centuries in Western Europe and the Americas, the movement dedicated to eliminating slavery, and, mainly responsible for creating the right conditions needed for ending the transatlantic slave trade and chattel slavery, was Abolitionism; also known as the abolition movement. Despite its cruelty and inhumanity, the slave system provoked little protest until the 1700s. Rationalist thinkers of the Enlightenment began to denounce it for its violation of the rights of man. Quaker, Mennonite Christians, and other evangelical religious groups criticized it on the grounds of Christian charity, based on the higher divine law of God.

By the late 1700s, moral disapproval of slavery was widespread as slavery was being vehemently denounced, directly and indirectly, from several international sources. During this period, anti-slavery reformers began to formally organize into groups eager to change the emotional climate and convert the hearts of men and women; and in so doing transform the prevalent social morays and laws of the land. Abolitionism as an organized movement began in Britain in the 1780s. In England, abolitionists worked to end the international slave trade and to free slaves in the British colonies. Slavery had never flourished in Britain itself. On the other hand, many British people had become rich through the slave trade. Aware that their fellow countrymen transported the greatest number of African slaves to the New World, the British abolitionists concentrated their efforts against the slave trade instead of slavery itself. They felt that the cessation of the trade would eventually lead to the termination of the institution.

English scholar Granville Sharp [1735, Durham, England; 1813, Fulham, London] was an early advocate of the abolition of slavery in Britain. Sharp was an philanthropist in the true sense of its' eighteenth century definition, that is, humanitarian in spirit while not necessarily involving monetary donations. As a humanist, he became involved in litigation with the master of a slave called Jonathan Strong. In 1767, the tribunal held that a slave remained in law the property of his owner even on English territory. Sharp devoted himself to overturning this judgment both with his writings and in the courts of law. It was eventually established in another important case he later took up – the case of James Somersett – that as soon as any slave set foot upon English soil, he or she became free. Sharp thus secured a legal decision in 1772 stating that Caribbean planters could not hold slaves in Britain, since slavery was contrary to English law. This decision, however, did not include slaves held in Britain's colonies. Although the decision only freed slaves who found themselves in Britain, it immediately affected the more than fifteen thousand slaves brought into Britain by their colonial owners. American slaves gained hope upon hearing this news, and some slaves even attempted to reach Britain as stowaways on transatlantic ships.

Sharp's untiring efforts for the abolition of slavery continued and eventually led to his founding of a society for the abolition of slavery in 1787. In that same year, Sharp helped settle about four hundred freed Black American slaves on African land where Freetown, Sierra Leone now stands. Land was obtained through negotiations with a local Black leader. The settlers suffered many hardships including hunger, disease, and warfare. The settlement almost died out before the Sierra Leone Company assumed responsibility in 1791 and replenished the colony with new settlers, including over twelve hundred Canadian Blacks who departed from Nova Scotia in early 1792. When Britain eventually made the slave trade illegal for its citizens in 1807, it viewed Freetown as a desirable base for naval operations against such trade. Consequently, in 1808, Sierra Leone was made a crown colony and British influence gradually spread inland. The British then forcibly freed captives from the slave ships of many nations, and settled them in the colony.

In 1821, Freetown became the seat of government for all of Britain's West Africa possessions, a position it retained until 1874. By 1850, more than fifty thousand former slaves, originally from many parts of Africa, had resettled there. The provision of churches and schools helped mold a common African Creole culture. In 1896, the British established a protectorate over an area that had almost the same borders as present-day Sierra Leone. Freetown became the nation's capital in 1961, the year of Sierra Leone's independence.

British anti-slavery attitudes had little consequence on the centers of slavery in the Caribbean. Turning their attention to these areas, British abolitionists began working in the late 1700s to prohibit the importation of African slaves into the British colonies. Under their leadership they succeeded in getting the slave trade to the British colonies, including Canada, abolished in 1807.

British politician, orator, reformer, and philanthropist William Wilberforce [1759, Hull, Yorkshire, England; 1833, London], was prominent from 1787 in the struggle to eradicate the slave trade and later to abolish slavery itself in British foreign territories. Educated at the University of Cambridge, Wilberforce's anti-slavery views were derived in part from evangelical Christianity, which he embraced in 1784. In 1780, he entered Parliament and became a leading Tory, noted for his eloquence. In 1787, he aided in the founding of the Society For Effecting The Abolition Of The Slave Trade, more commonly called the Anti-Slavery Society. Two years later, he spearheaded his first political campaign against the British slave trade. He also became the recognized leader and chief spokesman of the Clapham Sect.

The Clapham Sect was a group of wealthy evangelical Christians prominent in England from about 1790 to 1830. They campaigned for social reforms, including the abolition of slavery, and encouraged missionary work at home and abroad. The group was based at the Anglican Church of Clapham in South London. Its members included Wilberforce and many other members of the British Parliament. Their advocacy of various liberal issues and causes branded them with the sarcastic nickname of "Saints". They were responsible in large measure for the abolition of the slave trade and slavery in Great Britain.

In the British House of Commons, Wilberforce was a persuasive and persevering patron of anti-slavery legislation. A bill to end the slave trade passed in the House of Commons in 1792 but failed in the House of Lords. He achieved his first success in 1807, when a bill to abolish the slave trade in the British West Indies, Canada, and throughout the British Empire, became law. This statute, however, did not change the legal status of individuals enslaved prior to its enactment. In 1821, Wilberforce resumed the struggle with a call for the immediate emancipation of all slaves. Two years later, he helped organize and became a vice-president of the Society For The Mitigation And Gradual Abolition Of Slavery Throughout The British Dominions, more commonly called the British And Foreign Anti-Slavery Society. In 1825, Wilberforce retired from the House of Commons and turned over the parliamentary leadership of the abolition movement. In retirement, he continued to support the campaign against the foreign slave trade. The Emancipation Bill, or Slavery Abolition Act, he had long sought for was finally enacted one month after his death in 1833. This law abolished slavery and emancipated all slaves in Canada and throughout the British Empire. In order to facilitate the transitional period, compensation to owners of slaves was offered and apprenticeship arrangements were provided for the former slaves.

One of the first effective publicists of the British movement against slavery and the slave trade in the British colonies was abolitionist Thomas Clarkson [1760, Wisbech, Cambridgeshire, England; 1846, Ipswich, Suffolk]. Clarkson was an English cleric, but from 1785, he devoted his life to abolishing the slave trade. His 1786 publication entitled, "An Essay on the Slavery and Commerce of the Human Species", brought him into close contact with several opponents of slavery including Granville Sharp, William Wilberforce, and Josiah Wedgwood [1730, Burslem, Staffordshire, England; 1795, Etruria]. (Wedgwood was a famous English ceramic artist. As a potter, he became a leader in that industry during the greatest period of British pottery making. His works were among the finest examples of ceramic art. Wedgwood's daughter Susannah was the mother of Charles Darwin, making him the grandfather of the celebrated British naturalist.)

In 1787, Clarkson joined other leading abolitionists in forming the Anti-Slavery Society. The Society recruited Wilberforce as its parliamentary spokesperson and in 1788 succeeded in getting Prime Minister William Pitt [1759, Hayes, Kent, England; 1806, Putney], also known as William Pitt the Younger, to set up a select committee of the Privy Council to investigate the slave trade. During the previous year, the Society had achieved many successes including the establishment of Sierra Leone, created in part as a refuge for impoverished London Blacks. In 1792, Clarkson organized and journeyed with the Black settlers who sailed from Nova Scotia to join the fledgling West African settlement.

Clarkson visited several British ports to collect evidence of the causes and effects of slavery for his 1787 pamphlet, *A Summary View Of The Slave Trade And Of The Probable Consequences Of Its Abolition*. The facts that he collected were used in the anti-slavery parliamentary campaign led by Wilberforce. Limited progress was made during the early years of Britain's wars (1789-1815) with

Revolutionary and Napoleonic France. Many Parliamentarians believed that the slave trade provided essential wealth for Britain and valuable training for its' navy. When the 1807 law for the abolition of the slave trade finally was enacted, Clarkson's two-volume history of the trade was published. In part due to Clarkson's persistent efforts, Britain was joined, in 1815, by other European powers in officially condemning the trade. At the 1818 Congress of Aix-la-Chapelle, the nations that defeated France held meetings in order to help preserve the international peace established earlier by the Congress of Vienna at the end of the wars in 1815. During these meetings, however, measures for enforcing abolition of the slave trade were discussed without effect.

In 1823, Clarkson joined British politician and philanthropist Sir Thomas Fowell Buxton [1786, Castle Hedingham, Essex, England; 1845, near Cromer, Norfolk] and others, including William Wilberforce, in founding the British And Foreign Anti-Slavery Society. In 1825, Buxton succeeded Wilberforce as the House of Commons leader for the abolition of slavery in the British colonies. It was in this capacity that Buxton was partly responsible for the Abolition Act of 1833. Both he and Wilberforce were later honored by Canadian abolitionists when two early Black settlements were named after them.

The ideas Buxton expressed in his 1839 publication, *The African Slave Trade And Its Remedy*, convinced the British government to send an expedition in 1841 to the Niger River Delta. (Africa's third-longest river, the Niger flows through West Africa to empty into the Gulf of Guinea in present-day coastal Western Nigeria.) The expedition's goals were to make anti-slave trade treaties with the tribes of the area, to engage in other different kinds of trade, and to establish a missionary headquarters. The expedition suffered many deaths from disease and fever and was soon recalled. Although Buxton did not accompany the group, his own health was irreversibly damaged by the stress and anguish caused by the failure of the project.

Perhaps one of the most dramatic conversions to Abolitionism in Britain is that of Reverend John Newton [1725, Wapping, London, England; 1807]. Born the son of a commander of a merchant ship that sailed the Mediterranean, his mother died when he was 6 years old, and he had a rather unhappy life when sent away to school. Newton was eleven when he first went to sea with his father and made six voyages with him before the elder Newton retired.

While on shore leave in England, he met fourteen years old Mary Catlett, whom he called Polly. She enchanted him and remained in his thoughts throughout his adventures. Because of his overlong stay at her house on one of his visits in 1744, he was seized and impressed into service on a man-of-war, the H.M.S. Harwich. Finding conditions on board intolerable, he deserted. He was soon recaptured, however, and publicly flogged and demoted from midshipman to an ordinary seaman. At his own request, he was later exchanged for a merchant seaman and so returned to a life in maritime trade on a slave ship.

While buying slaves on the West African coast, near Sierra Leone, he had an argument with his employer and was made a servant of the slave trader. While working on a plantation, he received brutal treatment at the hands of his owner's wife. He was eventually rescued and returned to England in 1747 by a sea captain who had known his father.

In 1748, he became captain of his own slave ship. Once more at sea, he was caught up in a violent storm on a homeward voyage that led to his first prayers since his mother's death. This started the spiritual journey that would culminate in his Evangelism. Although he had had some early religious instruction from his mother, he had long since given up any religious convictions. His ship was spared during the severe storm convincing him that his prayers for help were answered. Later he reflected on what had happened and became convinced that God had helped him through the storm and that grace had begun to work for him. As a direct result of this Damascus-experience, Newton decided to henceforth subject his will to a higher power and devote his life to God. For the rest of his life, he observed the anniversary of his conversion. Although he continued in the slave trade for a time after his conversion, he was filled with contrition and saw to it that the slaves under his care were treated humanely.

In 1750, he finally married his childhood sweetheart Mary Catlett. They had no children. After a serious illness, he gave up seafaring in 1755. During his days as a sailor, he had begun to educate himself, learning Latin and other subjects. For the next five years, Newton was surveyor of tides, or Customs Officer, at Liverpool. There he came to know George Whitefield, deacon in the Church of England, evangelistic preacher, and leader of the Calvinistic Methodist Church.

Newton became Whitefield's enthusiastic disciple. During this period Newton also met and came to admire John Wesley [1703, Epworth, Lincolnshire, England; 1791, London], founder of Methodism.

Newton's self-education continued, and he learned Greek, Hebrew, and Theology. In 1764, he wrote of his adventure-filled experiences as a master of a slave ship in his autobiography, *An Authentic Narrative*. Later that year he decided to become a minister in the Church of England, and applied to the Archbishop of York for ordination. The Archbishop refused his request, but Newton persisted in his goal and was soon after ordained by the Bishop of Lincoln. He then accepted the curacy of Olney, Buckinghamshire. Newton quickly became a noted evangelical preacher and his church became so crowded during services that it had to be enlarged. He preached not only in Olney but also in other parts of the country.

In 1767, the poet William Cowper settled at Olney, and he and Newton quickly became friends. Cowper helped Newton with his religious services. They held not only a regular weekly church service but also began a series of weekly prayer meetings, for which their goal was to write a new hymn for each one. They collaborated on several editions of *Olney Hymns*, which achieved lasting popularity. The first edition, published in 1779, contained two hundred and eighty pieces by Newton including the world-famous hymn that celebrates his amazing transformation, "Amazing Grace".

Composed between 1760 and 1770 in Olney, "Amazing Grace" was possibly one of the hymns written for a weekly service. Although the hymn was not originally entitled "Amazing Grace", it later came to be known under that name. Through the years, other writers have composed additional verses to the hymn and possibly, verses from other Newton hymns have been added. The origin of the melody is unknown. Most hymnals attribute it to an early American folk melody, while others speculate that it may have originated as the tune of a song the slaves sang.

Newton was not only a prolific hymn writer but also kept extensive journals and wrote many letters. Historians accredit his journals and letters for much of what is known today about the slave trade during the 1700s. He also wrote some important theological works on Methodism.

In 1780, Newton left Olney to become rector of St. Mary Woolnoth, St. Mary Woolchurch, in London. There, he drew large congregations and influenced many people who would later crusade for the abolition of slavery, including William Wilberforce. Newton occupied part of his later life with work in the anti-slavery movement, becoming a confirmed abolitionist. He also toured the prisons in the Southampton area offering comfort to inmates. He continued to preach until the last year of life, although he was blind by that time.

By the mid-nineteenth century, most European nations had done away with slavery, save a few exceptions. Beginning in the fifteenth century, Hungarian and Romanian nobles, who needed laborers for their large estates, forced many Gypsies or Roma into slavery. In Romania, the enslavement of Gypsies did not end until 1855. Ironically, Great Britain, one of the key European powers that began and profited from the slave trade, became a leader in its demise. The abolition of slavery throughout Great Britain and its Empire in 1834 placed the British people and government at the forefront of the growing worldwide abolitionist movement. This international movement would eventually include most of the European powers and groups such as the Anti-Slavery Society of France. During the decades leading up to the Civil War, abolitionists worldwide exacted serious and constant pressure on the slaveholding policies of the United States government.

The tensions caused by slavery in the United States had already become apparent by the American Revolution, but they increased considerably in the nineteenth century, right up until the Civil War. The situation in the United States was more complex than elsewhere because slavery was a domestic rather than a colonial phenomenon. It had gradually developed into being the social and economic base of the plantation systems of eleven Southern states. Moreover, slavery had gained new vigor when highly profitable cotton based agriculture developed in the South in the early 1800s. Reacting to abolitionist attacks that labeled its peculiar institution as cruel and immoral, the South had intensified its system of slave control, especially after the Nat Turner revolt of 1831. By that time, American abolitionists recognized the failure of gradual persuasion. They subsequently turned to a more militant policy by calling for immediate abolition by law.

Quaker and Mennonite traditions, evangelical revivalism, and emancipation in Northern states from 1776 to 1827, all sparked interest in Abolitionism in the United States. (The state of Vermont was the first to outlaw human bondage in 1777.) The abolitionists differed from those of moderate anti-slavery feelings in that they called for an immediate cessation to slavery. The most zealous abolitionists refused to accept the validity of any laws that recognized slavery as an institution. They systematically violated the fugitive slave laws by organizing and operating the covert Underground Railroad, which hid and transported escaped slaves to the American free states and Canada. The activities and propaganda of the abolitionists made slavery a national issue. The movement, however, was both severely discredited in conservative Northern areas and fiercely opposed in the South.

William Lloyd Garrison

6.   AMERICAN ABOLITIONISTS

When Thomas Jefferson wrote the Declaration of Independence and included the words, "We hold these truths to be self-evident, that all men are created equal", some believe he fully expected the eventual abolition of that peculiar institution that was American slavery. Slavery would thrive for another eighty-seven years after 1776, and Jefferson himself would die a slave-owner. But the words and obvious implications of the Declaration of Independence need to be closely considered as one contemplates the century of bondage that endured despite a nation's founding document that invokes principles utterly inconsistent with human slavery.

From the beginnings of slavery in America, the practice had its detractors. During the 1700s the Religious Society of Friends, whose members are commonly called Quakers, and a few other Whites actively opposed the institution. One of the earliest American abolitionists was George Wythe [1726, Yorktown or Black River, Elizabeth City County, Virginia, USA; 1806, Richmond]. Wythe was a politician, jurist, Revolutionary patriot, signer of the Declaration of Independence, and early educational mentor to Thomas Jefferson. Unlike Jefferson, Wythe freed his own slaves and provided for them in his will. Men like Wythe, however, were often the exception to the rule.

The American Revolution's rhetoric of universal natural rights, including the right to freedom, called slavery into serious question. On the eve of the Revolution, the American colonies held five hundred thousand souls in bondage. Over five thousand African Americans fought along side the colonists expecting freedom as their reward. Upon war's end they were bitterly disappointed when denied their hard fought compensation. In the late eighteenth century, several slave-owning leaders of the American Revolutionary movement spoke out against slavery, including Jefferson and Patrick Henry [1736, Studley, Hanover County, Virginia, USA; 1799, Red Hill estate, near Appomattox and Brookneal]. When he died, George Washington's will provided for the manumission of his slaves upon the death of his wife. Many other Virginians followed suit during the first decades of the nation's independence. During this period, the number of free

Blacks in Virginia went from approximately two thousand to thirty thousand. Slavery and freedom nevertheless continued to exist side by side in the United States.

The abolition movement in the United States began publicly when the Society For The Abolition Of Slavery was formed in Philadelphia in 1775. The Society was lead by two Revolutionary patriots and signers of the Declaration of Independence. Benjamin Franklin [1706, Boston, Massachusetts, USA; Philadelphia, Pennsylvania, 1790] was named president of the Society, and physician Benjamin Rush [1745, Byberry (near Philadelphia), Pennsylvania, USA; 1813] was appointed secretary. In 1787, Franklin was elected president of the Pennsylvania Society For Promoting The Abolition Of Slavery. One of Franklin's last public acts prior to his death was to sign a petition to Congress in 1790 as president of the Society, requesting the abolition of slavery and the suppression of the slave trade. John Jay [1745, New York City, New York, USA; 1829, Bedford], a Revolutionary patriot and the first chief justice of the United States, was the president of the New York Manumission Society formed in 1785.

Following the Revolution, Northern states gradually abolished slavery. Southern evangelicals, along with some of the leading slave-owners of the Upper South, also thought seriously about freeing the slaves. The Virginia Abolition Society was formed in the 1780s to abolish slavery gradually through legislative action and through manumission. Despite these intentions and efforts, slavery flourished and gradually became solidly entrenched throughout the Southern states. At the start of the nineteenth century, America's eight hundred thousand enslaved African Americans outnumbered its one hundred thousand free Blacks. Directly or indirectly, slavery affected almost all Blacks in America. Every free African American seemed to have at least one relative or friend still in bondage.

Like other social reforms of the time, including temperance, women's rights and prison reforms, Abolitionism was initiated among the most radical Northern Whigs and rooted in the middle class religious revivals of the 1820s and 30s. Beginning in 1795 and expanding tremendously through the 1840s, a widespread and intense revival of interest in religion occurred in the United States, a phenomenon known as the Second Great Awakening. The First Great Awakening of the mid-eighteenth century had drawn on strict Calvinist theology, while the Second relied on the more liberal doctrines of Arminianism, which differed greatly to Calvinism by allowing human decisions in the salvation process. Arminianism was an important influence in Methodism. A still more liberal version of Arminianism went into the making of American Unitarianism. Unitarianism was a liberal religious movement that rejected the doctrine of the Holy Trinity. The movement spread throughout New England and the Eastern states, largely as an intellectual revolt from the rigid and dry teachings of Calvinism.

During the Second Great Awakening, preachers traveled the countryside spreading the word of God directly to the people in the spirit of evangelical benevolence, thus, bypassing the pompous church establishment and hierarchy. Bibles and other religious materials were distributed to the masses and interdenominational Sunday schools were started. The Second Awakening led to the founding of colleges and seminaries and to the organization of mission societies to aid the less fortunate. Large outdoor revival meetings took place as religion was given back to common folks. Certain evangelists emphasized free will, divine forgiveness for all, and the need of each person to freely accept or reject salvation.

Many converts naturally took up the cause of Abolitionism as their newly revived Christian duty. Although many Southerners were also reform-minded during this period, they disassociated themselves from the Northern reform movements, believing them to be tainted by Abolitionism.

As early as the 1780s, Blacks in Northern cities established hundreds of mutual aid and relief societies, churches, and fraternal organizations. Cooperative associations provided benefits for burials and support for widows, orphans, the ill, and the jobless. This help was generally denied to Blacks by White charitable missions. One of the first examples of such African American led groups was the Free African Society founded in 1787. Its co-founder was Richard Allen [1760, Philadelphia; Pennsylvania, USA; 1831], a pioneering Black abolitionist clergyman who later gained prominence as the co-founder of the first African Methodist Episcopal (AME) Church.

Soon after Allen was born, to enslaved parents, the family was sold to a farmer living near Dover, Delaware. There, Allen grew to adulthood and at seventeen, he became a Methodist convert. At twenty-two, he was permitted to preach. After the American

Revolution, Allen traveled through the Eastern states preaching to Blacks and Whites alike. In 1784, at the first general conference of the Methodist Episcopal Church at Baltimore, Allen was considered a talented candidate for the new denomination's ministry and was thus ordained as a Methodist minister. He succeeded in converting his owner, who allowed him to hire out his time. By cutting wood and working in a brickyard, Allen earned the money to buy his freedom in 1786 and went to Philadelphia where he joined St. George's Methodist Episcopal Church. There, he preached to the racially mixed congregation. As the number of African American worshipers increased, they were segregated and eventually denied their customary seats. One day, they were restricted to the gallery. When Allen and several others protested by kneeling to pray at the front of the gallery, they were forcibly moved back by several White parishioners. Rather than submit to further humiliation, they walked out of the church.

This episode of blatant racism prompted Allen and his followers, known as Allenites, to raise money to build an independent Methodist church for Black members. In 1787 he and his supporters, including Benjamin Rush, turned an old blacksmith shop into the first congregation of what would later become the AME Church.

Churches were among the first African American organizations established in Black communities. They were the central institutions serving each community's sacred, political, and social needs. Despite White opposition, some independent African American churches were organized in the South, generally with both free and enslaved members but with free clergymen. In the 1770s, early churches were established in the state of Georgia near the cities of Augusta and Savannah.

In Philadelphia during the 1790s, Richard Allen dedicated Saint Thomas Protestant Episcopal Church and the Bethel, meaning House of God, AME Church respectively. Mother Bethel, as it was commonly called, was one of the nation's largest Methodist congregations, with thirteen hundred members by 1810. Other African American congregations joined it in 1816 and won complete separation from the Protestant Episcopal Church. Together, these united Black congregations legally established the African Methodist Episcopal Church. African American Methodists from the Middle Atlantic states of New York, New Jersey, Delaware, and Maryland named itinerant minister Richard Allen the first bishop of this newly formed Protestant denomination. Other early African American churches included New York's African Methodist Episcopal Zion Church established in 1796, the Abyssinian Baptist Church founded in 1808, and Boston's African Baptist Church dedicated in 1805.

As bishop of the AME Church, a post he held until his death, Allen strove to make the Church a unifying force among American Blacks. He also intensified his efforts as an abolitionist and humanitarian. In 1792 and 1793, Allen helped organize Philadelphia's African Americans to nurse and bury yellow-fever victims. In 1830, he gathered forty delegates from free Black communities for the First National Negro Convention, which addressed African American concerns. The Convention adopted aggressive positions and denounced attempts to colonize American Blacks in Africa. It advocated slave rebellions, an end to segregation policies, and the boycotting of slave produced goods.

The United States prohibited the importation of slaves in 1808, though widespread smuggling continued until about 1862. With this victory, anti-slavery forces then focused on winning the emancipation of Blacks already in slavery on American soil. The upper Southern states of Maryland and Virginia, whose economies no longer needed all of its bondpeople, provided slaves to the new Western territories and to the deep Southern states. This kept the domestic slave trade flourishing. By this time, most Northern states had outlawed slavery, but the growing population of free Blacks within their borders caused serious anxieties. Freeing the slaves was one thing, what to do with them was another. This issue was hotly debated in concerned circles.

In 1816, a group of prominent White citizens, including slaveholders, founded the American Colonization Society, or AMS, in Washington, D.C. With support from the federal government, its mission was to re-settle free Blacks in Africa. Other groups advocated deportation to Latin America or the American West. Few, however, including the federal government, recommended full integration into American society.

The AMS would list amongst it's members: future President Andrew Jackson [1767, Waxhaw settlement, on the border between North and South Carolina, USA; 1845, Hermitage, Nashville, Tennessee]; author of the "Star-Spangled Banner", Francis Scott Key [1779, Frederick County, Maryland, USA; 1843, Baltimore]; and, James Monroe, fifth President (1817-1825) of the United States and the last of the so-called Virginia dynasty of American Presidents. Like many citizens of his time, Monroe believed the solution to the slavery problem was the colonization of freed bondpeople outside the boundaries of the United States. He supported and enforced an 1819 law that provided for the return to Africa of Blacks illegally captured and brought to the United States. He backed the activities of the AMS, which had acquired land in Africa, named it Liberia, and resettled freed Blacks there. In recognition of Monroe's support, the Liberian capital was named Monrovia, after him, in 1824.

The British orchestrated the first attempt for a West African colony for former slaves in 1787 at Saint George's Bay in present-day Sierra Leone. After it failed, a second attempt was made by British abolitionists, who, in 1792, founded Freetown in the same area. The example of Sierra Leone appealed to Americans interested in Black colonization, and in early 1822 the American Colonization Society succeeded in establishing its colony, Liberia, at nearby Cape Mesurado.

Prominent politicians and clergymen argued that Africans had been degraded in the United States, and even if emancipated, could never attain true full citizenship. The American Colonization Society's proposed solution to send free Blacks to the colony of Liberia seemed logical to many. There, it was hoped that manumitted Blacks might establish their own nation.

Although Blacks had long dreamed of returning to their homeland or ancestral continent, most African Americans were suspicious, rejecting the "back to Africa" movement and idea. Some argued that the intent of this organization was less to liberate slaves than to deport free African Americans. Understanding this, most Free Blacks opposed returning to Africa. Still, by 1827, the Society had taken over fourteen hundred volunteers, mostly free Blacks from the Upper South, to Liberia. By the Civil War, over fourteen thousand African Americans had emigrated there. Although the colonization of West Africa attracted more Black Americans than emigrated elsewhere except for Canada, it remained unpopular among Blacks because of its distance from the United States, its sponsorship by Whites, and its high sickness and mortality rates.

The first American publications totally devoted to abolishing slavery were written by Elihu Embree, a slave-owner living in the slave state of Tennessee. Embree demanded the abolition of slavery in a weekly newspaper published in 1819 in Jonesborough, and later in the monthly magazine that appeared in 1820, *The Emancipator*. It was not until the 1830s, however, that significant numbers of middle class Northerners began to campaign for the immediate emancipation of slaves and for their acceptance as equals into American society. Not all Northerners, however, supported the idea. Although slavery had been abolished throughout the Northern states, it remained economically important to them. Many New Yorkers were especially unsympathetic to abolitionists. The lucrative slave trade had used New York City as a port of entry before 1808, and Southern cotton was shipped in and out of the port up until the Civil War. Northern banks financed the cotton trade, while insurance and shipbuilding companies in the North had large stakes in the industry. Despite this type of resistance, or more often general indifference, the movement nevertheless slowly gained favor.

One of the key persons who began the abolitionist movement in the United States was the aggressive agitator, publisher, and social campaigner William Lloyd Garrison [1805, Newburyport, Massachusetts, USA; 1879, New York City]. Founder of the American Anti-Slavery Society, Garrison was a journalistic crusader who started a newspaper in Boston called *The Liberator*, which soon became the leading mouthpiece of American Abolitionism. His lifelong unwavering dedication to the cause helped lead the eventual successful abolitionist campaign against slavery in the United States. He became, to many of his time, the personification of the American abolitionist movement.

Garrison was the son of a wandering alcoholic Canadian seaman who abandoned his family when Garrison was two years old. He spent his childhood in abject poverty with his mother, a midwife, who reared him as a Baptist and inspired him with her knowledge of biblical verse. Garrison spent a few years in grammar school but was mostly self-educated. Indentured at the age of thirteen to the owner of the Newburyport Herald, he learned a trade and became an expert printer, compositor, and typesetter. As a printer working with machines, he referred to himself as a mechanic or craftsman. During his youth, he was influenced by Christian benevolence and became socially politicized and sympathized with the struggles of oppressed peoples for freedom. At age twenty-five he joined the abolitionist movement and embarked on a lifelong commitment.

Garrison attempted to arouse Northerners from their apathy on the issue of American slavery in articles written anonymously or under the pseudonym Aristides, in the *Herald* and other newspapers. In 1828-29, he further developed his views on the question of moral and social reform as editor of two newspapers – the world's first temperance paper, Boston's *National Philanthropist*, and the *Journal of the Times* published in Bennington, Vermont. In 1829, Garrison became partners with the itinerant Quaker abolitionist and editor Benjamin Lundy [1789, Hardwick, Sussex County, New Jersey, USA; 1839, Lowell, Illinois]. Lundy had been a saddlemaker who settled in Ohio in 1815. In 1821, he founded *The Genius Of Universal Emancipation*, an abolitionist journal that circulated principally among Scotch-Irish, Moravian, and Quaker freeholders in the Upper South. In 1828, he persuaded Garrison to become a coeditor of the journal and thus was the person responsible for enlisting Garrison to the cause of Abolitionism. Together they published their monthly periodical in Baltimore, Maryland.

As a pioneer of the anti-slavery movement in the United States, Lundy founded the abolitionist Union Humane Society in St. Clairsville, Ohio, in 1815. He organized other anti-slavery groups and published the *National Enquirer* and other periodicals. He also lectured and traveled widely, speaking against the expansion of slavery. He even journeyed to Southern Ontario to investigate the conditions faced by the newly settled fugitive slaves in the community of Wilberforce. He printed a detailed diary of the trip in his newspaper in 1832.

Lundy believed in gradual emancipation or gradualism, and Garrison at first shared his moderate views. Garrison quickly became convinced, however, that immediate and complete emancipation was necessary. His eloquent indictments of the slave trade aroused bitter acrimony in Baltimore, then a center of the domestic slave trade in the United States. He became a victim of political repression and was sued for libel by a Newburyport merchant slave trader who was engaged in the coastal slave trade. Garrison was fined, and, without money to pay the fine, was jailed for forty-seven days. This episode marked his young life and solidified his position as a martyr. After his release from prison, he ended his partnership with Lundy and returned to New

England. Lundy spent his last years in fruitless negotiations with the Mexican government, hoping to open areas of Texas for settlement by emancipated slaves.

In partnership with another abolitionist, Isaac Knapp, Garrison, by then a young man in his mid-twenties, launched a weekly newspaper called *The Liberator* in Boston on the first day of January 1831. The newspaper became the leading voice of American Abolitionism and the most uncompromising of American anti-slavery journals until it ended its mission in 1865. For years it was America's most influential anti-slavery periodical in the pre-Civil War period and was widely regarded as an authoritative voice of radical Yankee social reform in general. *The Liberator* had a circulation of approximately three thousand – of which three out of four subscribers were Black – but influenced a much wider audience. Editions were often made available for the perusal of citizens at town libraries, barbershops, and other public places. It was a sterling example of a personal newspaper dedicated to one man's vision and his unyielding espousal of immediate emancipation for the millions of Black slaves kept in bondage throughout the South.

The abolition movement gradually spread throughout the Northern states despite bitter and violent opposition by Southern slave-owners and Northerners who favored slavery. Owners considered slaves valuable economic assets, making voluntary manumission unthinkable. Garrison was profoundly convinced that slavery had to be abolished by the use of moral persuasion or "moral suasion". His core weapons were two documents, the Bible, and the American Declaration of Independence. He generally insisted that slavery would be abolished only when the mass of White Americans experienced a revolution in conscience or moral regeneration. Therefore, he crusaded for sustained programs of agitation that aimed to convert grass-roots public opinion in favor of Black emancipation and race equality. He appealed through *The Liberator* and through his speeches, especially those to the ecclesiastic authorities and clergy, for a practical and logical application of Christianity in demanding freedom for the slaves. His campaign created great opposition. In 1831, the state of Georgia offered a reward of five thousand dollars for his arrest and conviction under Georgia law. He also received a large quantity of abusive letters, several of which threatened him with assassination. Some Northerners objected to what they considered his extremist tactics. They also feared that the Southern planters might cut off the cotton supply for the textile industry. In 1835, Garrison's life was endangered by a lynch mob in front of Boston's Faneuil Hall, and, the Governor of Massachusetts considered extraditing him to Georgia on charges of sedition. Three years later he attended the National Anti-Slavery Convention Of American Women at the newly built Pennsylvania Hall in Philadelphia. The building was burned by a mob on the third day of the event. This episode publicly revealed to the nation that many Northerners were bent on preserving, throughout the free states, the idea of White supremacy and establishing strict criteria of "Whiteness" when it came to societal advantages and privileges, such as the right to vote and employment. In fact, many upper class Northerners, were connected in some way with the slavocracy of the South, by marriage, kinship, friendship, or inheritance.

In the North, Garrison's message of moral persuasion challenged moderate reformers to apply the principles of the Declaration of Independence to all people, regardless of skin color and race. Fearful slave-owners in the South, mistakenly assuming that *The Liberator* represented the majority opinion of Northerners, reacted militantly by defending slavery's positive qualities, as viewed by them. They also called for the enactment of stricter legislative measures to suppress all conceivable opposition to their peculiar institution.

Garrison's publication continued to change the direction of the American anti-slavery movement by insisting that abolition, rather than African colonization, was the answer to the problem of slavery. Like most of the abolitionists he recruited, Garrison was a convert from the American Colonization Society that was advocating the return of free Blacks to Africa. He now rejected colonization as a false reform and instead adhered to the principle of Immediatism, borrowed from English abolitionists, which was based on the concept of immediate emancipation. Immediatism condemned slavery as a national sin, called for its immediate eradication, and proposed plans for incorporating the freed slaves into American society.

Through *The Liberator*, which circulated widely both in England and the United States, Garrison quickly attained international recognition as the most radical of American anti-slavery advocates. He attacked, without mercy, Northern racism and segregation policies in schools, on trains, and other public places. He viewed integration of the races in the free North as a stepping stone towards full emancipation in the South. To Garrison's dismay, several Northern states were reacting harshly towards the increasing free Black population. Legislators passed strict laws, known as Black Codes, which limited the freedom of these Blacks to attend church, schools, carry firearms, vote, hold public office, sit on juries, and marry Whites. Some Codes even prohibited the entry of any new free Blacks into state territory.

In 1832, Garrison helped to organize the New England Anti-Slavery Society, the first such society in America. This organization and its evangelical reformers strongly believed that moral free will and Christian charity would eventually triumph against the forces of cruelty and power. The next year in Philadelphia, after a trip to England where he enlisted the aid of abolitionist sympathizers, Garrison played a primary role in creating the national American Anti-Slavery Society (1833-70). He helped organize the Society with delegates from similar state and local societies. He wrote its Declaration of Sentiments and served as its first corresponding secretary. He was also the Society's long lasting president from 1843 until 1865.

The American Anti-Slavery Society promoted the cause of immediate emancipation of slaves in the United States and acted as the main activist organ of the American abolition movement. The Society was the most militant of all the anti-slavery organizations to follow. The new movement's supporters included free Northern Blacks, and educated White Northeastern Quakers and Unitarians, making it the first truly integrated social movement. Generally, Abolitionism's largest base of support was among the evangelical middle class of New England, upstate New York, and the Old American Northwest or former Northwest Territory. Support within the working and upper classes was minimal.

Perceived as misguided fanatics by the general public, the abolitionists were relatively few in number with only about one hundred and sixty thousand by the mid-1830s. During the early 1840s, the movement slowly grew in the free states to over one thousand anti-slavery societies with over two hundred thousand members, with Black membership representing a majority. Members in the societies were recruited mainly from religious circles and philanthropic backgrounds including businessmen and professionals. Many members who came from the free Black population sat on the various administrative boards. These societies held meetings, adopted resolutions, signed anti-slavery petitions to be delivered to Congress, published journals, and enlisted subscriptions. They also printed and distributed propaganda in large quantities, aided runaways, negotiated with slaveholders, and sent forth lecturers and agents to deliver the anti-slavery message to Northern audiences. Fugitive settlements in Canada were often sponsored by these societies, which sent representatives into Canadian territory to provide encouragement, aid, and report their findings. The societies held public meetings that were most effective when featuring the eloquent and powerful testimony of former slaves. Militant in the battle against slavery, the societies' leaders were reviled in the South. The members of the societies were condemned, while their anti-slavery activities often met with violent public opposition. All too often, mobs invaded and broke up meetings, attacked speakers, and burned printing presses.

Abolitionists were aware that they constituted a political minority. They knew that the two main national parties, Democrats in particular, wanted to keep moral and sectional issues out of politics and would try to ignore the abolition movement. In response, the abolitionists decided to confront the party system as well as slavery with an ambitious goal of political transformation for the country. They organized a postal campaign in 1835, mailing massive amounts of anti-slavery protest literature. Southerners and most Northerners characterized this literature as subversive, and the ruling Democratic administration in Washington could no longer avoid the issue. In the next year, abolitionists began sending hundreds of petitions to Congress. Some of the petitions were against the annexation of the slave holding republic of Texas, while others demanded the end of slavery in Washington, D.C., or the abolition of the interstate slave trade. Each of these issues was within the constitutional jurisdiction assigned to Congress. In the process of organizing these campaigns, abolitionists turned themselves into an influential and cohesive movement. They also urged the federal government to debate slavery; an issue that most congressional representatives from both regions and both parties wished to avert. Democratic President of the United States (seventh President, 1829-37) and slave-owner Andrew Jackson, rather than officially censor the mail, simply allowed local postmasters to destroy mail that they judged subversive or dangerous. Democrats in Congress, with help from Southern Whigs, devised a gag rule whereby Congress tabled anti-slavery petitions without ever reading them. At the same time, Northern mobs began attacking abolitionists and their supporters as threats to social order and racial purity. These aggressive and illegal acts gave many abolitionists the ammunition they wanted. They could now connect the defense of slavery to assaults on the fundamental rights of free speech and of petition. These blatant abuses of power eventually enticed former President (sixth President, 1825-29) John Quincy Adams [1767, Braintree (now Quincy), Massachusetts, USA; 1848, Washington, D.C.], who had returned to federal government as a congressman from Massachusetts, to led the challenge against the so-called "gag rule". It was a battle that convinced many Northerners that Southern slavery corrupted republican government and threatened Northern civil liberties. Originally a small radical minority, abolitionists had finally helped force the country to face head on the contentious issue of slavery.

It was primarily as an editorialist, however, violently denouncing slave masters and their moderate opponents, that William Lloyd Garrison became prominent, influential, and feared. He refused to modify his severe attacks upon them. In 1837, in the wake of financial panic and the failure of abolitionist campaigns to gain support in the North, Garrison embarked on a bold new course. He challenged organized traditional religions, which as a group usually withheld formal support to Abolitionism, on the question of slavery. He cut all personal ties with institutional churches and became a Christian without a denomination, although he sympathized with Quaker philosophies. He renounced the relationships between church and state and embraced doctrines of Christian Perfectionism. These doctrines combined abolition, women's rights, and peaceful nonresistance with selected Biblical references. Garrison's spiritual mission was to encourage and justify the demise of a corrupt American society by advocating the disobedience of its immoral laws and disapproval of its institutions. As a pacifist, Garrison personally struggled with the duality of the Bible's spirit of Old Testament vengeance and New Testament Christian love, forgiveness, and charity.

As Garrison's demands on the Northern clergy went unchallenged and his criticisms of them increased, opposition to his stance developed within abolitionist ranks. A further cause of contention was Garrison's advocacy of equal rights for women in general, and, within the abolitionist movement. He based his support of women's rights on his desire for universal emancipation. The division was still further widened when Garrison later became convinced that the slavery clauses of the United States Constitution were immoral. Consequently, he believed it was equally immoral to take an oath in support of the Constitution. In 1840, he publicly burned a copy of the Constitution and condemned it as "a covenant with Death and an agreement with Hell". In 1842, Garrison took the even more controversial position that Northerners should disavow all allegiance to the Union, since the Constitution protected slavery. Throughout this decade, however, he and most of his associates upheld pacifist beliefs and insisted that slavery should not be abolished violently. This blend of pacifism and anarchism came to be known as the Garrisonian principle. It's motto of "No Union With Slaveholders", formulated in 1844, was a blatant demand for peaceful separation of the free Northern states from the Southern slave states.

By 1839, Garrison's increasingly personal definition of the slavery issue had hastened a crisis within the American Anti-Slavery Society. A majority of members strongly disapproved of both Garrison's no-government notions and the participation of women. Garrison and his supporters were clearly more radical than other members were. They believed that all good causes helped one another other. Many Northerners saw women activists as a threat to the status quo, leading to a breakdown in the American social order. In 1840, dissension reached its peak when Garrison and his followers voted a series of resolutions admitting women and insisted on sharing organizational responsibility with them. They also officially denounced the United States Constitution as supportive of slavery. The national organization split over these and other basic differences of approach.

The Society divided into two main groups, the radicals, and the gradualists. The split was induced by disagreements involving strategy and policy. The radical leaders of the Society included Garrison, Wendell Phillips, Lucretia Mott, Lydia Maria Child and John Brown [1800, Torrington, Connecticut, USA; 1859, Charlestown, Virginia]. They refused to adhere to a policy of gradual and legal emancipation of the slaves. This group retained control of *The Liberator* and the American Anti-Slavery Society.

In addition to Garrison, the three abolitionist leaders responsible for establishing the American Anti-Slavery Society were cleric Theodore Dwight Weld and brothers Arthur and Lewis Tappan. In 1839, Garrison's espousals of anticlericalism, perfectionism, radical pacifism, and women's rights drove these individuals, along with some less-militant members, away from the Society. This less radical wing, or gradualists, also included prominent abolitionist James Gillespie Birney. Together, they believed that emancipation could be accomplished legally by applying political and religious pressures. In 1840, led by the Tappan brothers, this group formed the rival American And Foreign Anti-Slavery Society, which advocated political action and moral persuasion. From then on, this new society, along with numerous state organizations, carried on most of the effective American anti-slavery agitation.

Businessman and philanthropist Arthur Tappan [1786, Northampton, Massachusetts, USA; 1865, New Haven, Connecticut] used much of his time, energy, and fortune in the fight to eradicate slavery. Following a pious Christian upbringing, Tappan moved to Boston at the age of fifteen to enter the dry goods business. Six years later he started his own company in Portland, Maine, and then in 1809 moved the business to the Canadian city of Montreal. Tappan struggled with the business both in Canada and the United States, to which he returned after the outbreak of the War of 1812. In 1826, he started a new firm with his brother Lewis in New York City. This business, a silk-importing company, was successful and both brothers became rich. A national financial panic in 1837 forced the Tappans to close their enterprise, but the brothers started another company when they opened the first commercial credit rating service in the 1840s. Arthur Tappan consistently used his money to support colleges, theological seminaries, and missionary societies. Conservative in his moral views, he founded the *New York Journal of Commerce* in 1827 to provide a newspaper free of immoral advertisements. He also supported movements for temperance, against the use of tobacco, and stricter enforcement of the Sabbath. Tappan, however, devoted himself primarily to the abolitionist movement during the latter part of his life. He helped start several abolitionist journals, and he was founder and first president (1833-40) of the American Anti-Slavery Society. Tappan initially supported the efforts of William Lloyd Garrison but split with him and the American Anti-Slavery Society when Garrison insisted upon connecting abolition with other reforms.

In 1839, abolitionists began to organize a legal defense for the African slaves from the ship Amistad. Over the next two years Lewis Tappan [1788, Northampton, Massachusetts, USA; 1873] led this effort and raised money for the education and legal defense of the Amistad slaves. He also published the *National Era*; a journal devoted to the cause of freeing the slaves.

With the passage of the Fugitive Slave Law of 1850, however, both of the Tappan brothers became more radical. They openly declared their determination to disobey the law and aid the Underground Railroad. They also developed a strong connection with Canada's anti-slavery efforts. They encouraged the Canadian abolitionist movement and the general resettlement of Black fugitives in Canada, and helped sponsor several settlements in Southern Ontario.

In addition to the Tappans, other conservative opponents of Garrison's inflammatory approach broke away. These politically minded abolitionists strongly disagreed with Garrison and his followers' adamant belief that political activity was both ineffective and sinful in the fight to end slavery. This faction, instead, believed in the political process to further anti-slavery goals. In 1939, they met in Warsaw, New York, to organize the Liberty Party (1840-48), the first anti-slavery political party in the United States.

Liberty Party backers realized that the abolition of slavery in the South would not happen through political action. The Party's goals, however, included efforts to dramatize the anti-slavery issue and pressure legislators into taking stronger anti-slavery positions. They wished to stop the interstate slave trade, and prevent slavery from spreading beyond the states where it already existed into the yet unsettled federal territories. The Party also demanded an end to slavery within the boundaries of the nation's capitol, Washington D.C., for both humanitarian and symbolic reasons. It was appalling to them that the seat of American freedom and justice was tainted with the presence of American slavery.

The party's first national convention took place at Albany, New York, in 1840. They nominated Kentuckian and former slaveholder James Gillespie Birney [1792, Danville, Kentucky, USA; 1857, Eagleswood, New Jersey] for president. Educated at the College of New Jersey, now Princeton University, Birney studied law and practiced in Danville. He was elected to the Kentucky legislature in 1816, and in 1818 he settled in Alabama, where he was elected to the legislature in the following year. He helped incorporate into the state constitution clauses that permitted the legislature to free slaves and to prohibit the selling of slaves brought into the state. In 1832, he gave up a successful law practice to work for the American Colonization Society, and supported the resettling of Blacks in Africa. He freed his inherited slaves in 1834 and during the following year moved to Cincinnati, Ohio, where he began, in 1836, publication of an anti-slavery newspaper, *The Philanthropist*. In 1837, he journeyed to Toronto, Canada, to investigate the conditions of fugitive slaves. In that same year he became executive secretary of the American Anti-Slavery Society, and three years later was vice president of the World Anti-Slavery Convention in London.

The Liberty Party nominated Birney for President in 1840. By this time, he had become a prominent moderate anti-slavery proponent. As the party's first national leader, he emphasized electoral activity as a means to end slavery. Despite a poor showing in the election, the Liberty Party nominated Birney as its Presidential candidate again in 1844. Although the Party polled only seven thousand votes in 1840, it raised that total to sixty-two thousand in 1844. The votes it garnered in 1844, especially in the state of New York, probably denied Whig candidate Henry Clay [1777, Hanover County, Virginia, USA; 1852, Washington, D.C.] from winning the presidency. Birney's career was abruptly ended by a severe permanent physical injury in 1845.

The next leader of the Liberty Party was a prominent senator, lawyer, and reformer in the anti-slavery movement, John Parker Hale [1806, Rochester, New Hampshire, USA; 1873, Dover]. Educated at Phillips Exeter Academy and Bowdoin College, he went on to study law and was admitted to the bar in 1830. He became a successful jury lawyer in Dover, New Hampshire, and was known for his oratory and his radical democratic principles. After a term in the state legislature, Hale was appointed United States district attorney in 1834, a position he occupied until 1841. The following year he was elected to the United States House of Representatives as a Democrat. As a congressman, Hale came to prominence as a crusader for the anti-slavery forces. In 1845, the Democratic Party refused to re-nominate him because he opposed the admission of new slave states into the Union. In 1846, running as an independent, Hale was elected to the United States Senate and served for sixteen years. His major accomplishment as a senator was the passage of a bill abolishing flogging in the Navy. It was his prominence in the anti-slavery movement, however, that led to his receiving the Presidential nomination of the Liberty Party. Early in 1848, the party nominated him at its convention in New York City. Later that same year, the Liberty Party met in Buffalo, New York, with other groups to form the new Free-Soil Party (1848-54). Hale withdrew his candidacy from the Presidential race when the two parties merged.

In 1852, Hale was the Free Soil Presidential candidate in an unsuccessful bid. Following this defeat, he resumed his private law practice. He returned to national politics in 1855, elected to fill the unexpired term of a deceased New Hampshire senator. In 1858, he won reelection to a full term in the Senate. By this time he had switched to the new Republican Party and was regarded as one of its leaders. During the Civil War he was chairman of the Senate Committee on Naval Affairs, and consistently supported the policies of President Abraham Lincoln. In 1863, Hale was accused of corruption concerning work he did for the navy. Although a senatorial investigation cleared him of any crime, his reputation was damaged and he was not nominated for another term. Shortly before his assassination, Abraham Lincoln appointed Hale minister to Spain (1865-69). Hale did not do well as a diplomat, however, and he was recalled.

The 1840 split within the national abolitionist movement left William Lloyd Garrison in control of a small group of loyal followers. The split denied him of the support of new anti-slavery converts and of the growing Northern reform community at large. In the two decades between the split and the Civil War, Garrison's influence decreased as his radicalism intensified. The decade prior to the War saw his opposition to slavery and to the federal government reach its peak. He refused to vote in government elections because he felt all political parties were corrupt. To Garrison, it did not matter if abolitionists voted, it was more important to make all voters abolitionists. He publicly opposed the federal government because it permitted slavery, and gradually became less opposed to violence as a means for ending the practice. He condoned violent resistance to the 1850 Fugitive Slave Law, supported the Underground Railroad, condemned the Kansas-Nebraska Act of 1854, denounced the 1857 Dred Scott decision, and lauded John Brown's 1859 raid on Harpers Ferry. In 1854, Garrison publicly burned a copy of the United States Constitution at an abolitionist rally in Framingham, Massachusetts. He later advocated the disunion of free states from slave states, and, in 1857, held an unsuccessful free state secessionist convention in Worcester, Massachusetts.

Despite his radicalism, by the 1850s, Garrison's new attitudes were, for the most part, mirrored by the abolitionist community at large. Belief in the use of violence against slave masters had replaced the earlier doctrine of moral persuasion. This was especially true during the maelstrom of controversy over extending slavery into the territory of Kansas. Ironically, abolitionists could claim ultimate success only after the triumph of Union forces in the Civil War. In the end, blood and bullets delivered victory, not pure idealism.

Because of radicals like Garrison, the abolition movement labored for many years under the negative perception that it threatened the harmony of North and South in the Union. It was further viewed as running counter to the American Constitution, which left the issue of slavery to the individual states. Hence, the majority of the Northern public remained unwilling to adopt abolitionist policy and was suspicious of abolitionist extremism.

A number of factors combined to give the movement increased credibility and momentum. Chief among these was the question of permitting or outlawing slavery in new Western territories. Northerners and Southerners began taking increasingly firm positions on opposite sides of that issue throughout the 1840s and 50s. There was also repugnance at the cruelty of slave catchers under the Fugitive Slave Law of 1850. During the 1850s, the anti-slavery question finally entered the mainstream of American politics. The voting public witnessed the emergence of influential national political parties including the Free-Soil Party and it's successor, the Republican Party.

In 1861, William Lloyd Garrison announced his support for war against the seceding Southern states. With the outbreak of the Civil War, he ceased to advocate disunion and predicted the victory of the North and the end of slavery. He supported his son's decision to volunteer to fight. Throughout the War, Garrison agitated for rapid and complete emancipation of the slaves.

The War forced Garrison to choose between his pacifist convictions and emancipation. In short, he made a major sacrifice of one set of principles in order to pursue another. Placing freedom for the slave foremost, he supported Abraham Lincoln consistently and in 1863 welcomed the Emancipation Proclamation as the fulfillment of all his desires. The Emancipation Proclamation removed the last division between Garrison and Lincoln, and Lincoln publicly praised Garrison's long and uncompromising crusade to eradicate slavery. The President invited Garrison to Charleston, South Carolina as a special guest for the ceremonial retaking of Fort Sumter in 1865.

The stress caused by the War years took its toll on Garrison. His son had fought as a Lieutenant in the Union Army's 54th Massachusetts Regiment (composed entirely of Black soldiers and known as the famous Glory Brigade), and his wife suffered a stroke in 1863. Garrison had married his wife, Helen Benson, in 1834. Helen was the daughter of a Quaker Baptist family from Providence, Rhode Island. Although not an activist, she had supported her husband in his endeavors and raised their seven children. She was largely responsible for giving him the stable family life he never knew as a child. To a certain degree, her wartime illness and resulting need for care crippled Garrison's ability to work following the War.

Like many Americans after the War, Garrison had to recover from both personal and national nightmares. His religious faith helped him come to terms with the devastation caused by the War. He decided the War was God's divine retribution against a sinful and hypocritical nation, severely compromised by its refusal to atone for the horrendous transgression of slavery. With some regrets, however, he acknowledged that the political revolution had occurred by bayonet rather than by moral reformation. In the end, he accepted the reality of military emancipation instead of his long desired goal of moral emancipation.

Ironically, emancipation brought to the surface the concealed conservatism in Garrison's plans for freed slaves. He was not prepared to guarantee their political rights immediately but did continue to insist on eventual Black equality and the creation of freedmen aid programs in the old slave states. In 1865, following the Civil War and the abolition of slavery, he advocated dissolution of the anti-slavery societies and tried unsuccessfully to dissolve the American Anti-Slavery Society, from which he resigned. With the ratification of the amendment that constitutionally abolished slavery in the United States, Garrison published the last issue of *The Liberator* in December 1865. He publicly announced that his vocation as an abolitionist was ended.

Garrison spent his last years regularly supporting the Republican Party and continuing to support pacifism. During this period, he became prominent in a variety of reform campaigns including free trade, suffrage for American women, justice for Native Americans, and prohibition of alcohol and tobacco. The American Anti-Slavery Society, along with most anti-slavery societies, was formally dissolved in 1870, when the adoption of the amendment to the American Constitution secured the right to vote for African Americans.

The man who spearheaded the American Anti-Slavery Society's drive for constitutional amendments was abolitionist leader, political reformer, and lawyer Wendell Phillips [1811, Boston, Massachusetts, USA; 1884]. Phillips was educated in Boston at Harvard University and Harvard Law School. His father, a prominent judge, was Boston's first mayor. At an 1837 public meeting in Boston's Faneuil Hall, he delivered an address rebuking the proslavery mob that had murdered the anti-slavery newspaper editor Elijah Parish Lovejoy, in Alton, Illinois. His oration became one of the most famous speeches in history for its protest against mob rule. He immediately achieved wide recognition as one of the most handsome and eloquent anti-slavery lecturers. Phillips subsequently lectured in many parts of the country against slavery and became known as the "Golden Trumpet" of Abolitionism. His oratorical vigor helped popularize the anti-slavery cause. His best known speeches were "Toussaint L'Ouverture", and "Burial of John Brown".

Unyielding in his opposition to slavery, Phillips gave up his law practice in 1837 to join William Lloyd Garrison's group of abolitionists. His reform career spanned forty-seven years during which he contributed many articles to *The Liberator* and married Ann Terry Greene, a disciple of Garrison's. Phillips exerted powerful leadership in the American Anti-Slavery Society. He ignored the many threats of violence made against him and fought courageously against any individual, institution, or law that he believed blocked abolition. He denounced the federal Constitution for its toleration of slavery and favored ending slavery even at the cost of breaking up the Union. During the Civil War, he severely criticized the administration of President Lincoln for taking a moderate position on slavery and the emancipation of the slaves, and he opposed Lincoln's reelection in 1864.

In 1865, Phillips broke with Garrison over the issue of dissolving the American Anti-Slavery Society. Garrison felt that the mission of the Society had been fulfilled. Phillips, who wished the

Society to continue, succeeded Garrison as its president. As president, he led the fight for the passage of constitutional amendments favoring basic rights for Blacks. In 1870, after the amendments passed, the Society was dissolved. Thereafter, Phillips lectured on a variety of issues, including abolition of capital punishment, prohibition of alcoholic beverages, higher taxation of the rich, and woman suffrage. He also condemned the history of Indian ill treatment by White men in the United States, and, became interested in improving conditions and rights for workers. In 1870, the Prohibition and Labor Reform parties nominated Phillips for governor of Massachusetts. Unsuccessful, he nevertheless won almost fifteen percent of the vote.

During the decades leading up to the Civil War, opposition to the abolitionist movement was not only located in the South but was a strong force in the North. The North's economy and many Northern businessmen benefited directly or indirectly from slavery. Many in the White Northern population felt unsure that Blacks could properly assimilate into American society. They also worried that their privileges as White citizens and the principle of racial supremacy were threatened by abolitionist demands for equal rights for Blacks. In their opinion, White entitlement meant freedom for all but not equality for all.

Northern abolitionist and their activities were often made targets of violence perpetrated by White Northerners. The written word was a powerful tool for the abolitionist cause. Rhetoric and violent aggression, however, often victimized its authors and messengers. One such victim was White abolitionist, clergyman, and newspaper editor Elijah Parish Lovejoy [1802, Albion, Maine, USA; 1837, Alton, Illinois]. Following an education at Waterville College (now Colby College) and Theological Seminary in Princeton, New Jersey, Lovejoy was ordained a Presbyterian minister in 1833. Shortly thereafter, he became the editor of the *St. Louis Observer*; an influential Presbyterian weekly published in St. Louis, Missouri. He was strongly disliked by proslavery groups in St. Louis for writing anti-slavery editorials. In 1836, under the threat of violence, he was forced to move his presses across the Mississippi River to Alton, Illinois, where he established the *Alton Observer*. Although supporters of slavery wrecked three of his presses, Lovejoy continued to attack slavery and helped organize the Illinois Anti-Slavery Society. On November 7, 1837, a mob gathered to destroy his newest press and Lovejoy was shot and killed trying to stop them. His death shocked many Americans and subsequently accelerated the growth of the abolitionist movement throughout the nation. His brother Owen Lovejoy [1811; 1864] also supported anti-slavery activities in Illinois and as member of Congress from 1857 to 64. He was an early supporter of Abraham Lincoln.

Cassius Marcellus Clay [1810, Madison County, Kentucky, USA; 1903, Whitehall] was a Black statesman and abolitionist, educated at Yale College. He was the son of a slaveholder, but he learned to despise slavery and preached against it. Deeply influenced by William Lloyd Garrison, Clay became a passionate and dedicated anti-slavery advocate. A lifelong resident of Kentucky, he entered that state's legislature in 1835, but was defeated in 1841 because of his opposition to slavery. During his three terms in the Kentucky legislature, he strongly recommended gradual emancipation for African Americans. He continued his crusade against slavery in the anti-slavery weekly *True American*, a newspaper he founded in Lexington, Kentucky in 1845. His opinions on slavery and his fervid nature earned him a reputation as a combatant rebel. He carried two pistols and a knife because of threats on his life, and he guarded his home and office with a cannon. When his printing equipment was destroyed by a proslavery mob, he continued to publish the paper from Cincinnati, Ohio. Later, after moving to Louisville, Kentucky, he changed its name to the *Examiner*. Although he had opposed the invasion of Texas in 1846, he was among the first to volunteer to fight in the Mexican-American War (1846-1848), and served with distinction. In 1847, he was taken prisoner of war for a short time. In 1854, he was one of the founders of the Republican Party and later worked for Abraham Lincoln's election in 1860. His friendship with Abraham Lincoln brought him the position of American minister to Russia, from 1861 to 69. Shortly before his death, Clay was declared legally insane.

Another noted target and victim of anti-reformer violence was a White New England school teacher named Prudence Crandall [1803, Hopkinton, Rhode Island, USA; 1890, Elk Falls, Kansas]. Born of Quaker parentage, Crandall established in 1831 the Canterbury Female Boarding School for White girls in Canterbury, Connecticut. Two years later, she admitted an African American girl for the first time. The parents of the other students threatened to withdraw their daughters from the school. Faced with the violent resistance of her community, Crandall closed the school.

Later that year, with the help of William Lloyd Garrison, she reopened with twenty Black girls as students and converted her school to a teacher-training institute for young African American women in the Northeast. The school was exclusively for Black girls, or as she put it "young ladies and little misses of color". Many citizens of Canterbury objected and tried to discourage Crandall and her students. The community tried to close the school by boycott, abuse, insult, threats, and enforcement of an obsolete vagrancy law. Public meetings were called, petitions were circulated, and a few months later the "Black Law" of Connecticut was passed. This legislation prohibited anyone from setting up or establishing any school for the education of nonresident African Americans, or to teach in any such school without the permission of local authorities. For resisting this law Crandall was arrested, imprisoned, tried, and condemned. Leading abolitionists contributed money for her defense in court. In 1834, the court of errors reversed the decision on a technicality. Soon afterward, she decided to abandon her project when a local mob attacked the school and partially destroyed her house. The affair served to further intensify the animosity between the slavery and anti-slavery factions. After marrying the abolitionist Reverend Calvin Philleo, Crandall moved to the Midwest, where she became active in the women's rights movement. She spent the remainder of her life in Illinois and Kansas.

Despite the tireless efforts made by anti-slavery advocates in the arena of public opinion, the American abolitionist movement was largely unsuccessful in advancing its cause with legislators and in the courts. In 1840, the movement won a rare legal victory in a federal district court in Connecticut, a state in which slavery was legal. In the next year, the United States Supreme Court upheld this landmark decision, known as the Amistad Case. Consequently, abolitionists would finally claim to feel the first warm winds of change.

Joseph Cinque

7. AMISTAD

A slave rebellion known as the Amistad mutiny occurred on board a slave ship named La Amistad, off the coast of the Spanish colony of Cuba. The slave ship entered American waters and was seized off the coast of Connecticut. Fifty-three African captives who rebelled were captured and tried in the United States. The Court ruled that the Africans aboard should be returned to their homeland and not returned to Cuba as slaves. Ironically, the word amistad means "friendship" in Spanish.

While not particularly significant for its legal principles, the surprising victory for the anti-slavery forces brought great attention to the Amistad Case in the United States. It also had important political and legal repercussions in the American abolitionist movement. The facts of the case, enveloped in judicial minutia and legal interpretations, expose the complexities surrounding the practice of human bondage before the Civil War.

The Amistad saga began in June 1839 when Spanish planters Pedro Montez and José Ruiz purchased fifty-three Africans in Havana, Cuba, a Caribbean center for the slave trade. The Africans – forty-nine adult men, three girls, and one boy – had recently been kidnapped in West Africa and transported to Cuba illegally by Portuguese slave traders. This was done in violation of all bans on international slave trading and treaties then in existence. In order to establish their status as legal slaves in Cuba, Montez and Ruiz obtained fake identification papers, showing the captives had been born in Cuba. They then placed the illegally abducted Africans on the Spanish schooner, La Amistad, and set out with them on a transshipment sea voyage to another part of Cuba. Upon arrival, Montez and Ruiz planned to sell their captives to plantation owners.

One of the captives was Joseph Cinque [circa 1811, Sierra Leone; circa 1852-79]. He is believed to have been born Sengbe Pieh in the Mende region of West Africa. While in his twenties, he was captured by four Black strangers as he walked along a well-traveled path. His wife and three children were unaware of what had happened and probably feared that animals might have killed him. Cinque later thought his captors may have been from a rival tribe or perhaps debt collectors. After being forced to march for days to reach the coast, he boarded the Portuguese slave ship Tecora along with hundreds of other captives. Unsanitary conditions and lack of food caused many to die during the two-month traumatic voyage to Cuba. Because it was illegal to import slaves into Cuba, the prisoners were smuggled in during the night. Slavery itself was legal there, so efforts were made to pass off the new arrivals as Cuban-born slaves. Sengbe Pieh was given the Spanish Christian name Joseph Cinque and soon found himself bound for Puerto Principe (now Camaguey), Cuba, aboard the Amistad. Because the prisoners did not speak Spanish, they had extreme difficulty understanding what was happening. The cook on the schooner gave Cinque the impression that they were being taken somewhere to be turned into dried meat and eaten.

On the second day of July, after a few nights at sea, Cinque decided he had nothing to lose by trying to get free. He found a nail and hid it until he could use it to free himself and others from their iron collars and chains. On a stormy night, the ship's unwilling passengers freed themselves from their restraints and rebelled. Led principally by Cinque and armed with sugarcane knives they found on board, the slaves killed the ship's captain Ramón Ferrer and took over the vessel. Three other crewmembers, including the cook, either died during the uprising or jumped off the ship attempting to reach shore by swimming or by lifeboat. One slave died during the revolt.

The slaves did not kill Ruiz and Montez because they believed the two men could navigate the ship and sail them home to Sierra Leone, Africa. They also spared the life of the cabin boy who was a Cuban-born slave. For almost two months, the injured Ruiz and Montez steered the ship in a wide circle. They sailed the ship east during the day, as if headed for Africa; however, at night they turned north, hoping to be rescued by reaching one of the southern ports of the United States. Supplies were scarce, and ten of the Africans died after mistaking liquid medicine for a beverage. After zigzagging on the Atlantic Ocean, the ship reached American waters between the coasts of Connecticut and Long Island, near Montauk Point, New York. La Amistad was almost entirely out of water and food, and some of the Africans had died. In late August, two fishermen by the name of Henry Green and Peletiah Fordham started to bargain with the Africans to sell them provisions. Green and Fordham planned to bring the ship into port and claim it for salvage, and request the court to award them compensation for recovering the ship and its human and material cargo. Before they could do so, and while Cinque and some others went ashore to gather supplies, Lieutenant Thomas R. Gedney at the helm of the American Coast Guard ship U.S.S. Washington, boarded La Amistad. He then ordered the vessel towed to New London in the free slave state of Connecticut. On board, Gedney found the cabin boy and thirty-nine surviving African mutineers. Montez and Ruiz were freed, while the Africans were imprisoned in New Haven, Connecticut.

Gedney rapidly filed a legal claim for salvage in the district court in Connecticut. The two fishermen also filed a salvage claim. Ruiz and Montez filed a claim as the owners of the slaves, asking the court to turn over the vessel and its cargo of slaves to the Spanish government. Furthermore, William Holabird, the district attorney in Connecticut, filed a claim on behalf of the federal government contending that the Africans should be handed over to the custody of the United States government. Initially, Holabird declared the government wanted to return the slaves to Africa because they had been imported into the United States in violation of various federal laws prohibiting the slave trade. Holabird amended his claim, however, after consulting with the administration of President Martin Van Buren [1782, Kinderhook, New York, USA; 1862]. Eighth President of the United States (1837-41) and one of the founders of the Democratic Party, Van Buren had close ties with a proslavery faction of the Party. He preferred the return of the Africans to the island planters and expected his secretary of state John Forsyth [1780, Fredericksburg, Virginia, USA; 1841] to make that happen. Spain, and its eleven year old queen, Isabella II, had been exerting diplomatic pressure on Van Buren to do just that. Therefore, in an additional filing to the court, Holabird stated that the Africans should be returned to Ruiz and Montez under the terms of the 1795 Pinckney Treaty between the United States and Spain. In the Pinckney Treaty, Spain recognized the boundary claims of the United States under the 1783 Treaty of Paris, the treaty that closed the American Revolutionary War. Simultaneously, Holabird requested that the adult Africans be detained for prosecution and charged with murder, piracy, and mutiny on the high seas. If the court upheld that claim, the Africans could be returned to Cuba for trial. While the district court sorted out these competing claims, accusations, and assertions, the Africans were kept in a prison in New Haven.

Anti-slavery forces immediately seized upon this drama to seek justice for the Africans and, on a higher plain, challenge the yet unbroken wall built by the slavocracy. Abolitionist networks were activated as they publicized the plight of the Amistads – as the Africans from the vessel came to be known – in newspapers and public meetings. They also began to organize a legal defense for them. Black communities and anti-slavery advocates mobilized to raise money. They produced a theatrical play in New York, held anti-slavery events, and sold portraits of Joseph Cinque, the anointed leader of the captured Africans. The Amistad Case became an international cause celebre for American abolitionists while Cinque became an effective symbol and speaker for abolitionist causes.

During the two-year ordeal, New York businessman and philanthropist Lewis Tappan, along with other abolitionists, rallied public sentiment and raised funds for the prisoners' defense. These dedicated New England abolitionists stirred public sympathy for the African captives against the American government's proslavery stance. They also raised money for the education of the Amistads. Theology students often visited the jail to teach them English and Christianity.

The Amistad Committee, a union of four missionary societies organized to support the landmark Amistad Case, later developed into the American Missionary Association, or AMA. The AMA was officially founded in Albany, New York, in 1846. Membership in the Association was open to all non-slave-holding Christians. Led by Lewis Tappan and other prominent abolitionists, the AMA was an ecumenical and interfaith organization that worked to develop educational opportunities for African Americans and other minorities in the United States. The nondenominational society itself was incorporated in 1846 by the merger of three missionary anti-slavery societies whose goal was to establish missions for freed slaves overseas. In its early years, the association ran missions in Puerto Rico, Hawaii, and Thailand. It also ministered to Native Americans in North and South Dakota, Asians in Alaska and along the Pacific Coast, and rural inhabitants in the South.

The AMA was the first American organization of its kind to support efforts among escaped slaves in Ontario. The AMA called its efforts in Canada the Canada Mission. It sent money and missionaries to Ontario, and it opened schools and aided settlement. Its presence in Southern Ontario was widespread, but sometimes resented as a foreign intrusion. Its many efforts met with mitigated success, causing it to withdraw from Canada during the Civil War years.

During the 1850s and onward, the AMA concentrated primarily on abolitionist activities and the establishment of educational institutions. When the Union armies began freeing slaves during the Civil War, the AMA opened schools for them. The organization established approximately five hundred schools throughout the South for freed slaves in the decades following the War. These schools were actually open to all students and often functioned as integrated institutions during the Reconstruction period (1865-77).

As the South recovered from the devastating effects of the War and developed public school systems, the AMA donated its elementary and secondary schools to the public systems and instead focused on developing and expanding colleges for African Americans in the South. Ten predominantly African Americans colleges arose from the AMA's efforts including Berea College in Berea, Kentucky, which was the first to be opened in 1855, and Howard University in Washington, D.C.

A Connecticut attorney, Roger Sherman Baldwin, was primarily in charge of the Amistads' defense. New York lawyers Seth P. Staples and Theodore Sedgwick, and the leading anti-slavery attorney in Boston, Massachusetts Ellis Gray Loring, assisted Baldwin. In September 1839, the abolitionist attorneys applied to Justice Smith Thompson [1768, Amenia, New York, USA; 1843, Poughkeepsie] of the American Supreme Court for a writ of habeas corpus challenging the government's attempt to return the prisoners to Cuba or to prosecute them for murder. Justice Thompson held that – because whatever crime the Africans had committed took place on the high seas on board a Spanish ship – the American courts had no authority to investigate the affair. This ended the government's attempt to prosecute the rebels for murder. Although the murder charges were dismissed, the Amistads continued to be imprisoned. Justice Thompson refused to release them until the district court in Connecticut determined their status. The focus of the case then turned to salvage claims and property rights.

Working to resolve the various legal claims, District Court Judge Andrew T. Judson began to render decisions that were generally favorable to the Africans. First, he determined that because they were not subject to prosecution for their mutiny on the ship, they could not be kept in prison. He ordered the United States marshal to find a better place to lodge them and to make sure they had adequate provisions, clothing, and medical care. He then ruled that since slavery did not exist in Connecticut, the Africans could not be considered property and Gedney could claim no salvage rights in them. The remaining question for Judson was the status of the Amistads. If they were African-born and had been transported to Cuba illegally, then they should be liberated. If they were legally slaves in Cuba, then he was prepared to turn them over to Montez and Ruiz.

The trial to decide the status of the Amistads finally began in January of 1840. Prosecutors argued that the mutineers were subject to the laws governing conduct between slaves and their owners. To avoid return to Cuba, the defense had to show that the Amistads had been born in Africa and only recently transported to Cuba, in violation of various international bans on the slave trade. While slavery was legal in Cuba, importation of slaves from Africa was not.

The Amistads did not speak Spanish, which suggested their African birth. However, the real crux to the defense was the testimony of the Amistad rebels themselves. Initially, this seemed impossible because no one around was able to communicate with them and no one knew what language they spoke. Josiah W. Gibbs, a linguistics professor from Yale College, solved this problem. Gibbs spent time with the Africans and learned how to count in their language. He then went to the wharves in New York City and stopped every Black sailor he could find, counting for them in the Amistads' language and hoping to find someone who spoke it. Eventually Gibbs encountered James Covey, a sailor on a British naval ship, and Charles Pratt, both natives of West Africa who had been kidnapped and enslaved earlier in their lives. Both men spoke English and Mende, the language of the Amistad rebels. Covey testified at the trial about life in Africa and translated for the Amistads. When Cinque took the stand, he proved an eloquent speaker. Pratt testified that only people who had lived in West Africa could know the culture and geography that the Amistads described. Covey and Pratt's testimony helped show the court that the Amistad mutineers were native Africans who had been illegally kidnapped and transported to Cuba.

Upon hearing all the evidence, Judson held against the federal government. He ruled that the Amistads were not merchandise, but instead were victims of kidnapping and had the right to escape their captors in any way possible. He ordered that the Amistads be delivered to the President of the United States to be transported to Africa. He also awarded Gedney salvage rights for one-third the value of the vessel itself. He then ordered the ship and all its goods returned to Cuba, but only after the Spanish government had paid Gedney his salvage claim. Since the cabin boy had been legally a slave in Cuba, Judson ordered that he be returned to Cuba.

President Van Buren was shocked and infuriated by the court's decision. In anticipation of a favorable ruling, he had ordered a Navy ship sent to Connecticut to return the Amistads to Cuba immediately after the trial. A candidate for reelection that year, Van Buren anticipated a ruling against the defendants and hoped to gain proslavery votes by removing the Amistads before abolitionists could appeal to a higher court. The American government appealed Judson's decision to the United States Supreme Court. The pressure to appeal the decision came primarily from Van Buren, who was still allied with the proslavery majority in the Democratic Party. The government argued that the Africans should be returned to their Spanish owners, under the treaty signed with Spain.

Congressman and former President John Quincy Adams, eldest son of second President John Adams, acted on his anti-slavery convictions and joined Baldwin to argue the Amistad case before the nation's highest court. In his pre-presidential years, Adams was one of America's greatest diplomats, formulating, among other things, what came to be called the Monroe Doctrine. In his post-presidential years, as a Congressman from 1831 to 1848, he conducted a consistent and often dramatic fight against the expansion of slavery. His role in the Amistad affair was significant. He argued eloquently for the Amistad rebels and spoke at great length about the nature of international law and the treaty obligations of the United States. In March 1841, by a majority vote of eight to one, the Supreme Court agreed with the trial court by upholding the main gist of the lower court's decision. Speaking for the Court was Justice Joseph Story [1779, Marblehead, Massachusetts, USA; 1845, Cambridge], the youngest man ever appointed to the Supreme Court of the United States and also one of the Court's greatest legal scholars. He recognized that if the Amistads had been born in Cuba, and thus were legally enslaved there, the treaty with Spain would require the United States to return them to Cuba.

The bench concluded, however, that the Amistads never were the lawful slaves of Montez and Ruiz, or of any other Spanish subjects. The Court decided that the Amistads were natives of Africa who had been kidnapped and unlawfully brought to Cuba, in violation of the laws and treaties of Spain. The Supreme Court thus finally freed the Amistads after a two-year confinement. The Court did so on the grounds that they were kidnapped in an illegal slave trade and had acted in self-defense. In short, the Supreme Court ruled that people escaping illegal slavery had the right to fight to regain their freedom.

After upholding Judson's decision on the freedom of the Amistads, the Supreme Court reversed his order that they be returned to Africa at government expense. Instead, the Court ordered the United States marshal to release them from captivity and have them sent to a community in Connecticut. With help from abolitionist and missionary groups who raised money, the liberated Amistads set sail for Africa. Cinque and thirty-four surviving Mendean men, women and children – the others having died at sea or while awaiting their trial – returned home to Africa in November 1841. Along with them were a translator and five Black and White teachers and missionaries who intended to establish a Christian mission. Together, they traveled aboard the ship Gentleman and arrived in Freetown, Sierra Leone, in mid-January 1842. This remained the only documented instance when kidnapped Africans reached the New World and were legally allowed to return home.

Spain continued to insist for years that the United States pay reparations for the Cuban transport ship. The American Congress intermittently debated the Amistad case, without resolution, for more than twenty years, until the Civil War began.

The effect of the Amistad case and its influence on the development of the American abolitionist movement should not be underestimated. The Amistad is generally considered the most important legal case dealing with slavery before the Dred Scott case of 1857. The trial epitomized the clash between freedom and slavery in the United States. The Amistad trials came at an important time, when slavery continued to expand in the American South and abolition by moral persuasion had apparently failed. The trials changed America and transformed the anti-slavery movement. Abolitionists used the trials to publicize the evils of slavery. Many Americans learned about the cruelties of the slave trade from the testimony of Cinque and the other captives. The trials encouraged abolitionists to shift their tactics from persuasion to political and legal agitation. That agitation would arouse increasing numbers of Americans against the immorality of slavery.

As the idea of Abolitionism gradually expanded and gained momentum, an important group of reformers from the world of letters joined the fray. In 1851, a major literary event greatly influenced the future of the United States and shook the very foundations of the South's peculiar institution.

UNCLE TOM'S CABIN

HARRIET BEECHER STOWE

Uncle Tom's Cabin book cover

Harriet Beecher Stowe

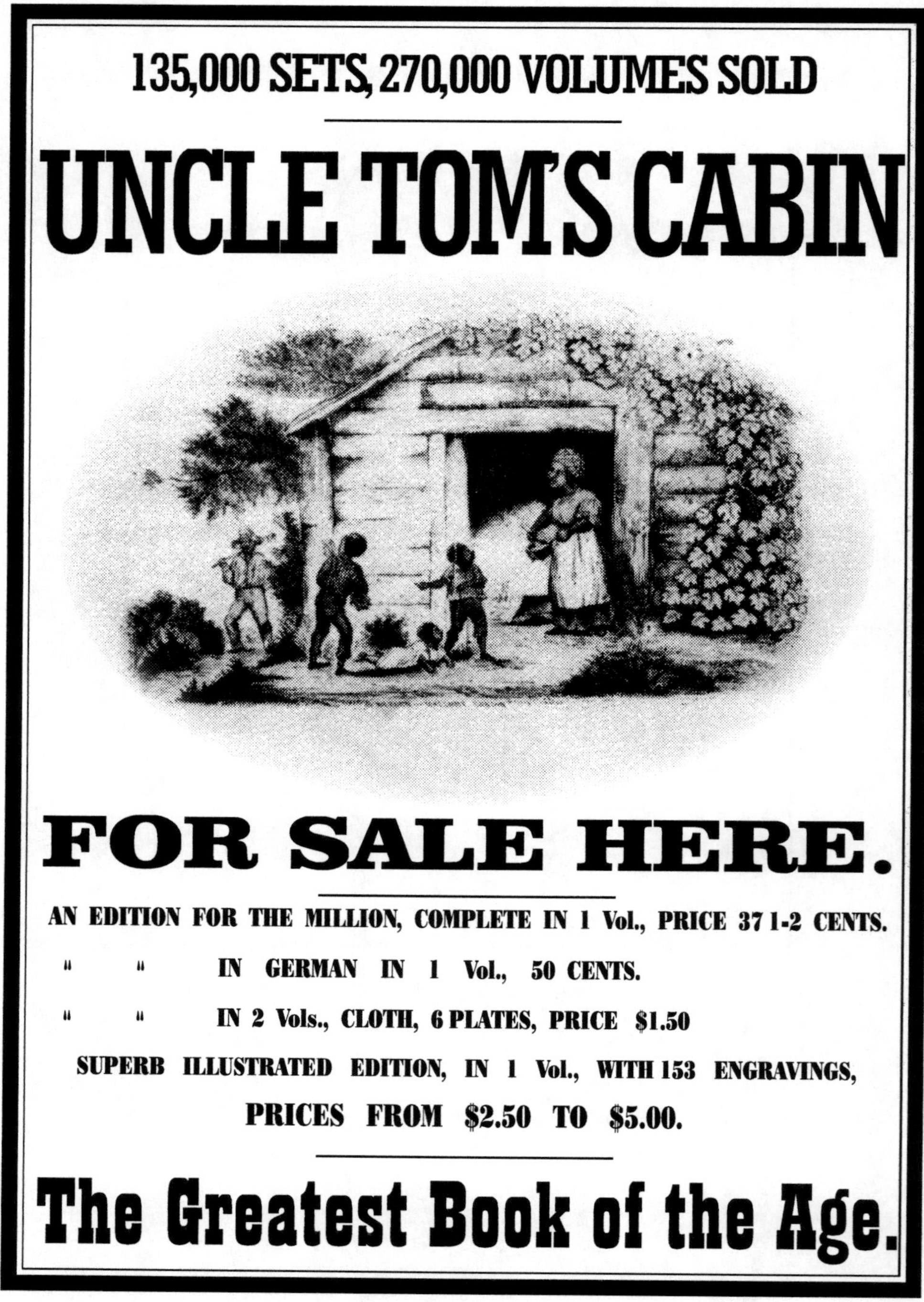

Uncle Tom's Cabin advertisement

8. UNCLE TOM'S CABIN

When Abraham Lincoln was introduced to Harriet Beecher Stowe, he allegedly remarked, "So you're the little lady who caused this big war."

Harriet Beecher Stowe [born Harriet Elizabeth Beecher, 1811, Litchfield, Connecticut, USA; 1896, Hartford] wrote an anti-slavery novel entitled *Uncle Tom's Cabin; or, Life Among the Lowly*, that was published serially in a newspaper in 1851 and in book form the year after. It was widely read in the United States, Canada, and abroad. Its pages aroused many to join the cause of abolition, while others vehemently rejected its indictment of slavery. Stowe's novel increased fractional feeling over slavery and intensified sectional differences. It was a powerful condemnation of slavery and one of the most influential books of its kind in American literature. The novel intensified the disagreement between the North and the South. Many believe it crystallized the anti-slavery movement in the United States and was among the causes of the American Civil War.

Stowe was born into a distinguished nineteenth century American family that made significant contributions to the religious and cultural life of the United States. Descendants of an Englishman who settled in 1638 at New Haven, Connecticut, the Beechers were reared in an atmosphere of learning, strict religious commitment, and sensitivity for social issues.

Stowe was the daughter of a prominent Presbyterian minister, Lyman Beecher [1775, New Haven, Connecticut, USA; 1863, Brooklyn, New York]. Beecher was one of the most representative figures of American religion during his time. He graduated from Yale University in 1797. He then entered Yale University's divinity school, completed his studies in 1799, and was ordained. After ministries in New York, Connecticut, and Boston, in 1832 he became a theological professor and president of Lane Theological Seminary in Cincinnati, Ohio, serving from 1832 until his resignation. His beliefs proved too mild for Ohio Presbyterians and was accused of heresy, but later acquitted. He resigned the seminary position in 1850 and went to live with his son Henry in Brooklyn, New York. Throughout his career, he promoted revivalism. He often led revival meetings at which he preached against excessive drinking, dueling, Unitarianism, and slavery. His most influential publication was 1832's *A Plea for the West*, which praised the potential of the frontier while warning of what he called the dangers of Roman Catholicism. His three marriages produced thirteen children. A contemporary called Lyman Beecher "the father of more brains than any other man in America".

Harriet Beecher Stowe's eldest sister, Catharine Esther Beecher [1800 East Hampton, Long Island, New York, USA; 1878, Elmira], was well known in her own right as an educator, lecturer, author, and advocate for the importance of women's roles in both educational and domestic work. She was an early advocate of education for women in the homemaking profession, and was strongly opposed to the women's suffrage movement.

Four of Harriet's brothers followed in their father's footsteps to achieve national reputations as clergymen and educators. One of these brothers, Henry Ward Beecher [1813, Litchfield, Connecticut, USA; 1887, Brooklyn, New York], was an abolitionist and one of the most eloquent, dramatic, and witty clergymen and orators of his day. Educated at Amherst College and at the Lane Theological Seminary, Henry served as a preacher to Presbyterian congregations in Indiana at Indianapolis and Lawrenceburg. In 1847, he became the minister of the Plymouth Church of the Pilgrims in Brooklyn. The Church quickly became an important center of activities of abolitionists. He kept this position for the remainder of his life and became one of the most celebrated pulpit orators and lecturers in American history. He attracted and mesmerized large audiences in the United States and England with his brilliant sermons and leadership at services and revival meetings. Although his theological views were generally orthodox, he tried to reconcile the Bible and evolution. His pronouncements on such controversial causes as the biological theory of evolution and scientific historical study of biblical texts made his speeches original and timely. As his liberalism grew, he was among the few clergymen to abandon notions about miracles, future punishment, Christ's divinity, and support Charles Darwin's theory of evolution.

The growing abolitionist movement increasingly included militants drawn from the ranks of the clergy, such as Henry Ward Beecher. He was one of the earliest and best-known proponents of the abolitionist agenda and was active in support of women's rights. From 1861 to 1863 he was editor of the *Independent*, a political and religious periodical principally devoted to these causes, and from 1870 to 1881, he edited a similar publication, *The Christian Union*, later named *The Outlook*. His published works included novels, magazine articles, lectures, and reprinted sermons.

In 1874, Henry's former friend and successor as editor of the *Independent*, the journalist and writer Theodore Tilton, brought suit for damages against him, charging that Henry had committed adultery with his wife. The Beecher-Tilton scandal had been precipitated by radical feminist, publisher, and first American woman Presidential candidate Victoria Claflin Woodhull [1838, Homer, Ohio, USA; 1927, Norton Park, Bremons, Worcestershire, England]. Woodhull and her sister were indicted for sending obscene material through the mails after they printed in their newspaper that Reverend Beecher had committed adultery with a parishioner. A sensational trial ended in a hung jury, leaving Henry's reputation uncleared, despite the support of his congregation. Although later investigations, including an inquiry by a council of Congregational churches, fully exonerated him, his later years remained marred by the scandal.

Edward Beecher [1803, USA; 1895, Brooklyn, New York] was another of Harriet's brothers and the third child of Lyman Beecher. He graduated from Yale University in 1822 and taught for four years before becoming minister of Boston's Park Street Church. In 1830, he went to Illinois to become president of Illinois College at Jacksonville.

As a member of the anti-slavery movement, he was associated with newspaper editor Elijah Lovejoy. After Lovejoy was killed in a riot in Alton, Illinois, Edward wrote a booklet entitled *Narrative of Riots at Alton*, which became one of the more famous anti-slavery works of the period. In 1844, he returned to the parish ministry in Boston and edited, for several years, a magazine called the *Congregationalist*. From 1855 to 1871, he was preacher of a church in Galesburg, Illinois. He then returned to Brooklyn and served a Congregational church until he died.

Harriet Beecher Stowe was educated at the academy in Litchfield and at Hartford Female Seminary founded by her sister Catherine. From 1832 to 1850, she lived and taught in Cincinnati, Ohio, where her father served as president of Lane Theological Seminary. There she took an active part in the literary and school life until 1836; contributing stories and sketches to local journals and compiling a geography schoolbook. That same year she married Reverend Calvin Ellis Stowe, a clergyman, seminary professor, and a member of the Lane faculty. He encouraged her literary activity and was himself an eminent biblical scholar. He was a Northern Whig and great school reformer who was a proponent of a system of tax supported public schools. He and others proposed public school systems that were centralized at the state level and that made attendance mandatory. These learning institutions were geared to teaching manners, civility, and patriotism, along with reading, writing, and arithmetic. In addition to being a passionate social reformer, Calvin Ellis Stowe was also a devoted opponent of slavery.

Harriet Beecher Stowe's life experienced privation and anxiety, due largely to her husband's precarious health. Despite this, she wrote continually and in 1843 published her first book entitled *The Mayflower; or, Sketches of Scenes and Characters Among the Descendants of the Pilgrims*. Many of Stowe's subsequent works dealt with New England in the late 1700's and early 1800's. She lived for eighteen years in Cincinnati, separated only by the Ohio River from a slave-holding community where she often visited plantations. This proximity to Kentucky gave her firsthand knowledge of the South. She encountered fugitive slaves, and learned about life in the South from friends and from her own visits there. Her years in Cincinnati provided her with many of the characters and incidents for *Uncle Tom's Cabin*. In 1850, her husband became professor at Bowdoin College and moved his family to Brunswick, Maine.

While living in Brunswick, Stowe drew upon her recollections, all of which originated in her lifelong hatred of slavery, to write the story of *Uncle Tom's Cabin*. She also used real people as models for her main characters, Eliza, and Uncle Tom. The story was initially written for serial publication in the *National Era*, a Washington, D.C. abolitionist magazine. As a serial, the story was well received but attracted little unusual attention. The success of the book, however, was unparalleled and achieved tremendous popularity. Seven million copies were sold worldwide within ten years, and it was translated into more than twenty foreign languages. Its publication brought Stowe unprecedented overnight success.

The main character in *Uncle Tom's Cabin* is Uncle Tom, a dignified old African American slave. The story describes Tom's experiences with three slave-owners. Two of them, George Shelby and Augustine St. Clare, treat Tom kindly. However, the third, Simon Legree, abuses Tom and has him brutally beaten to death for refusing to tell where two fugitive slaves are hiding. A subplot of the novel tells about the family of slaves, George and Eliza and their baby, who flee to freedom in Canada. In one famous passage, Eliza, clutching her baby, escapes across the frozen Ohio River from pursuing slave catchers. Two other characters in the book are Topsy, a mischievous African American girl, and Little Eva, St. Clare's young daughter. The death of Little Eva provides the reader with another celebrated passage.

Following the Civil War, *Uncle Tom's Cabin* became known mainly through abridgments of the book and by plays based on the novel. These versions, however, often distorted the original story and characters. By the late nineteenth century, most people believed that *Uncle Tom's Cabin* dealt primarily with the death of Tom and Little Eva, Topsy's antics, and Eliza's escape. The term "Uncle Tom" came to stand for a Negro who, for selfish reasons or through fear, adopts a humble manner to please White people. Actually, the book portrayed Tom as a brave man who dies rather than betray two fellow slaves. The novel is melodramatic and sentimental, but it is more than a melodrama. It re-created characters, scenes, and incidents with humor and realism. It analyzed the issue of slavery in the Midwest, New England, and the South during the days of the Fugitive Slave Law. Few people realized that Simon Legree, the cruel villain, was a Northerner, and that Augustine St. Clare, a Southerner, recognized the evils of slavery.

Many felt the novel presented a realistic account of American life a decade before the Civil War. Stowe created a vivid picture of Southern life, with Tom being sold from one master to another. *Uncle Tom's Cabin* also provides a good description of the upper Midwest as seen by George and Eliza as they fled northward into Canada. Though the story depicts some of the kindly and patriarchal aspects of slavery, it emphasizes the dark and cruel side.

Uncle Tom's Cabin was groundbreaking at many levels and had a lasting impact on American literature and politics. The book's melodramatic events and dialogue cast the slavery issue in sharp terms of good and evil. Stowe's novel stimulated tremendous anti-slavery sentiment in the United States and convinced many Americans, especially in the North, to support the abolitionist movement. When published, the book was a political and cultural phenomenon. It created a far-reaching emotional response that played a major role in turning the problem of slavery into a moral issue. The novel did much to solidify militant anti-slavery feelings in the North and stirred outrage in the South. As a result, Stowe's name quickly became vilified in the South.

In the novel, Stowe provided dramatic examples of the evils of slavery and demonstrated how the peculiar institution corrupts otherwise benevolent slave-owners. Certain passages in the novel, embedded with references to the New Testament and the crucifixion of Jesus Christ, demonstrated how Stowe, the daughter of a clergyman, used her Christian perspective to promote the abolition of slavery.

In the South, *Uncle Tom's Cabin* was viewed by many as a book of propaganda. Stowe's depiction of slavery in the Southern states contributed towards the growth of the North's and, to a certain extent, the world's negative perception of Southern antebellum society, and its institution of bondage. In response to Stowe's hugely popular international book, some Southern authors tried to defend slavery with fictional works of their own. Caroline Lee Hentz's 1854 novel *The Planter's Northern Bride*, depicts an educated and genteel Southern slave-owner who travels to the North with one of his slaves. Both the master and the narrator respond to criticisms of slavery by arguing that Southern slaves receive better treatment than factory laborers in the North and in Europe.

In Canada, Stowe's novel first appeared serially in major publications across the country, and then sold thousands in book form. It made abolitionists of many Canadians. The alleged prototype of Uncle Tom, Reverend Josiah Henson, was living with his wife Nancy at the colony of Dawn, near Dresden, Ontario. Many people felt Henson was immortalized by Harriet Beecher Stowe as her model for the leading character in *Uncle Tom's Cabin*.

In 1853, Stowe reinforced her story by publishing another book entitled *A Key To Uncle Tom's Cabin*, containing an impressive accumulated array of documentary evidence and testimonies in support of her attack upon slavery. Meanwhile, the dramatic stage adaptation of *Uncle Tom's Cabin* played to capacity audiences. Economic, social, and racial tensions in American society before the Civil War period often found a way into popular drama, most successfully in the various theatrical adaptations of *Uncle Tom's Cabin*. Sentimental versions of the book filled so many professional stages that this material was performed more often than any other American play of the time. An 1852 adaptation by George Aiken was the most enduring version. When most people thought of the book's famous characters – Uncle Tom, Little Eva, Topsy, and Simon Legree – they were not recalling the book, but were thinking instead of Aiken's play of 1852, or of crude and violent spectacles called *Tom Shows*, which played in small towns in the North. Aiken's play and the *Tom Shows* only faintly suggest Stowe's book. Although Blacks were sometimes part of the cast, the major actors were usually White, with dark skin makeup. Black performers were often allowed only stereotypical roles, if any, in productions by major companies. *Tom Shows* were in the tradition of American blackface minstrel shows started in the 1830s, which used White entertainers with exaggerated Negro make-up depicting the "happy slave". These shows, presented in theatres throughout the North to White audiences, were demeaning to all African Americans of that period, especially the free Northern Blacks who were struggling to maintain their dignity and attempting to carve a place for themselves in conventional society.

Uncle Tom's Cabin, like most of Stowe's novels, was considered by some to be rambling in structure, but rich in pathos and dramatic incident. It was one of the best examples of the so-called sentimental fiction that enjoyed popularity in the United States during the nineteenth century. Sentimental authors focused on domestic scenes, and their work evoked strong emotions. Like Stowe, many of these writers were social reformists, but they were criticized for creating overly idealized characters.

The sentimental novel is an important form of American fiction that developed out of the responses of White novelists to the abuses of slavery. The most famous and historically most significant work of American sentimental fiction was *Uncle Tom's Cabin*. Sentimental fiction aimed to arouse pity for the oppressed and offered a natural form for authors writing about the evils of slavery. In Stowe's book and in books that followed in this tradition, pity for the oppressed did not require revolutionary change but rather called for an outpouring of Christian love and benevolence. Sentimental fiction evoked this Christian sympathy from Northern White women in particular, by showing how the slave system defiled the most basic bonds of humanity, such as that between mother and child. One can thus argue that sentimentality played an important part in hastening the Civil War.

When Stowe made a journey to Europe in 1853, she was celebrated in England and welcomed by the English abolitionists. Later, however, British public opinion turned against her with publication in 1869 of a magazine article, "The True Story of Lord Byron's Life", and the book published the year after, *Lady Byron Vindicated*. It told of Lady Byron's separation from her husband, the famous poet, Lord Byron.

Stowe's account was based on Lady Byron's talk with her in 1856 and detailed her accusation that the poet had had an incestuous love for his sister. Of her later books, this one proved to be the most shocking to her contemporaries.

In 1856, she renewed her attack against slavery and published a two-volume novel entitled *Dred: A Tale of the Great Dismal Swamp*. When *The Atlantic Monthly* magazine was established in 1857, Stowe found a ready vehicle for her writings. By this time, she was living in nearby Andover, Massachusetts, a center of the anti-slavery movement. She found other outlets for her writing in the *Independent of New York* and later the *Christian Union*, of which papers her brother Henry was editor. She was also published in the magazine *Lady's Book*, the first periodical in the United States to devote its contents entirely to matters of interest to women. Stowe was a noted feminist and supported the National American Woman Suffrage Association. She worked with the association to advance women's rights on both the state and federal levels.

By the time she died, Stowe had long been recognized at home and abroad as one of America's foremost literary celebrities. In her latter years, Stowe led the life of a woman of letters, writing romantic novels dealing with New England life in the eighteenth and early nineteenth centuries. She also wrote short stories and many studies of social life in both fiction and essay. Stowe also published a small volume of religious poetry and toward the twilight of her career gave some public readings from her writings. She made her final home in Hartford, Connecticut. Harvard University's Schlesinger Library at Radcliffe, specializing in American women's history, houses many of her original papers.

As influential as it was, *Uncle Tom's Cabin* was but one of many works of American literature that advanced the anti-slavery cause. During the nineteenth century, poetry was a popular form of literature and an effective means of protest. The most famous American poets of the epoch were called the Fireside Poets or the Schoolroom Poets, because their works were often read "by the fireside" at home or in school. These sentimental poets concerned themselves with feelings and called for social reforms, including abolition.

One such humanitarian poet was John Greenleaf Whittier [1807, Haverhill, Massachusetts, USA; 1892, Hampton Falls]. Whittier was born on a farm and was of Puritan and Quaker ancestry. He had little formal education, but he attended Haverhill Academy for two terms. Largely self-educated, his best-known poems fell into two groups, those attacking slavery, and those praising the charms of New England country life. Whittier's earliest works, including his 1831 *Legends Of New England In Prose And Verse*, were pastoral evocations of the rugged farm life of New England. Whittier's simple, direct, and sentimental style made his poems, such as 1854's "Maud Muller", very popular. The Scottish poet Robert Burns influenced Whittier. Like Burns, Whittier wrote ballads on rural themes. His poetry also shows the influence of his Quaker religion and rural New England background. In two 1857-58 ballads entitled "Skipper Ireson's Ride" and "Telling the Bees", Whittier showed his interest in the people, customs, legends, and settings of New England. A deeply religious man, Whittier followed the Quaker faith of his parents and was known as the Quaker poet.

His father convinced him that it was impractical to expect to earn a living writing poetry, so he turned to journalism. His earliest work attracted the attention of William Lloyd Garrison, at the time editor of the *Free Press* newspaper in Newburyport, Massachusetts, who asked him to contribute articles. Whittier thus began a long career as contributing editor, journalist, essayist, and poet. As a Quaker deeply concerned with politics and social welfare, Whittier was active in politics and the anti-slavery movement from 1833 to 1863. He agreed with Garrison's anti-slavery politics, and committed himself to the abolitionist cause in his celebrated 1833 pamphlet *Justice And Expediency*. This fiery pamphlet made him prominent in the abolitionist movement. He was a delegate to the anti-slavery convention in Philadelphia in 1833, and he served a term in the Massachusetts legislature. He became a well-known lobbyist both in Boston and in Washington, D.C. From 1836, he lived in Amesbury, Massachusetts with his mother, aunt, and sister.

Whittier was a founder of the Liberty Party in 1839, and participated in the founding of the Republican Party in 1854. As one of the leading supporters of the Liberty Party, he edited in 1854-55 the *Middlesex Standard*, a paper published by the Liberty Party in Lowell, Massachusetts. He was also chiefly responsible for editing the *Essex Transcript*, another of the Liberty Party's publications.

For more than three decades, Whittier devoted himself to the eradication of slavery in the United States. He called for the abolition of slavery in newspaper articles while the abolitionist cause dominated his poetry. He dedicated one such poem to Canadian abolitionist Alexander Milton Ross. His numerous fiery anti-slavery poems were published in an 1846 collection entitled *Voices Of Freedom*. One powerful poem, entitled "Massachusetts to Virginia" and published in 1843, criticized the slave state, Virginia, for betraying the Founding Fathers' democratic principles and love of liberty. Whittier's finest political poem is considered to be 1850's "Ichabod", a word which comes from the Hebrew word meaning inglorious. It attacks Senator Daniel Webster [1782, Salisbury (now Franklin), New Hampshire, USA; 1852, Marshfield, Massachusetts] for his part in the passage of the Compromise of 1850. Whittier objected to the compromise because it required that fugitive slaves be returned to their masters. Yet he used a dignified, restrained tone that makes Ichabod seem less a criticism of Webster than an expression of sympathy for him.

By 1843, Whittier had broken with Garrison, but he continued to support the anti-slavery movement and its political candidates, including Abraham Lincoln. His writings continued to be significant during the Civil War. Barbara Frietchie [1766; 1862] is the name of a woman who supposedly acted bravely to protect the Union flag against Confederate troops in 1862. The incident is known mainly because it was dramatized in Whittier's 1863 poem, "Barbara Frietchie". It tells of Confederate General Stonewall Jackson leading his troops through Frederick, Maryland, during the Civil War. When Jackson ordered the Union flags shot down, Barbara Frietchie defied the General by waving the Stars and Stripes from an upper window of her home while exclaiming: "Shoot if you must this old gray head, but spare your country's flag," she said. The ninety-year old woman's patriotic bravery embarrassed Jackson, who replied with the order: "Who touches a hair of yon gray head, Dies like a dog! March on!" he said.

With the end of the Civil War, Whittier's poetry returned to pastoral themes. Often considered his masterpiece and most popular work is the 1866 nostalgic narrative poem "Snow-Bound", for which he achieved a national reputation. This long poem is an affectionate description of Quaker life and tells of a family marooned in their farmhouse by a blizzard. Based on the poet's childhood memories, this poem is representative of his moralistic, sincere, yet emotional style.

In old age, Whittier was paid homage with various accolades. Both his 70th and 80th birthdays were celebrated as literary events. In 1887, the town of Whittier, California was named in his honor.

Another prominent author who expressed his strong anti-slavery beliefs in his writings was Henry Wadsworth Longfellow [1807, Portland, Maine (then in Massachusetts), USA; 1882, Cambridge, Massachusetts]. Longfellow was the son of Stephen Longfellow and Zilpah Wadsworth Longfellow. His mother, Zilpah Wadsworth Longfellow, was the daughter of Peleg Wadsworth, a Revolutionary War general. From early childhood, it was evident that he was to be drawn to writing and the power of words. His father was eager to have his son become an attorney. However, Henry asserted his ambition in a letter to his father explaining that he eagerly aspired to become an author. He was educated at Bowdoin College in Brunswick, Maine and after graduating at age eighteen he traveled abroad and studied languages in Europe in preparation for a teaching career. He was a professor of modern languages at Bowdoin from 1829 to 1835. In late 1835, during a second trip to Europe, Longfellow's wife of four years, Mary Storer Potter, suffered a miscarriage and died in Rotterdam, Netherlands. A few months later, Longfellow returned to the United States and began teaching at Harvard University.

In 1843, he married Fanny Appleton who became the mother of his six children. Their extremely happy married life ended in 1861 when she tragically died, after accidentally setting her dress afire when a package of her children's curls, which she was sealing with matches and wax, burst into flame. She was fatally burned despite Longfellow's efforts to smother the fire with his hands and a rug. Fanny was buried on the eighteenth anniversary of her marriage to Longfellow, but Longfellow was too severely burned and mournful to attend her funeral.

After retiring from Harvard in 1854, Longfellow devoted himself exclusively to writing. As a New England poet, Longfellow had gained public recognition beginning in 1839 with his initial volume of poems. His 1842 *Poems on Slavery* described his opposition to slavery and forms an illuminating contribution to the tradition of American political poems. He made Nova Scotia famous in his notable 1847 long narrative poem, "Evangeline". This partly fictional poem recounts how French colonists, called Acadians, were driven from their homes in Nova Scotia by British troops during the French and Indian War. The poem gave part of the province the nickname Land of Evangeline.

In 1850, Longfellow published another collection of poems entitled *The Seaside And The Fireside*. The title suggests two of the settings that conveyed some of the author's most characteristic themes, the sea, and the family circle. This volume contains "The Building of the Ship", which draws on Longfellow's familiarity with shipbuilding in Maine for its primary subject matter. The newly built ship symbolized the nation, especially in the final stanza, which he began with the lines "Thou, too, sail on, O Ship of State! Sail on, O Union, strong and great!" A decade later, President Abraham Lincoln was deeply moved by these lines.

Longfellow was one of the most widely published and most famous American poets of the 1800s. He was among the first American poets to use native themes, writing about life in America and the American landscape. He influenced the poetic taste of generations of readers throughout the English-speaking world. Combining gentility with the common touch, he was equally successful in lyric and narrative poetry and during his later years became an expert of the sonnet. Ballads like "The Wreck of the Hesperus" and 1863's "Tales of a Wayside Inn", containing the well-known poem "Paul Revere's Ride", were familiar to every schoolchild, and "Evangeline" became the first enduringly successful long poem written in the United States. His exploration of Indian lore in "The Song of Hiawatha" showed his skill in the use of American subject matter, and as a pioneer in the teaching of modern languages, he helped introduce Americans to the literature of Europe. Longfellow also translated poetry from eighteen languages. He was one of the most popular of American poets, primarily for his simplicity of style and theme and for his technical aptitude, but also for his role in the creation of an American mythology. His works were translated into many languages, and he became known and celebrated throughout the Western world as the grand old man of American letters.

Longfellow's last visit to Europe in 1868-69 was a triumphal tour during which he received honorary degrees from both Oxford and Cambridge, and was chosen a member of the Russian Academy of Science and of the Spanish Academy. In 1884, two years after his death, he became the first American writer to be honored with a bust in the Poets' Corner of Westminster Abbey in London.

Poet and ardent abolitionist James Russell Lowell [1819, Cambridge, Massachusetts, USA; 1891, at Elmwood, in Cambridge] played an important part in the cultural life of the United States during the 1800s. A man for all seasons, he worked in many areas as an author, essayist, editor, diplomat, literary critic, lecturer, teacher, scholar, reformer, and diplomat. Lowell was from a prominent and gifted

Massachusetts family. The Lowells of New England included, among others: the founder of the first textile mill in the United States, Francis Cabot Lowell [1775, Newburyport, Massachusetts, USA; 1817]; jurist John Lowell; an astronomer and founder of the Lowell Observatory, Percival Lowell; one of Harvard University's most influential presidents, Abbott Lawrence Lowell [1856, Boston, Massachusetts, USA; 1943]; and two celebrated twentieth-century poets, Amy Lawrence Lowell [1874, Brookline, Massachusetts, USA; 1925] and Robert Traill Spence Lowell [1917, Boston, Massachusetts, USA; 1977].

James Russell Lowell attended classical school in Cambridge, where he read a great deal but neglected formal studies. He pursued his education at Harvard Law School, graduating in 1840 as class poet. Lowell was admitted to the bar that same year but disliked the law and gave it up three years later. By 1844, his literary work had gained him fame that led to the offer of a professorship at Harvard. Lowell accepted but asked to go to Europe for a year to renew his knowledge of modern languages. On his return, he married Maria White, a poet, abolitionist, and devotee of social causes. During their marriage, he settled down to a life dedicated to teaching and writing. Throughout these years, he wrote much on abolition. Maria died in 1853, and in 1857, he married Frances Dunlap.

As an author, he followed his conscience on humanitarian and social issues. In the early 1840s, Lowell's first volumes of poems were published and he founded a short-lived literary magazine, *The Pioneer*. During the second half of the decade, Lowell contributed to several abolitionist publications, including the *National Anti-Slavery Standard*, which he helped edit, and the *Pennsylvania Freeman*. In 1846, he wrote for the *Boston Courier* the first of the *Biglow Papers*, a series of satirical verses in Yankee dialect purporting to be by Hosea Biglow, a young New England farmer. In the *Biglow Papers*, Lowell used humor for social criticism. The work consisted of poems and prose notes that served as a vehicle for expressing Lowell's opposition to United States involvement in the Mexican-American War. Hosea Biglow, the chief character, is an uneducated but practical-minded New England farmer who speaks in a rural New England dialect. Lowell's amusing treatment of this dialect earned him a lasting place among leading American humorists. In 1848, the first series of *Biglow Papers* was collected in book form.

In 1855, Lowell succeeded the American poet Henry Wadsworth Longfellow as professor of modern languages at Harvard, serving until 1876. From 1857 to 1861, he served as the first editor of *The Atlantic Monthly*, the oldest general periodical published in the United States. *The Atlantic Monthly* was the voice of liberal Boston when it was launched from the Old Corner Bookstore, which quickly became a gathering place of famous nineteenth-century writers. From 1863 to 1872, Lowell was coeditor of the *North American Review*. Under his leadership, both magazines achieved major literary and intellectual importance.

Meanwhile, Lowell continued writing significant poetry. He delivered his "Commemoration Ode" at the memorial services in 1865 for the Harvard Civil War dead. He published in book form in 1867 the second series of *Biglow Papers*, which reflected his anti-slavery position and his support of the North during the War. He also wrote outspoken articles on social issues, including the guarantee of full rights of citizenship to African Americans.

Following the Civil War, Lowell became increasingly active in politics. He was a delegate to the Republican National Convention in 1876 but refused a request to run for Congress that year. Lowell supported the Republican Presidential candidate, Rutherford B. Hayes. When Hayes became President, Lowell was appointed American minister to Spain. Lowell occupied this position from 1877 to 1880 and then served as minister to Great Britain until 1885. During his years in Spain and Britain, Lowell became a well-liked figure in European society and a spokesperson for American ideals of democracy. He worked to raise European esteem of American culture. His efforts on behalf of American authors brought them international attention for the first time.

In 1885, Lowell retired to Elmwood, the family home where he had been born. He lived quietly for the rest of his life but occasionally spoke at public events. At the time of his death, he was generally considered as a major international literary figure and the most distinguished man of letters in the United States.

One of the first anti-slavery books produced in the United States was published in 1833 and written by abolitionist, teacher, author, and editor Lydia Maria Frances Child [1802, Medford, Massachusetts, USA; 1880, Wayland]. As a pioneering women editor she founded in 1826 the first magazine for children published in the United States, *Juvenile Miscellany*. In 1828, she married Boston lawyer and ardent abolitionist David Lee Child [1794; 1874]. She became involved in Abolitionism in 1831, when she met William Lloyd Garrison. In 1833, Child wrote her best-known work, *An Appeal in Favor of that Class of Americans Called Africans*, which related the history of slavery and denounced the inequality of employment and education for African Americans. It was the first such work published in book form, and succeeded in inducing many people to join the abolitionist movement.

For three years she was editor, and later coeditor with her husband, of the *National Anti-Slavery Standard* (1840-1849), the weekly publication of the American Anti-Slavery Society. She wrote a series of letters supporting John Brown after he led his historic raid at Harpers Ferry in 1859, and later transcribed the recollections of slaves who had been freed. As a direct result of their anti-slavery activities, which included using their home as a Station for the Underground Railroad, Lydia and her husband were ostracized, and her children's magazine failed. Nevertheless, she continued her efforts in support of civil rights for African Americans and women, writing many fictional and nonfictional works devoted to these subjects.

Anti-slavery historian, journalist, and diplomat Richard Hildreth [1807, Deerfield, Massachusetts, USA; 1865] was another of the highly regarded abolitionist novelist. After graduating from Harvard University in 1826 he practiced law in Boston from 1830 to 1832, and then worked as editor of the *Boston Daily Atlas*. Hildreth authored one of the first anti-slavery novels in 1836 entitled *The Slave: or Memoirs of Archy Moore*. It was very successful, and in 1852, a revised version entitled *The White Slave: or Memoirs of a Fugitive*, briefly rivaled the popularity of *Uncle Tom's Cabin*. Hildreth's 1854 book, *Despotism In America*, made an incisive analysis of Southern United States' society under slavery. His most significant work was a six-volume *History of the United States*. In 1861, President Abraham Lincoln appointed Hildreth the American consul to Trieste, Italy.

Celebrated writer and naturalist Henry David Thoreau [1817, Concord, Massachusetts, USA; 1862], influenced by William Lloyd Garrison, passionately called for an end to slavery in his speeches and literature. He attacked the practice in his 1854 essay "Slavery In Massachusetts". His strong views were summarized in one potent phrase: "The law will never make men free, it is men who have got to make the law free". He also defended fiery abolitionist John Brown's raid at Harpers Ferry in an 1859 publication entitled *A Plea for Captain John Brown*. In 1866, "A Yankee in Canada, with Anti-slavery and Reform Papers" was published in Boston. Thoreau expanded his protests against slavery by lecturing against the Fugitive Slave Laws and by aiding escaped slaves in their flight to freedom in Canada.

Thoreau was graduated from Harvard University in 1837 and failed at a teaching job before running a private school with his brother from about 1838 until his brother fell ill in 1841. From 1841 to 1843 Thoreau lived in the home of lecturer, poet, and essayist Ralph Waldo Emerson [1803, Boston, Massachusetts, USA; 1882, Concord], the leading exponent of New England Transcendentalism. It was during this period that he decided to devote his life to writing. Unable to support himself through his writing, Thoreau worked for a stint as a laborer, including a time in his family's pencil factory, and as a surveyor. During this period, in the latter 1850s, he traveled extensively, recounting his adventures in essays such as his 1866 piece entitled, "Quebec".

Thoreau adhered to the philosophy of transcendentalism, with its emphasis on mysticism and individualism. The movement stood for the individual as rebel against the established orders of society. Thoreau was a man unto himself who looked at society and government and found them lacking in nearly every respect. He often-launched attacks on the prevalent social institutions he considered immoral. Essentially a philosopher of individualism, Thoreau placed nature above materialism in private life and ethics above conformity in politics. He believed in simplicity and saw God in nature's wonders. He was a pioneering ecologist and advocate of national parks.

His faith in the religious significance of nature led to his celebrated 1854 work entitled *Walden; or, Life In The Woods*. In *Walden*, Thoreau presented a detailed written study of his experiment in living close to nature while isolated along Walden Pond. The book explains how in 1845 he built a cabin, on land owned by Emerson, in the woods on the shore of Walden Pond in Massachusetts and lived there alone. He read, worked the land for his food, entertained visitors, and recorded his observations and experiences in journals. His style showed a sensitive response to the root meanings, images, sounds, and subtle nuances of words.

During his Walden stay, Thoreau chose to spend a night in jail rather than to support the Mexican-American War by paying his 1846 poll tax. The experience marked a turning point for Thoreau. He vowed not to support a government that permitted slavery and condemned what he saw as the United States' imperialist war against Mexico. He clarified his position in perhaps his most famous social protest and testament to freedom, his 1849 essay "Civil Disobedience" – originally titled, "Resistance to Civil Government". In this essay, Thoreau discussed his doctrine of passive resistance, a method of protest that later was adopted by Indian leader Mohandas Gandhi and Martin Luther King, Jr.

Thoreau spent much of his life in or near the anti-slavery hotbed of Concord. Long ill with tuberculosis, Thoreau died after a futile journey in 1861 to Minnesota in search of better health. He is buried in Sleepy Hollow Cemetery in Concord along with Emerson

The abolitionist cause also attracted educators and philosophers such as Amos Bronson Alcott [1799, Wolcott, Connecticut, USA; 1888]. Alcott was the father of celebrated author Louisa May Alcott, the second of four daughters borne by his wife Abigail. He and his family were poor until his daughter Louisa May became a literary success.

As an educator, Bronson Alcott developed a radical method of teaching young children by means of conversation. In 1834, he established a school at Boston in which his new egalitarian system of teaching was employed. The school was criticized by the press and considered by the public as a revolutionary innovation. His method of teaching was far in advance of his time and won him few pupils. In 1839, he closed the school and later moved to Concord, Massachusetts. Thereafter, he became widely known as a lecturer, women's-rights proponent, and anti-slavery advocate. As a prominent abolitionist, he opposed the Mexican-American War because he felt it resulted from a desire by the American government to extend slavery into Texas.

As a philosopher, Bronson Alcott was a leader of the philosophic doctrine of transcendentalism. In 1841, he helped found the socialist Brook Farm Institute Of Agriculture And Education, a cooperative experimental community. Brook Farm was established in West Roxbury, now part of Boston. Members of the transcendentalism movement founded the farm to develop a union between intellectual growth and manual labor. To achieve this goal, they operated a school on the farm. The members of the group were to contribute equally to the work and to share equally in the proceeds from the work and from the social and educational opportunities. In 1847, the community was abandoned after the central building burned.

Louisa May Alcott [1832, Germantown, Pennsylvania, USA; 1888, Boston, Massachusetts] is best known for Little Women, her popular Civil War era story of the development of four sisters into young women set in New England. She also wrote approximately two hundred and seventy other works, making her one of America's best-loved children's novelist. Her adult novels were less popular.

As a result of her father's involvement in a number of financially disastrous utopian schemes, the family was continually in desperate need of money. The experiences of the March girls in Little Women (Jo, Meg, Beth, and Amy) recall those of the young Alcott sisters. When the family moved to Concord, their neighbors and friends included literary giants Thoreau and Emerson. To help her family, Alcott worked as a seamstress, servant, and schoolteacher, finally turning to writing. She sold her first story in 1852, and other salable fiction rapidly followed. By 1860 she had also published a book of fairy tales and had become a regular contributor to *The Atlantic Monthly*.

In 1862, during the Civil War, Louisa Alcott served as a nurse in the Union hospital at Georgetown, now part of Washington, D.C. The poignant letters she wrote home telling of her hospital experiences were published in 1863 under the title *Hospital Sketches*. The publication rewarded her financially and won her notoriety. Her first serious novel appeared the next year.

Alcott became a respected and financially successful novelist with her largely autobiographical *Little Women*, published in 1868. Her new found wealth enabled her to pay off all the family debts and allowed for a long tour of Europe with her sister May. Her work was now in demand, and sequels soon followed including *Little Men*, written in Rome, Italy and published in 1871.

Throughout her life, Alcott worked for the abolition of slavery. As her fame grew, she also gave her support to the temperance and the woman's suffrage movements. She never married. Her last years were spent in sickness, but she continued to write until her death. She died on the day of her father's funeral.

African American involvement in the anti-slavery crusade was substantial. The abolitionist movement attracted many Black leaders, writers, and former slaves from the fledgling free Black communities. These free Blacks had either been born free, escaped slavery, or obtained manumission by the freeing of masters or self-purchase. Many Northern free Blacks worked independently or alongside White abolitionists in demanding freedom for the slaves. Numerous articulate former slaves wrote influential and powerful poems, plays, short stories, autobiographies, and novels, which provided a unique view into the African American experience. Most slaves were denied by law and practice the opportunity to learn to read and write. The achievement of literacy, and especially the publication of written works, demonstrated to many people that African Americans had the talent and ability to create material of literary merit and achieve the same accomplishments as Whites.

The earliest surviving works of Black American literature date from the mid-eighteenth century and were written by Africans brought to America as slaves. The oldest example is considered to be a poem written in 1746 by Lucy Terry Prince [circa 1730, West Africa; 1821, Sunderland, Vermont, USA] entitled "Bar's Fight". In addition to being a pioneering African American poet, she was also known for her extraordinary oratorical skills.

Born in West Africa, enslaved, and brought to Rhode Island, Prince was sold at the age of five to a Massachusetts resident, Ebenezer Wells. Baptized soon after, she was taught to read and write by her owner. At age sixteen, she was witness to a Native American raid against White settlers that took place in a field outside of Deerfield, Massachusetts. Her famous 1746 poem describes the victims and survivors of the raid. The poem was preserved and handed down orally until its publication in 1855 by American editor and author Josiah Gilbert Holland [1819, Belchertown, Massachusetts, USA; 1881] in his *History of Western Massachusetts*.

While Prince's reputation as a poet rests on a single poem, her reputation as an orator follows from two unusual events. She married Abijah Prince, a free African American who purchased her freedom, and moved to Vermont in 1756. They were the parents of six children. When one of her sons was ready to seek higher education, Williams College rejected him because of his race. Incensed by this injustice, Lucy reputedly pleaded her case for several hours in front of the college trustees, quoting both the law and the Bible. Although unsuccessful with the trustees, a few years later Lucy appeared before the United States Circuit Court. When a land dispute between the Princes and their neighbors could not be solved in the local judiciary, it went to the Circuit court. Dissatisfied with her lawyer, Isaac Ticknor, later Governor of Vermont, Prince pleaded her own case and won, earning the praise of the presiding judge.

Jupiter Hammon [circa 1711, Oyster Bay, New York, USA; circa 1806] gained fame as a Black poet and the first published Black American writer. His biblically inspired, hymnlike verse defined his role as a founder of the Black American literary tradition.

Hammon was a slave his entire life, and served several generations of the Lloyd family in Lloyd's Neck, Long Island, New York. During the Revolutionary War, he lived with his owners in Hartford, Connecticut. The family later returned to New York State. Many of his writings neither condemn, nor even mention slavery. Instead, they praise Christianity in the same manner as the evangelical hymns that were his models. Although his words were not deliberately radical, they nonetheless represented a radical act.

His masters were affluent, and the few documents of his life with them show that he was a favorite servant who worked as a clerk in their family enterprise and was trained both as a craftsman and as a farmhand. He was also permitted to attend school, and his formal education helped shape his development as a poet. Like his owners, Hammon was a devout Christian, and was influenced by the religious revivals taking place in eighteenth century New England. His writing reflects his deep spirituality.

Hammon became the first known Black American to publish a piece of literature when the eighty-eight line poem "An Evening Thought; Salvation by Christ, with Penitential Cries" appeared in 1761. The poem was written on Christmas Day, 1760, and like his other works, showed intense religious fervor. Hammon's subsequent publications included a 1778 poetical address to Phillis Wheatley, another early African American author, and "An Evening's Improvement", which included the verse dialogue "The Kind Master and Dutiful Servant".

In his speech "Address To The Negroes Of The State of New York" which he presented at the African Society in New York in 1786, Hammon clearly expressed in this speech his opinions on slavery. As an individual, he claimed he did not wish to be free, causing some to speculate that he felt it was his personal duty to endure slavery with patience. Hammon did, however, add that he believed slavery was unjust, and urged owners to free the young. The speech was reprinted twice for a Pennsylvania abolitionist society.

Black poetry at the time of the American War of Independence retained its concern with the burning issues of the Revolution, including liberty, equality, independence, and identity. It also expressed Black experiences of divided loyalties between their African ancestry and culture, and their tenuous American reality. Several of the nation's early leaders believed that African slaves were intellectually inferior to Whites. Thomas Jefferson and others wrote extensively on the subject. It was generally believed that Black Africa was uncivilized and illiterate, often ignoring hard evidence to the contrary. In fact, great Black civilizations and cultures had flourished throughout the so-called Dark Continent for thousands of years.

Phillis Wheatley [circa 1753, Senegal, Africa; 1784, Boston, Massachusetts], a Boston colonial bondwoman, vehemently challenged these prevalent racist assumptions and stereotypes. Captured in Africa by slave traders at the age of eight, Phillis was transported to the American colonies and sold to John Wheatley, a wealthy merchant tailor of Boston, Massachusetts, who bought her as a servant for his wife. She was educated by her owners and taught English, ancient Greek, and Latin. She also studied geography and history. She began writing poetry at the age of about fourteen. In 1773, she accompanied a member of the Wheatley family to England, where she gained widespread attention in literary circles. Her book entitled *Poems On Various Subjects, Religious And Moral*, was published that year in London. Her poetry reflected both the influence of Alexander Pope and her study of Latin. It became the first Black American work of literature to be widely distributed.

Wheatley was deeply religious. Several of her poems expressed her satisfaction at becoming a Christian in American society, while others were about more worldly issues. In one poem, Wheatley contrasted her status as a slave with the demand of the American Colonies for independence. In another, she honored George Washington. Like the White patriot poets, Wheatley wrote in eighteenth century literary forms. However, her highly structured and elegant poetry nonetheless expressed her frustration at enslavement and desire to reach a paradise where the color of her skin and social position would no longer restrain her. She is generally recognized as the first important African American poet. Her poetry, along with that of other slaves, began a powerful Black American tradition in American literature.

After returning from England, Wheatley returned to Boston and became an accomplished poet. She was freed following the deaths of the

Wheatleys. In 1778, she married John Peters, a free Black man. Her reputation as a poet soon declined, however, and she died virtually unknown.

Many early Black writers focused on expressing Christian sentiments rather than proving the equality of African Americans or ending slavery. However, beginning in the late 1700s, Black writers increasingly used their poetry, fiction, and autobiographical material to challenge inequality, injustice, and enslavement. During the nineteenth century, African American poets wrote about the abolition of slavery and the emancipation of its victims. They often intentionally expressed themselves with irony and ambiguity so that different audiences heard different messages. White abolitionist poets, from their more privileged social position, could afford to be more direct and confrontational about the enslavement issue.

The first Southern Black poet was George Moses Horton [circa 1797, Raleigh, Northampton County, North Carolina, USA; 1883, Philadelphia, Pennsylvania], often called the first African American professional man of letters. Born into slavery, Horton was the property of three generations of the same North Carolina family before Emancipation in 1865. He had no formal education, but began creating poetry by composing verses in his head. He was taught by his mother to read and write, and began to compose poems while working on the campus of the University of North Carolina. Horton, who was enslaved for most of his life, made money, even as a bondman, by creating poems for university students. These early patrons commissioned him to compose love poems for their sweethearts. Horton had not yet learned to write, but he dictated while the students transcribed. Students paid him for his verses, between 25 and 50 cents per poem, and they occasionally compensated him with books.

White novelist Caroline Lee Hentz noticed Horton's talents and helped him improve his writing skills. Several professors at the university helped him publish his work in a number of newspapers. He became the first Black person in the South to publish a book, receiving local notoriety, but his creative potential was continually frustrated by the limits on his freedom. Known as the "Colored Bard" of North Carolina, Horton wrote of his desire for freedom in a book entitled *The Hope Of Liberty*, written in 1829. His work was issued in the hopes of raising enough money to buy his freedom. Horton's last collection was published at the end of the Civil War, when he became legally free.

Many of his poems dealt with traditional subjects such as love, religion, and death, but some, especially in later years, expressed anti-slavery themes. When freedom came for Horton, he was seventy years old and no longer able to pursue the career he might have had. He moved north to Philadelphia and is thought to have remained there until he passed away.

African American reformer, lecturer, and author Frances Ellen Watkins Harper (born Frances Ella Watkins) [1825, Baltimore, Maryland, USA; 1911] devoted her life to Abolitionism, the rights of freed slaves, the temperance movement, and women's suffrage. She was a prolific writer and dynamic speaker who stirred audiences by reading from her frankly propagandist poems.

Harper was born of free parents who died when she was only two years old, after which an uncle reared and educated her. She began to write poetry as a young girl and began lecturing in 1854. She spoke vigorously against enslavement throughout the Northeastern United States and Canada. In 1860, she married Fenton Harper, a farmer, and then gave up lecturing until after his death in 1864. She published several volumes of poetry, four novels, as well as many essays, stories, and letters. These works satisfied both her desire for artistic expression, and her support for Black emancipation and women's rights. Her use of long narrative verses in rhymed tetrameter served her elocution style very well as her themes focused on the value of self-sacrifice and life in the South. Written in witty and ironic African American vernacular, her works were peopled with socially committed Black characters.

Harper was a devout Christian who became involved in radical politics. Her passionate abolitionist and early feminist poems called both Blacks and Whites to action against injustice. She began writing in the mid-nineteenth century and was one of the first widely noted African American authors. She was particularly recognized for her poems on Black suffering, which were often published in abolitionist newspapers including *The Liberator*. Most of Harpers poems dealt with anti-slavery and racial themes, but she also wrote about a variety of other subjects. She became the leading African American poet of her time, despite the fact that contemporary literary critics rarely found her work brilliant or original. During her later years, Harper became known for her lectures supporting women's suffrage and opposing the consumption and sale of alcohol. From 1883 to 1890, Harper served as superintendent of activities among African Americans for the Woman's Christian Temperance Union.

African American poets usually borrowed the language and style of the largely White, mainstream United States. In using conventional language, these African American authors showed their White audiences how differently anthems of freedom and liberty sounded from the viewpoint of those who had been denied the promise of equality.

The poet James M. Whitfield [1822, New Hampshire, USA; 1871] was born a free Black American. His poetry attracted the interest of Black leader Frederick Douglass, and by 1850, Whitfield's poetry was familiar to readers of *The Liberator*, and other anti-slavery publications. In 1853, Whitfield published his work entitled *America and other Poems*. The book was a critical success, but sales were not sufficient to enable him to abandon his trade as a barber to write poetry full-time. Filled with harsh imagery, his work was an ironic and bitter analysis of slavery in a supposedly free nation.

Apart from poetry, early Black literature successfully explored other forms. Independent African American theater flourished in Northern cities for a brief time in the 1820s. A Black acting troupe called the African Theater was founded in New York City by dramatist William Henry Brown. The troupe produced plays by Shakespeare as well as Black plays, including the first play by an African American writer, *The Drama Of King Shotaway*, written by Brown in 1823. His play was based on a slave insurrection on the island of Saint Vincent in the West Indies. By the 1830s, White officials had closed African American theaters, claiming they instigated disorderly conduct.

Boston pamphleteer David Walker [1785, Wilmington, North Carolina, USA; 1830, Boston, Massachusetts] was an African American dedicated to the anti-slavery movement. Born a free man, his father had been a slave and his mother a free woman. In 1827, he settled in Boston and opened a second-hand clothing business. He became a leader in Boston's Colored Association, which condemned slavery. Self educated; Walker wrote for and helped distribute *Freedom's Journal*, the first Black newspaper in the United States. After traveling through the South and observing the condition of slaves, Walker wrote and published in 1829 a famous radical anti-slavery pamphlet called *An Appeal to the Colored Citizens of the World, or David Walker's Appeal*. In it he denounced slavery and urged American slaves to fight for their freedom and proper place in American society. Its publication was considered insurrectionary and marked the start of the radical anti-slavery movement in the United States. His pamphlet was the strongest attack on slavery made up to that time by an African American author. Walker detailed in clear terms the horrors that many Black slaves suffered at the hands of their White owners.

David Walker's Appeal shocked leaders in several Southern states. As a result, they prohibited the distribution of the pamphlet and of all anti-slavery literature in general. Three Southern states, Georgia, Louisiana, and North Carolina adopted a policy of imposed illiteracy, accordingly enacting laws making it illegal to teach Blacks to read and write. Walker, a used clothes merchant, smuggled his pamphlets into the slave states by sewing them into the lining of jackets worn by Black sailors. Consequently, Walker received threats against his life and Southern officials put a price on Walker's head of one thousand dollars dead or ten thousand dollars if captured alive. Not long after, Walker suddenly died under mysterious circumstances, reportedly of poisoning. Many abolitionists believed he was murdered.

The abolition movement brought about the greatest development in nineteenth-century American literary biography, the slave narrative. This unique American literary genre recorded another side of life in America. These works represented the embodiment of the slaves' perspective. The narratives consisted of a former slave's memoir of daily plantation life, his sufferings as a slave, and his eventual escape from bondage to freedom. The narratives contained many humorous anecdotes of the deception and pretenses that the slave was forced to practice in order to ingratiate himself with the owner. They also described expressions of religious fervor and superstition, but, above all, a pervasive longing for freedom, dignity, and self-respect.

The first example of the slave narrative appeared in Boston in 1760 entitled, *A Narrative of the Uncommon Sufferings and Surprising Deliverance of Briton Hammon, A Negro Man*. This was followed by other early examples, including 1784's *A Narrative of the Lord's Wonderful Dealings with J. Murrant, A Black, Taken Down From his own Relation*. African-born Olaudah Equiano's [circa 1750, Benin, kingdom of Benin, present-day Nigeria; 1797, England] autobiography is considered to be one of the most important early slave narratives from the perspective of a former bondman. In recording the history of his own kidnapping, sale, and enslavement, the African who would become known as Gustavus Vassa, also provided a history of slavery in North America.

Equiano was the son of an elder in Benin. His status, however, did not protect him from being kidnapped in 1756 by White slave traders, and sold into slavery while still a child. His African name, Olaudah Equiano, was changed first to Jacob and then to Michael and finally to Gustavus Vassa by his captors. Sold to a British naval officer in Virginia, Vassa saw military action in Canada and on the high seas before returning to England in 1762. He had been promised at the least a bonus of money and at the most his freedom, but he was sold again, first to a captain of merchant vessels in Montserrat and then to a storekeeper in Philadelphia, from whom he purchased his freedom. He settled in England, converted to Christianity, and traveled extensively in the service of the abolitionist cause.

Equiano's two-volume autobiography – *The Interesting Narrative of the Life and Adventures of Olaudah Equiano, Or Gustavus Vassa, The African, Written by Himself* – was a powerful contribution to the anti-slavery crusade. His title alone made a significant statement. With it he reclaimed his African identity, Olaudah Equiano, and subordinated the slave name Gustavus Vassa. His book described the many injustices he suffered, including, the several inhumane months as a captive in Africa, followed by his arduous passage to Barbados on a slave ship. The book was first published in England in 1789 followed by an American edition published in 1791.

The slave narrative gained popularity during the nineteenth century, as slavery became an important topic of political discussion. Their publication was encouraged by the abolitionists. The narratives, many of them based on oral testimonies, quickly multiplied. Although some of these accounts were factual autobiographies, many others were influenced or sensationalized by the author's desire to arouse sympathy for the anti-slavery cause. In some instances, the narrative was fictitious. An example of this was a work entitled *The Autobiography of a Female Slave*, written by Mattie Griffith in 1856.

The slave narrative reached its peak with Frederick Douglass' (original name Frederick Augustus Washington Bailey) [1818, Tuckahoe, Talbot County, Maryland, USA; 1895, Anacostia, Washington, D.C.] classic 1845 autobiography, *Narrative of the Life of Frederick Douglass, An American Slave*. His narrative created a masterpiece of the genre providing unsettling commentary and vivid details on the nature of slavery. The novel demonstrated how slaves were often deprived of contact with their families and made victims of harsh treatment. Accounts such as these energized the abolitionist movement and were an effective setback to those who asserted that slaves were content. Douglass' book was revised and enlarged several times for two later editions: *My Bondage and My Freedom*, published in 1855; and, *The Life and Times of Frederick Douglass*, published in 1881 and revised in 1892. In these accounts, he described his experiences as a slave in the South and as a fugitive in the North. He also described life as a free African American before the Civil War and depicted his rise to national prominence during and following the War. While depicting his life as a slave and his struggle toward freedom, Douglass emphasized the primary role that literacy played in opening opportunities for Blacks. He symbolically referred to his ability to write his own life story as the ultimate act of an emancipated man.

Frederick Douglass was one of the most eminent human-rights leaders and the most celebrated Black journalist, orator, reformer, and abolitionist leader of the nineteenth century. His oratorical and literary brilliance thrust him into the forefront as a leading spokesman of the American anti-slavery movement as he campaigned for the end of slavery. In later life, he continued to work for full civil rights for African Americans and he became the first African Americans citizen to receive high rank appointments in the United States government.

Douglass was born the child of an unknown White man and a Black slave by the name of Harriet Bailey. Like most slaves, his owner did not reveal his birth date, and slave mothers new little about conventional calendars. The absence of birth dates often added to a slave's low sense of self-worth and identity. Douglass would be troubled all his life about his unknown date of birth and in vain tirelessly searched for any records that could help. Following his death, records were found which confirmed that his birth took place in February 1818.

Douglass was born a slave because by law children followed the status of their mothers. He was forcibly separated from his mother at an early age and never knew her well, although she did walk long distances to visit him until she died when he was only nine. He initially lived with his grandparents on a Maryland plantation and then was placed under the care of a woman called Aunt Katy, who raised slave children on the plantation of Colonel Edward Lloyd. At seven, Douglass was sent to his owner, Captain Aaron Anthony [; 1823], at a nearby plantation. There he met for the first time his brother and two sisters. At the age of eight, he was sent north across the Chesapeake Bay to Baltimore to live as a house servant with the family of Hugh and Sophia Auld, who were relatives of his owner. Sophia Auld defied state law by teaching Douglass to read from the Bible until her husband forbade such instruction; believing that learning would make Douglass unfit for slavery. Frederick had already learned basic literacy skills and secretly used books belonging to Sophia Auld's son to further teach himself. He also continued his education secretly with the help of White schoolchildren in the street.

At age thirteen, he bought his first book, *The Columbian Orator*. This work contained speeches denouncing slavery and oppression. The study of this book deepened his hatred of slavery and convinced him of the injustice of enslavement as well as the natural right of all people to be free. The book also taught him public speaking techniques that would later make him a great orator.

At age sixteen, the Aulds found Douglass becoming too independent, so they returned him to his owner. There he was made to work on the plantation as a field hand and forced to submit more readily to slavery. When Douglass was about seventeen, he was sent by his owner to work for Edward Covey, a known slave breaker who specialized in breaking the spirit of uncooperative slaves. Covey had Douglass punished and beaten daily for the slightest violation of the rules. After almost six months, Douglass stood up to Covey, wrestling him in a fight. Following that episode, Covey never again attempted to mistreat Douglass. Douglass later described his confrontation with Covey as the turning point of his life as a slave. Before the conflict, Douglass considered himself worthless, but after it, he wrote passionately about attaining manhood. Covey returned Douglass to his owner, who then sent him back to Baltimore and hired him out as an apprentice in a shipyard. He learned the ship caulker's trade, which involved making ships watertight, and learned to write by tracing letters on the prows of these ships.

Douglass had once tried to escape with three others in 1836, but the plot was discovered before they could get away. Now, two years later, he obtained papers supplied by a free African American seaman and, dressed as a sailor just returning from sea duty, boarded a train from Baltimore and fled to New York City. Once in New York, Douglass made his way to the home of David Ruggles [1810, Connecticut, USA;

1849], one of the leading African American abolitionists in the nation and publisher-editor of the anti-slavery magazine, *The Mirror Of Liberty*. In order to elude slave hunters, Ruggles helped him decide on a new name, Frederick Johnson, and also helped him contact his fiancée, Anna Murray [USA; 1882, Anacostia, Washington, D.C.], a free African American from Baltimore. She arrived a few days later, and married Douglass.

The couple went to New Bedford, in the free state of Massachusetts. New Bedford was known as a haven for fugitive slaves despite its typical Northern prejudice and discrimination. There, Douglass hoped to find work as a ship's caulker. He got a job as a caulker, but the other men refused to work with him because he was Black. Due to racial discrimination, he was forced to work for three years as a common laborer holding unskilled jobs, among them collecting rubbish and digging cellars. Douglass struggled to provide for his wife and first newborn child. The couple eventually had five children, including two sons who served in the Union Army during the Civil War. The children's education was a priority for Douglass who believed strongly that education translated into power. To his dismay, his wife remained illiterate all her life.

Douglass joined the New Bedford African Methodist Episcopal Zion Church and eventually became a licensed preacher. His sermons to the congregation honed his oratorical skills. During this period, he felt that his surname, Johnson, was too common. He decided to change it to Douglass, the name of a character in the 1810 poem, "The Lady Of The Lake", by Scottish writer Sir Walter Scott.

While in New Bedford, Douglass began to read the anti-slavery newspaper *The Liberator* and soon joined William Lloyd Garrison's followers in New Bedford. In 1841, he attended the Massachusetts Anti-Slavery Society convention in Nantucket, where he was invited to describe his feelings and experiences as a slave and explain what freedom meant to him. His unrehearsed statements were so heartfelt and naturally eloquent that he was unexpectedly launched into a new career as a compelling speaker for the Society. His fiery address made such a profound impression that the Society hired him as a full-time lecturer. In this position, and later as an agent for the larger American Anti-Slavery Society, he traveled throughout much of the segregated North, speaking at anti-slavery assemblies, giving public lectures, and aiding to recruit members for the societies. In 1841, Douglass campaigned in Rhode

Island against a proposed new state constitution that would deny African Americans the right to vote. In 1843, he traveled through the East and Middle West to address a series of anti-slavery meetings known as the One Hundred Conventions. Abolitionist women at these events often organized concerts and fairs to raise money for anti-slavery efforts.

Douglass campaigned tirelessly against bondage, but also for the civil rights of free African Americans. He spoke at several meetings that were broken up by White mobs, but he continued to speak out as a strong abolitionist. Despite insults, heckling, mockery, and violent personal attack, Douglass never wavered in his dedication to the anti-slavery cause. In the early 1840's, he protested against segregated seating on trains by sitting in cars reserved for Whites. He had to be literally dragged from the White cars. Douglass also protested against religious discrimination. He walked out of a church that kept African Americans from taking part in a service until the Whites had finished participating. Through these and other controversial actions, Douglass quickly became a leading abolitionist, campaigning tirelessly for the end of slavery and inequality in the United States.

Frederick Douglass had become one of the most famous orators of the time. His eloquent words about his life as a slave were a powerful weapon against the institution. However, as his oratory grew more polished, audiences began to question whether he had ever been enslaved. To counter skeptics, who doubted that such an articulate spokesperson could ever have been a slave, Douglass felt impelled to write his autobiography in 1845. Before the Civil War, former slaves who wished to tell their stories found access to publishers through connections with White abolitionists. Douglass was no exception, for his book included a preface, written by William Lloyd Garrison, which encouraged the reader to trust the writer.

Douglass' narrative was one of the most effective accounts authored by an escaped slave and quickly became a classic in American literature as well as a major source about the institution of slavery from the slave's perspective. In his book, he revealed the names of his former masters and described every aspect of his life in bondage. Douglass, however, left out details about his method of escape so as not to jeopardize similar attempts by other slaves. He published the details of his life as a slave despite the danger of his recapture under the provisions of the Fugitive Slave Laws; which allowed owners to seize runaway slaves and return them to bondage. Due to his increasing celebrity,

Douglass feared that his identity as a runaway slave would be revealed when the book was published, and that his owners would hire slave catchers to return him to Maryland. Therefore, in 1845, Douglass left on a two-year anti-slavery speaking tour of Great Britain and Ireland. His oratory skills made a great impression overseas and helped win many new friends for the abolitionist cause. He was greatly criticized back home, however, for whispering the fault of one nation in the ears of another.

In 1847, after English Quakers raised money to buy his freedom, Douglass returned to the United States. Now legally free, he started his own anti-slavery newspaper; managed and edited solely by African Americans. This he did to showcase Black intellectual talents and to disprove the proslavery argument that African Americans were intellectually inferior by nature. He moved his family to Rochester, New York, a hotbed of anti-slavery activity led by various women's rights groups. There he began publishing a weekly paper called *The North Star*. This publication later became *Frederick Douglass' Weekly* and was followed by *Douglass' Monthly*, which originated as a supplement to the *Weekly*. Douglass published and edited his newspapers almost continuously from 1847 through 1863, and he rapidly gained prominence as an influential journalist. Subscribers from the United States, Canada, and around the world helped finance his publications. Julia Griffith, whom he had met in England, moved to Rochester to work with Douglass. She oversaw his business concerns. The two maintained a close personal relationship for many years.

In his papers, Douglass supported the rights of free African Americans and slaves, condemned discrimination, and championed a number of other causes, most notably women's rights. In 1848, Douglass participated in the first women's rights convention held at Seneca Falls, New York, and throughout his career, he promoted women's equality. In the 1850's, Douglass charged that employers hired White immigrants ahead of African Americans. He even accused some abolitionist business executives of job discrimination against African Americans. In his famous speech, "The Mournful Wail of Millions", delivered in Rochester on July 4, 1852, Douglass denounced the celebration of independence while people were still enslaved. He also led a successful attack against Rochester's segregated schools. Douglass hoped that African Americans would no longer be employed only as servants and laborers. He proposed that schools be established to train them to become skilled artisans.

William Lloyd Garrison disagreed with the need for a separate, Black aligned press. He argued that Douglass' oratorical skills would be wasted running the business. Until he returned from the British Isles in 1847, Douglass had supported the opinions of Garrison, who favored ending slavery through the force of moral persuasion. Garrison also opposed any political action that indicated acceptance of the Constitution of the United States, which he and his supporters considered an immoral, proslavery document. In Britain and later in Rochester, however, Douglass met political abolitionists, who felt that it was possible to use the political system to combat slavery. They organized the anti-slavery Liberty Party, and called for the election of abolitionists to public office. Garrison called for the North to secede, if necessary, to free itself from the moral curse of slavery. In contrast, Douglass became convinced that this course of action would only abandon slaves to their owners. Douglass also rejected Garrison's pacifist philosophy that slaves must not actively resist their oppression. Douglass believed in the right of slaves to rebel and the right of fugitives to resist re-enslavement. His home in Rochester was a Station on the Underground Railroad and he personally joined other abolitionists in helping many of these fugitive slaves to reach safety in Canada, choosing St. Catharines, Ontario as his preferred reception center. Garrison denounced Douglass as a traitor to the cause, and the two men broke their friendship over this issue and drifted apart.

Douglass believed in politics as a legitimate weapon for social change. From 1848 through the 1850s, he politically allied himself and worked closely with the abolitionist Liberty Party led by James G. Birney. He supported its unbending demands for the total eradication of slavery. Occasionally, Douglass also supported the larger Free-Soil and Republican parties, which promised only to prevent the extension of slavery to new territories and states. Douglass also became a friend of abolitionist John Brown, who advocated the use of armed force to help free slaves. Douglass did not reject violence as a weapon against slavery. He believed it not wrong for slaves, or their friends, to hunt, harass, and even strike down the traffickers in human flesh. Yet, Douglass refused to join or support Brown in an attack planned on the federal arsenal and armory at Harpers Ferry in October 1859, and specifically advised against the raid. He warned Brown that seizing the armory would be considered an attack on the Federal government and could prove disastrous. After Brown was captured in the raid, Douglass faced charges that he was an accomplice and fled to Canada and then England to avoid possible arrest for treason. He returned to the United States, travelling again through Canada, about six months later upon receiving news of the death of his youngest child and after tensions over the John Brown incident had eased.

In the spring of 1860, not long after his return to the United States, Douglass began campaigning in the national Presidential election. At first he supported Gerrit Smith [1797, Utica, New York, USA; 1874, New York City], a leading antislavery crusader who provided financial backing for John Brown's activities. Later he came out in support of Abraham Lincoln and campaigned for him during his successful Presidential bid. After the outbreak of the Civil War, Douglass became a consultant to Lincoln urging him to expand his war goals beyond the stated objective of preserving the Union. Douglass argued that slavery was the true cause of the conflict and that the Union should make the abolition of bondage its main goal. He applauded President Lincoln's final Emancipation Proclamation of 1863, which freed slaves in the rebellious states, but expressed his disappointment that not all slaves had been freed. Douglass also called for the Union Army to recruit slaves and free African Americans; advocating the War be made a direct confrontation against slavery. He helped recruit two regiments of African Americans soldiers, the Massachusetts 54th and 55th. His own sons, Lewis and Frederick, were among the first to enlist for these all Black regiments. These regiments went on to serve the Union with decorated distinction in battle. When the African American troops were given lower wages and fewer chances for promotion than White soldiers were, Douglass met with Lincoln to request equal treatment for them. As the War progressed, President Lincoln conferred with Douglass as a representative of his people. By the end of the War, more than two hundred thousand African Americans had served in the United States Army and Navy.

Following the War, Douglass became a leading spokesman for improving the situation of former slaves and fought for their full civil rights. He supported the Negro Suffrage movement and labored for the passage of constitutional amendments securing African American rights. Later he saw that Southern African Americans had returned to virtual slavery under a post-war farming system called sharecropping. He attacked this system and urged that the federal government grant land to Blacks. Southern Confederate monuments and reunions during the decades following the War appalled Douglass. He felt the country was reuniting, but not the races. He condemned segregation policies and spoke out against lynching. Yet, he discouraged Blacks from leaving the South for greener and safer pastures out West. Instead, he believed Blacks should remain and demand equality and opportunity. Many in the Black community disagreed with Douglass on this issue and accused him of being out of touch with post-war Black realities.

In the 1872 national Presidential election, Douglass was the vice-presidential candidate on the Equal Rights Party slate led by the feminist Victoria Claflin Woodhull, the first woman ever to run for the presidency. In that same year, Douglass moved to the nation's capital after his Rochester home was burned under suspicious circumstances. In Anacostia near Washington D.C., he purchased a large and luxurious house that he called Cedar Hill. There, he increasingly became recognized as the premier leader of the country's African Americans and was deemed the Sage of Anacostia.

Douglass remained loyal to the Republican Party, despite its declining dedication to African American causes after Reconstruction. His own commitment to reform never diminished and he vigorously continued to support the women's rights movement. He held several government positions, serving as assistant secretary of the Santo Domingo Commission in 1871, United States marshal for the District of Columbia from 1877 to 1881, and as recorder of deeds for the District from 1881 to 1886. He pursued his active role in public service from 1889 to 1891 as United States minister and consul general to Haiti.

Controversy arose during the later years of Douglass' life. In 1882, his wife of forty-four years died. Although his marriage with Anna was not perfect, her passing nevertheless saddened him. In 1884, he married his White secretary and suffragette Helen Pitts. Some African Americans, and many Whites, criticized him for marrying outside his race, but he categorically rejected that his actions should be confined by his skin color. For Douglass, the marriage symbolized one more victory in his lifelong battle against racial discrimination. In fact during his first marriage, Douglass had often sought emotional comfort and intimacy with close White female friends including feminist Ottilie Assing. Assing was a German woman living in the United States and working for a German publication as a journalist. She interviewed Douglass, wrote articles on his activities, and translated his autobiography in German. Their liaison lasted three decades. On her death, Assing provided for Douglass in her will.

With Helen, Douglass recaptured a zest for life temporarily lost after the death of his first wife. Together, they engaged in social activities and traveled to Europe and Northern Africa. Douglass remained an active reformer literally until the day he died, when he collapsed in his Washington home after attending the National Council Of Women's suffrage meeting as an honored special guest. He had been warmly welcomed onto the speaker's platform but refused to speak. Helen lived on and vigorously preserved his reputation and legacy.

Along with Frederick Douglass's written account of his life, Harriet Ann Jacobs' [1812, Edenton, North Carolina, USA; 1897, Washington, D.C.] book is one of the two classic American slave narratives. Edited by Lydia Maria Child who donated her services, Jacobs' wrote the most significant major antebellum autobiography of a Black women.

She was born a slave and became a fugitive in the 1830s. By the time she was in her early twenties, Jacobs had borne two children, at least in part to discourage the sexual advances of her then master, James Norcom. In retaliation, Norcom banished Jacobs from Edenton to one of his country plantations. His threats to do the same to her children caused Jacobs to act. Her father, Daniel, had by then secured his freedom and lived in Edenton, where he labored as a carpenter. Jacobs believed that if she succeeded in escaping, Norcom would be willing to sell her children to Daniel, thus allowing them to avoid becoming plantation slaves. Her strategy worked when, in 1835, she escaped from the Norcom plantation. For the next seven years, Jacobs remained hidden by various family and friends in a small cramped loft in her grandmother's barn. Finally, she managed to escape to the North where she was reunited with her children, and then began working with abolitionists. She even worked in the abolitionist bookstore above Frederick Douglass' newspaper printing press.

Jacobs recorded her triumphant struggle for freedom in an autobiography that was published under a pseudonym in 1861. Her novel, *Incidents in the Life of a Slave Girl*, offered a different but no less horrifying portrayal of the evils of slavery. Jacobs' book recounted the history of her family, including the grandmother who hid her from her owner for seven years, a brother who escaped and spoke out for emancipation, and her two children she rescued and sent North. Hers was the only autobiography about the unique hardships suffered by women slaves. She described the humiliation of slavery and the sexual oppression and abuse experienced by young female slaves. She recalled tense relations with her owner, who was determined to make her his concubine, her owner's jealous wife, and the future congressman who fathered her children but broke his promise to free them. She portrayed a supportive free Black and slave community, and several sympathetic Whites including a slave mistress who cared for her. In addition, she told of a Northern woman who employed her, helped her avoid capture, and eventually bought her freedom.

Along with Douglass and Jacobs, numerous African American authors told their own stories of bondage and escape in books. Others focused on describing the plight of African Americans in general and denouncing what they believed to be an evil institution and stain on the nation's character. One important literary work of the latter kind was authored by Black army officer, physician, journalist, and social reformer Martin Robinson Delany [1812, Charles Town, Virginia (now West Virginia), USA; 1885, Xenia, Ohio]. The son of free Blacks, Delany was trained as a doctor at Harvard University, and practiced medicine in Pittsburgh. In 1852, he invented a device that would assist railroad locomotives in climbing and descending inclined planes but was denied a patent. In that same year, he started a medical practice in Pittsburgh, Pennsylvania. He spent most of his time, however, fighting against enslavement. He worked for the Underground Railroad and wrote for the *North Star* newspaper, the anti-slavery newspaper owned by Frederick Douglass. In 1852, he wrote his most important work: *The Condition, Elevation, Emigration, and Destiny of the Colored People of the United States*. In this book, Delany took the position of Black nationalism and argued for a separatist state for African Americans. In 1854, he helped organize the National Emigration Convention to discuss his proposal for the resettlement of Blacks in Africa.

In 1856, Delany moved to Canada and from Chatham, Ontario, continued his abolitionist activities. He supported John Brown's initiatives and participated in Brown's 1858 meetings held in Chatham. He also became the chief advocate of resettlement in West Africa. He believed integration of the races unlikely and undesirable. In 1858, he organized the Niger Valley Exploring Party with other Chatham abolitionists. The following year, he traveled to Africa and signed a treaty with a local leader for the settlement of unoccupied land in Niger. He then encouraged free African Americans and Canadians to move to Africa but quickly lost enthusiasm when the Civil War's naval blockades and disruptive effect on the sea routes destroyed his plans.

At the beginning of the Civil War, Delany published *Blake*, a fiction novel about a free Black man who organizes a slave rebellion. He then left Canada and put aside his writing to join the Union army. Delany was one of seventy-five African American officers in the Union army and served as a surgeon during the War. He became the first African American to earn the rank of major. Following the War, he worked for three years in the Freedmen's Bureau, a United States War Department agency established in 1865 to aid newly emancipated slaves after the Civil War. He subsequently became active in South Carolina politics but made a political miscalculation in 1876 by supporting former Confederate General Wade Hampton [1818, Charleston, South Carolina, USA; 1902], whose election as governor opened the door for a return to White supremacy in that state.

While the narrative was the most popular form of Black literature during the nineteenth century, Blacks also described slave life in fiction. These stories were similar in content to slave autobiographies. William Wells Brown [1815, near Lexington, Kentucky, USA; 1884, Chelsea, Massachusetts] was the first Black American author to publish a full-length fiction novel. Brown was born to an African American slave mother and a White slaveholding father. He grew up near St. Louis, Missouri where he served various owners. During his youth as a slave, he was variously employed as house servant, steamboat steward, and field hand on a hemp and tobacco farm. After twenty years in slavery and one unsuccessful and severely punished attempt at escape, Brown emancipated himself by making his way to Cincinnati, Ohio. There he adopted the name of a Quaker, Wells Brown, who helped him when he was a runaway. He had originally planned to settle in Southern Ontario following his escape but was frustrated by a frozen Lake Erie blocking steamboat passage across. Consequently he settled in the Southern Great Lakes region, spent the next two years working on a Lake Erie steamboat, and actively assisted dozens of slaves to escape to Canada. In the summer of 1834 he met and married Elizabeth Spooner, a free African American woman. Together they had three daughters, one of whom died shortly after birth. Two years after his marriage, Brown moved to Buffalo, where he began his career in the anti-slavery movement. He regularly attended meetings of the Western New York Anti-Slavery Society, welcomed anti-slavery lecturers at his home, spoke at local anti-slavery gatherings, and traveled to Haiti and Cuba to investigate emigration possibilities. Brown even traveled to Nova Scotia and central Canada in 1861 as an immigration agent for Haiti, trying to recruit African Canadians to join an emigration scheme to the Caribbean Island. Although fifteen hundred Blacks attended four meetings, he claimed no more than fifty would emigrate. While in Canada, he also visited Black settlements and reported his disappointment in their level of success. His opinion, however, was obviously biased towards these non-Haitian settlements.

Brown's abolitionist career was marked in the summer of 1843 when the city of Buffalo, New York hosted a national anti-slavery convention and the National Convention Of Colored Citizens. Brown attended both meetings, joined several committees, and became friends with a number of Black abolitionists, including Charles Lenox Remond and Frederick Douglass. Brown joined these two in their appeal to the power of moral persuasion, their rejection of anti-slavery violence, and their boycott of political Abolitionism. Brown's growing commitment to the abolitionist movement, his increasing sophistication as an orator, and his expanding reputation in the abolitionists community brought an invitation to speak before the American Anti-Slavery Society at its 1844 annual meeting in New York City. Three years later, he was hired as a Massachusetts Anti-Slavery Society lecture agent and moved to the Boston area.

By 1847, having taught himself to read and write, he had published his popular and highly dramatic autobiography: *Narrative Of William W. Brown, A Fugitive Slave*. In addition to his work as a lecturer for the abolitionist movement and temperance reform, Brown began a successful writing career. As a writer, he was the first African American to have a play and a travelogue published. The publication of those works, as well as a compilation of anti-slavery songs, established his reputation as the most prolific African American man of letters of the mid-1800s. Through his writing, he hoped to build sympathy for the anti-slavery agenda.

In 1849, he embarked on a lecture tour of England and remained abroad for five years. The length of his extended stay was determined by personal and political factors. Like Frederick Douglass before him, Brown was exhilarated by the relative freedom and equality Europe offered a Black man. During his lengthy speaking tour, he advocated the abolition of slavery. He also had time to write and enjoy the benefits of a reform minded strata of British society. He was also attempting to recover from the end of his marriage. In any case, once the American Fugitive Slave Law was enacted in 1850, it was risky for an escaped slave to return to the United States. Concern for Brown's safety prompted English abolitionists to purchase his freedom in 1854. His anti-slavery lectures in Europe inspired his 1852 book, *Three Years in Europe*, which was later expanded and renamed *The American Fugitive in Europe*. He published his only play in 1858 called *The Escape or A Leap for Freedom*. This melodrama was about two slaves who secretly married. Brown's historical writings included several books containing detailed descriptions about slave life, racism, and Abolitionism. His works revealed his growing anti-slavery militancy.

Brown's only fiction novel, *Clotel or The President's Daughter*, was the first written by a Black American author. Published in Britain in 1854, the book was a satire of race matters in antebellum America and gave a fictional account of slave children allegedly fathered by American President Thomas Jefferson with his slave Currer. *Clotel*, the fictional daughter of Jefferson, serves as the main character of the book, in which Brown combined historical fiction, national legend, and the increasingly divisive subject of race. It was intended to underscore the distance between American ideals of liberty and the actual living circumstances of Black American slaves.

After the Civil War, Brown fulfilled his lifelong desire to become a physician. During the remainder of his life, he lived in the Boston area and produced three major volumes of African American history. He also continued to lecture, write, and travel extensively.

Harriet E. Wilson's [circa 1828, Milford, New Hampshire, USA; circa 1863, Boston, Massachusetts] book, *Our Nig*, was the first fiction novel published in the United States by a Black American author and the first book authored by an African American woman. *Our Nig* was also known as: *Sketches from the Life of A Free Black, in a Two-Story White House, North; Showing That Slavery's Shadows Fall Even There.*

In 1850, Harriet was living with the Samuel Boyles family in the town of Milford. The next year, she married Thomas Wilson, a free man who passed himself off as an escaped slave from Virginia so he could lecture on the horrors of slavery. Shortly after the birth of their son, George Mason Wilson in 1852, Thomas left them. Harriet Wilson, who was unable to work due to the physical and emotional abuse inflicted by her employers, lost custody of her son. She began writing to earn enough money to reclaim him. Her son died five months after her book's Boston publication in 1859.

Our Nig is a largely autobiographical novel that explicitly compares the racist conditions suffered by an African American indentured servant in the North to slavery in the South. Using the slave narrative as a model, Wilson indicted Northern treatment of African Americans.

The chief character of the novel, Frado, has a Black father and a White mother. A theme of abandonment begins when Frado loses both parents. Her mother leaves, and her father dies. She is then left to the mercy of a cruel mistress who abuses her. She escapes and supports herself as a milliner, marries, but again is abandoned, this time by her husband. The novel ends tragically with Frado and her baby homeless and destitute.

Wilson wrote the novel to alleviate her poverty. She appended endorsements of her good character written by White friends, and appealed to her readers for financial aid. She alienated both Northern women and abolitionists, however, by exposing the horrors of slavery and racial prejudice in Northern households. Possibly because of its controversial stand, the novel was published at the writer's own expense and sold poorly. Wilson died not long after the novel appeared, and her work fell into obscurity.

The spoken word was often used by abolitionists to advance their cause. Powerful and effective speeches by Black American orators were sometimes more influential than books. Few proved this better than uncompromising mystic, preacher, feminist, and abolitionist Sojourner Truth (originally named Isabella Baumfree Van Wagener) [circa 1797, Hurley, Ulster County, New York, USA; 1883, Battle Creek, Michigan].

The circumstances surrounding her liberation are vague, but her surname was taken from Isaac Van Wagener, who was reportedly the last of her several owners. She was born into slavery but apparently ran away when her owner refused to acknowledge New York State's emancipation act of 1827, which freed all of the state's ten thousand men, women, and children still held in bondage. After settling in New York City, where she worked as a domestic servant, she became closely associated with a Christian evangelist named Elijah Pierson. She became involved with his religious cult but, disillusioned, broke with it in 1843. A mystic who heard voices she believed to be God's, that same year she experienced what she regarded as a command from God to preach. Obeying her voices, she took the name Sojourner Truth, adopting her new name as symbolic of her spiritual mission, and thereafter began preaching in the streets of New York City and along the eastern seaboard. She took up the struggle for Black emancipation and women's suffrage, becoming a leading African American woman orator. Her early speeches were based on the belief that people best show love for God by love and concern for others. She was exposed to the anti-slavery movement, which she ardently embraced, and for the next few years, she toured the country speaking in its behalf; thus becoming the first African American woman orator to speak out against slavery.

An illiterate all her life, she nevertheless could quote the Bible word for word. An imposing six feet tall with a deep rich voice, she stirred audiences around the country with her charismatic presence and oratorical skills. Her growing reputation and personal magnetism often attracted huge crowds to her informal lectures and appearances. Her quick wit and inspiring faith helped spread her fame as she traveled widely through New England and the Midwest on lecture tours. She supported herself by selling copies of her book, *The Narrative of Sojourner Truth*, which she had dictated to a friend.

Discovering the women's rights movement in 1850, she adopted their cause and became an advocate of women's issues. She made a famous speech entitled "Ain't I a Woman?" at a convention on women's issues in 1851 in Akron, Ohio. She made that speech in response to Protestant ministers' claims that men deserved greater privileges than women because of man's superior intellect and because God had chosen Jesus to take the form of a man. The speech was retold in written form by Frances D. Gage thirty years after the convention and became a classic of American literature.

During the Civil War, Sojourner solicited gifts for African American volunteer regiments, and President Lincoln received her as his guest in Washington, in the White House in 1864. She served in Washington as a counselor to freed slaves and worked to improve living conditions for African Americans there. She also helped find work and homes for slaves who had escaped from the South to Washington. In the 1870's, she tried to persuade the federal government to set aside undeveloped lands in the West as farms for African Americans. Her plan for a Negro State in the West won no government support. She continued to give her speaking tours across the nation until 1875, continuously advocating equality for African Americans and for women. In 1997, the United States spacecraft Mars Pathfinder landed on the planet Mars carrying on board a small rover named Sojourner, in honor of Sojourner Truth; the word sojourner meaning traveler. Homage was thus accorded, in this unique way, to a woman who had, more than a century earlier, traveled the United States in the name of justice and equality.

In addition to the spoken-word, African Americans slaves also used music and lyrics to orally express their plight. Many of these songs are now recognized as the forerunners of more modern Black American musical forms including spirituals, the blues, and ultimately, jazz. The intent of this slave music and the human suffering that lay behind it conveyed a strong message to those who listened. Joshua McCarter Simpson, from Ohio, was one such African American poet whose memorable songs of emancipation were set to popular tunes and sung by runaway slaves.

Although the American political establishment was rarely sympathetic to abolitionist agendas, several Black activists worked with various political organizations dedicated to the abolition of slavery. One such African American was Charles Lenox Remond [1810, Salem, Massachusetts, USA; 1873]. Remond worked passionately for the anti-slavery cause by traveling throughout the Northern United States and Europe testifying against slavery and organizing moral and political opposition. Remond was the first Black person to speak at public meetings in support of Abolitionism and was the American delegate to the 1840 World's Anti-Slavery Convention in London. At the 1858 Convention of Colored Citizens of Massachusetts, Remond proposed the militant suggestion that Southern slaves should resort to insurrection.

Another passionate Black abolitionist was Henry Highland Garnet [1815, New Market, Maryland, USA; 1882, Liberia]. Born a slave in Maryland, he escaped as a young boy with his family in 1824 to New York. There, he obtained an education including fourteen years of formal schooling, ending with his graduation from Oneida Institute in Whitesboro, New York, in 1840. Three years later, Garnet was ordained as a pastor and appointed preacher of the Liberty Street Presbyterian Church in Troy, New York. Later, he led congregations in New York City, the Jamaican city of Kingston, and Washington, D.C.

Before entering the clergy, Garnet had identified himself with the organized anti-slavery movement, speaking at the annual meeting of the American Anti-Slavery Society in 1840. The same year, he attended the first annual meeting of the American And Foreign Anti-Slavery Society. He became a leading advocate for racial equality during the mid-1800s and traveled throughout the United States and the British Isles lecturing against the slave trade. He often wrote and spoke of the role Blacks played in the American Revolution, and the accomplishments of Haitian revolutionary leaders such as Toussaint L'Ouverture. At the National Negro Convention of free African Americans held in Buffalo, New York in 1843, Garnet delivered his most famous speech "An Address to the Slaves of the United States". In his speech, Garnet urged slaves to protest for their lives and liberties and called upon them to rebel and kill their owners. He added that it would be better for slaves to die seeking freedom than to live in bondage. Many of the delegates to the convention considered Garnet's words too radical, resulting in him losing support. His call for slave resistance in any form, including violence, stunned the country. His speech was actually delivered as a resolution, which the convention failed to adopt, by one vote. Four years later, another national convention adopted a similar resolution by Garnet. Prominent abolitionists, such as Frederick Douglass, initially opposed Garnet's call to resistance. Yet, as the Civil War approached, and especially after the enactment of the Fugitive Slave Act of 1850, more abolitionists began to side with Garnet and his notion of violent resistance.

Garnet supported the idea of Black emigration from the United States and visited Canadian Black communities in 1848. What he saw in Canada did little to convince him that Blacks could find equality anywhere in North America. He instead called for closer ties between African Americans in the United States and Africa and called upon Blacks to immigrate to Africa. In 1858, Garnet founded the African Civilization Society with the mission of encouraging Blacks to immigrate to Africa. Although the Society dissolved before the end of the Civil War, Garnet maintained interest in Africa. Near the end of the War, Garnet addressed the House of Representatives, encouraging an end to slavery. In 1881, he was appointed American minister and consul general to the African nation of Liberia, where he died.

In the final analysis, despite the long struggle carried on by the abolitionists, the Civil War provided the ultimate victory for the American anti-slavery movement. After the War, many abolitionists joined the struggle to win political and social equality for Blacks. They became leading spokespersons for improving the situation and conditions of former slaves. They also worked for the passage of the Thirteenth, Fourteenth, and Fifteenth Amendments to the United States Constitution. These landmark amendments finally banned slavery, made all people born in the United States citizens, and prohibited racial discrimination in voting.

George Brown

9.   CANADIAN ABOLITIONISTS

In Canada, although much smaller in numbers, abolitionists worked along side their American counterparts throughout the decades leading to the Civil War. The goals were similar and the sense of urgency was the same. During these years, the general sentiment in Canada, while not necessarily pro-North, was generally anti-slavery.

The African slave trade reached Canadian territory with the first waves of European settlement early in the seventeenth century. Slavery existed throughout Canada for over two hundred years. During this period, chattel slavery was an accepted custom and laws were often passed to ensure its legal status. In New France, opposition to the practice was not prevalent. The colony's Roman Catholic Church was not active in opposing slavery as such, and it's clergy sometimes owned slaves themselves. The clergy in New France, however, did not publicly promote slavery, as did many Protestant clergy in the United States. The French Church instead seemed content with encouraging slave laws and regulations that were more humane. In short, the Church in New France generally adhered to the prevalent racial thoughts and morays of that epoch and thus accepted slavery as a social reality.

By the late eighteenth century, opposition to the institution of slavery was slowly growing among the people of Canada. Canadian slaves generally worked as personal domestic servants or on the wharves. A few settlers had many slaves, but more than twenty was considered unusual. This made the challenge to eradicate slavery far simpler than it was in plantation economies, where its labor was much more important. Some English speaking Canadians disliked the practice because of its association with the Americans. French Canadians, who often were relegated to a lower economic class, saw no direct pecuniary benefits in it for them. In general, Canadian public opinion did not support slavery as being necessary, practical, economically sound, or moral. Although fervent condemnation of slavery by both English and French Canadians was generally lacking, their indifference or mild tolerance towards it, or measured support of abolition, helped create a climate conducive towards ending the practice.

Between 1763 and 1790, British rule in Canada strengthened the colony's general legal structure and in some ways, defined the legality and practice of slavery. Beginning in the late eighteenth century, various Canadian legislators and courts began to limit, then abolish slavery despite vigorous opposition from slave-owners. Slavery technically remained legal in most of Canada, however, until it was abolished for the entire British Empire in 1834. By the 1820s, the practice was virtually ended throughout Canada by the combination of judicial and legislative limitations on its applicability and expansion.

Slavery as an institution in Canada first began to decline steadily during the 1790s. Although the British Imperial Acts of 1732 and 1790 sustained slavery and provided for the sale of slaves, many of its provisions were repealed by the Imperial Act of 1797. Many owners slowly began to pay wages to their slaves and gradually free them. Slavery retained, however, enough public support to prevent elected assemblies from taking decisive action. Instead, individual judges acted by judicial legislation against the institution. By the late eighteenth century, public opinion began to turn against slavery and the fledgling Canadian abolition movement started to win a string of important victories.

Ontario was the first province to officially challenge the practice of slavery and the only one to successfully legislate its abolition. Ontario's first Lieutenant Governor (1792-96) John Graves Simcoe [1752, Cotterstock, England; 1806, Exeter] had been a supporter of political reformer and abolitionist William Wilberforce in England. Simcoe challenged the legality of slavery for Ontario and as a direct result had slavery declared illegal by the House of Assembly in 1793. Simcoe, a loyalist, objected to slavery on religious and constitutional grounds. Opposed by Ontario's slave-owners, Simcoe proposed a compromise that freed no slaves but prevented the introduction of new ones. Ontario's Act to abolish slavery proposed only gradual emancipation, but was the first of its kind in the British Empire and set precedents later copied by the mother country. The Act declared that, henceforth, no person could be enslaved, but those already in bondage would continue to be slaves until their death. Indentured servitude could not last longer than nine years, and no new slaves could be imported into Ontario. All children born into slavery would find freedom at twenty-five years of age, but their own children would be free at birth. Until freed, owners had to provide adequately for their slaves.

Unlike Ontario, slavery was not abolished in the other Canadian territories but by the early 1800s, the courts had limited its expansion. In

Quebec, both the press and the courts attacked slavery. The *Quebec Gazette* newspaper began printing, as of 1790, anti-slavery poetry, stories, and other literature in both English and French. Two Philadelphia printers, former slave-owner William Brown [circa 1737, Nunton, Scotland; 1789, Quebec City, Canada] and his partner Thomas Gilmore, installed the first presses in Canada and immediately founded the *Quebec Gazette* in 1764 as the province of Quebec's first periodical. They also published Canada's first books. Journalist and politician John Neilson [1776, Balmaghie, Scotland; 1848, Quebec City, Canada], at the age of 21, succeeded his brother Samuel at the helm of the *Quebec Gazette*, which he ran for 50 years. Although of conservative views, he championed the cause of the French Canadians and continued to publish anti-slavery literature.

In 1793, the Quebec assembly attempted to pass a law to end slavery but opposition from slave-owners blocked its passage. Subsequent court decisions between 1797 and 1803, however, undermined the legal right to the possession of slaves by limiting its expansion and challenging its validity and very existence. One of the first initiatives was taken by the Chief Justice of the King's Bench in Montreal Sir James Monk [Massachusetts, USA;]. Monk arrived in Halifax, Nova Scotia from Massachusetts in 1749. Following his legal training in Halifax, he was called to the Bar in 1774. Beginning in 1794, he became Chief Justice in Montreal and a member of Quebec's Legislative and Executive Councils. In 1798, he freed two Black women slaves on technicalities, but more importantly, declared in his judgment that slavery did not exist in the province of Quebec. He also warned slave-owners that he would apply his interpretation of the law to all future cases. The slave-owners of Montreal responded in 1799 with a petition presented to the House of Assembly by Joseph Papineau. On behalf of the owners, Papineau argued that slavery was legal in Quebec, referring to various Ordinances and Acts. This petition resulted in a bill, similar to that passed in Ontario, which would have recognized and regulated slavery, limited its duration, and prohibited slave imports. Introduced in 1800, the bill failed passage. Similar bills tabled during the next few years met with the same fate. Later court decisions affirmed Monk's position but the legality of slavery in Quebec remained in a gray zone until its official abolition by the British Parliament in 1834.

Quebec's ambiguous stance towards slavery was mirrored in the Maritime colonies. There, resistance to the eradication of slavery came from all sides. In 1781, despite its small slave population, the Parliament of Prince Edward Island legislated that slaves could not be freed by conversion to Christianity. Nova Scotia's House of Assembly declared in 1787 that slavery did not exist in the colony, but its continued practice proved otherwise. The most effective and sustained challenge against slavery came in New Brunswick in 1800, spearheaded by lawyer Ward Chipman [1754, Marblehead, Massachusetts, USA; 1824, Fredericton, New Brunswick, Canada]. A graduate of Harvard College in 1770, Chipman assisted the Loyalist forces during the American Revolution and later helped organize the movement which led to the founding of New Brunswick in 1784. He became the colony's Solicitor General, drafted the charter for the city of Saint John, and as clerk of the Crown, served as crown prosecutor in most criminal cases for twenty-five years. It was during this period as Solicitor General that Chipman decided to challenge the legality of bondage in New Brunswick by preparing a thorough legal, historical, and moral statement against slavery. His arguments in defense of a Black slave named Nancy Morton in 1800 did not win her freedom but contributed to the gradual disappearance of legal slavery in the colony.

An Assemblyman from 1785-95, Chipman was named to the colony's executive council in 1806 and became a judge of the Supreme Court in 1809. As an appointed British agent to commissions established to determine the boundary with Maine, he successfully upheld New Brunswick's claim to much of the disputed territory. In his later years, he briefly administered the government of the colony and helped settle newly arriving Black refugees in 1815. He was, without any doubt, one of the most influential of New Brunswick's founding fathers.

Britain outlawed the slave trade throughout its Empire, including Canada, in 1807. Slavery itself was outlawed when the British Parliament passed a law abolishing the practice in all British North American colonies, on August 28, 1833. The law came into effect August 1, 1834. Henceforth, slaves became free upon entering Canadian territory, a fact quickly seized upon by abolitionists sympathetic to American slaves.

Transported by the Underground Railroad, Southern Ontario held a large concentration of Black residents who had settled in the area. It was these African Canadians, along with nearby sympathetic Whites, many of whom were Baptists and Quakers, who together formed the nucleus of Canada's abolitionist movement. Although religious organizations contributed to the welfare of resettled Blacks and their communities, not all Canadian churches agreed on how to deal with the influx of fugitive Blacks and the abolition movement. Baptists were the first to denounce slavery beginning in the late 1830s. Many Canadian churches however, including the Methodists and Presbyterians, were resisting such action so as not to sever ties with their neutral or pro-slavery American religious counterparts who helped finance their church activities. Controversy also touched the interdenominational groups, such as the Young Men's Christian Associations. Several Canadian YMCA chapters split with the American body during the 1850s and 60s due to American resistance towards inclusion of Blacks as members. Another group, however, the American Missionary Association, was the first of many foreign missionary organizations to aid the efforts among the fugitives slaves in Canada.

Before 1850, Canadian anti-slavery organizations were local in influence and nature. The nation's first prominent national body was founded at a public meeting at Toronto's city hall, presided by the mayor of the city in early 1851. The newly created Anti-Slavery Society of Canada became the leading voice of Canadian Abolitionism and assumed an international character through its alliances with other prominent foreign societies. A few months after its creation, the Society hosted an event in Toronto that included Frederick Douglass, who frequently lectured in Canada, and other prominent international abolitionists speaking to a crowd of two thousand. Leading American abolitionists often visited Canada and solicited support for their cause.

The Society was started as a response to the passing of the Fugitive Slave Act of 1850, and later opened a branch in Montreal and several others across Southern Ontario. Its membership included Protestant ministers, liberal businessmen, professionals, and Black abolitionists. The Society aided fugitives arriving in Canada and gave them money, food, clothing, and shelter until they were settled. It then helped them find a job and a home. The Society disbanded following the Civil War in 1867.

Benjamin Drew, a Boston abolitionist acting in cooperation with officers of the Canadian Anti-Slavery Society, visited various towns of Ontario in 1854, interviewing many fugitives from the slave states and copying their statements. For reasons of safety, he protected the identity of his informants and used fictitious names. John P. Jewett, the prominent, abolitionist publisher of Boston who had unexpectedly made a fortune from printing *Uncle Tom's Cabin* in 1852, attested for the integrity and intelligence of Drew. In 1856, he published Drew's book: *A North-Side View Of Slavery, The Narratives Of Fugitive Slaves In Canada*. The testimony included in the book tended to stress well-known gross abuses suffered by bondpeople in the slave states, however, some of the former slaves offered new and fresh insights into the working of the plantation system. For instance, many were from border states where owners systematically sold light-skinned slaves to states further South and kept the darker slaves, thereby preventing them from heading North undetected. For example, Ellen Craft, a light-skinned female slave, dressed as a man and passed herself off as a White master accompanied by his Black slave attendant. Her attendant was actually her dark-skinned husband, George. She concealed her female voice by claiming she was mute, and hid her illiteracy by putting her arm in a sling to avoid having to sign her name. In 1848, she and her husband left Macon, Georgia, train station and successfully traveled to Philadelphia by rail and steamship. They moved on to Boston and were later spirited by abolitionists overseas to England, fearful of the 1850 Fugitive Slave Law. The couple returned to Georgia after the Civil War and converted a plantation to a freedmen's school.

Despite its many and various activities, the Canadian Anti-Slavery Society's true impact was mainly symbolic. Lacking funds, members, and political clout, its influence gathered limited strength outside of Ontario. Unlike the United States, the issue of slavery never preoccupied elections in Canada and no national political party was closely connected with the anti-slavery movement. The Society, nevertheless, attracted prominent citizens as members. For example, the Society had elected Dr. Michael Willis as its first President. Willis had immigrated to Canada from Scotland in the 1840s. In 1847, he accepted the position of Professor of Theology in Knox College, Toronto. Leader of the local Free Church Presbyterian community, he channeled his energy towards socials causes including the issue of slavery. His dealings with the American Anti-Slavery Society led to a life long friendship with American abolitionist Gerrit Smith. His wife, Agnes, was an executive member of the women's auxiliary of the Anti-Slavery Society of Canada, known as the Toronto Ladies' Association for the Relief of Destitute Colored Fugitives. This Association provided food, shelter, and employment to former slaves.

Another of the Society's prominent executive committee members was journalist, politician, and ardent abolitionist George Brown [1818, Alloa, Scotland; 1880, Toronto, Ontario, Canada]. Brown was the powerful editor of one of Canada's most influential and important newspapers, *The Toronto Globe*. Raised in Edinburgh, Brown immigrated with his father Peter to New York in 1837. They moved to Toronto in 1843 and began a newspaper for Ontario Presbyterians called *The Banner*. The following year, he founded *The Toronto Globe* to support reform efforts for responsible government. He helped win the Reformers' victory of 1848, and built his *Globe* into a dynamic force in Ontario. From the *Globe*'s inception, he showed an interest in the plight of Blacks in Canada. Brown, along with his father and two siblings, Gordon and Isabella, formed the core of the Toronto anti-slavery movement. His brother-in-law, Isabella's husband Thomas Henning, was an early Canadian abolitionist and first secretary of the Canadian Anti-Slavery Society, as well as a member of the *Globe*'s editorial staff until 1854.

Brown's *Toronto Globe* was less radical than William Lloyd Garrison's *The Liberator*, but nevertheless provided the Canadian abolitionist movement with an influential forum and powerful voice against slavery, Canadian bigotry, and American institutional support of the Southern slavocracy. In the early 1850s, the *Globe* printed extracts of *Uncle Tom's Cabin* and editorially chastised supporters of the American Fugitive Laws. During this time, Brown entered the political arena, which would favor him for the next three decades. Black voters contributed to his initial electoral victories. He gradually became one of Canada's most prominent politicians and helped led the nation through the 1850s, the Civil War, and the forging of the eventual Canadian Confederation. Ironically, a recently dismissed *Globe* employee assassinated Brown. His killer, whom Brown had never met, was amongst other things, mocked by co-workers as being partially Black.

In addition to the *Globe*, many other Canadian newspapers and periodicals supported the abolition crusade. Amongst these were some that took strong positions, while others were less forceful in opinion. A few held widespread influence but most were local or fringe at best. The anti-slavery papers were matched in numbers by proslavery publications. These publications represented a large element in Canadian society that did not want to interfere in its southern neighbor's backyard. They collectively questioned and sometimes opposed efforts towards Black integration and resettlement in Canada, and furthermore, disagreed with the idea that Black Canadians should be treated as equals.

In short, Abolitionism in Canada was a poor cousin to the American movement, but it did offer vocal, moral, and limited financial support towards its efforts. More importantly, it helped expose and counter certain Canadian prejudices and eased the traumatic arrival of thousands of Black refugees disembarking the Underground Railroad.

Harriet Tubman

THE LIFE OF JOSIAH HENSON

FORMERLY A SLAVE

Josiah Henson book cover

William King

10. UNDERGROUND RAILROAD

The Underground Railroad, also called the Liberty Line, Freedom Train, and the Road to Freedom, was the symbolic name for an organized fugitive slave escape system existing in Canada and throughout the free states north of the Mason-Dixon Line in the period before the Civil War. The Underground Railroad was perhaps the most dramatic protest action against slavery in the United States.

The activities of clandestine escape networks began in the 1500s, and were later connected with organized abolitionist operations of the nineteenth century. In the decades preceding the Civil War, increasing numbers of discontented slaves escaped to places of safety in the Northern states and in Canada via the Underground Railroad. Legend has it that in 1831, a frustrated Kentucky slave owner chasing one of his escaped slaves exclaimed that the fugitive must have escaped on an underground road. This story spread and adopted a new term associated with the latest means of modern transportation in the 1830s, the railroad. Thus the term Underground Railroad came into use. The term first appeared in print during the 1840s.

Escaped slaves from the South were secretly helped by hundreds of sympathetic and often anonymous Northern men and women. This loose network of anti-slavery Northerners, mostly free Blacks and White Quakers, illegally helped fugitive slaves reach places of safety in defiance of the American Fugitive Slave laws. Free Black leaders and sympathetic Whites in numerous communities formed Vigilance Committees to organize resistance to slave-catchers and cooperate with the Railroad network. Most escaped slaves remained in Northern communities, but some fled to Black settlements in Canada, where they were usually safe from recapture.

Originating in the 1780s under Quaker patronage, the activity acquired legendary fame after the 1830s. Though neither underground nor a railroad, it was thus named because its activities had to be carried out in secret, using disguise or darkness, and because railway terms were used to describe the system in order to hide the true nature of the operation. Various routes were called Lines or Tracks; stopping places were called Safe Houses or Stations; a point of arrival at the end of the line was called a Terminus or Terminal; those who helped the slaves along the way were Conductors and Station Masters; their charges or freed slaves were known as Packages, Passengers, Cargo, or Freight; and, people who helped runaways by donating food, money and clothing were referred to as Stockholders. The network of routes extended in all directions throughout the Northern states and into Canadian territory. Canada was considered beyond the reach of fugitive-slave hunters, and offered freedom, security, and potential land ownership to Blacks.

Before runaways reached safe or friendly Northern territory, they usually traveled alone and without help. The difficult escape from South to North was often executed with few directions. Most Southern slaves had never been to the North and had only a vague idea where it was. Their information depended on what they could overhear in the owner's house, or in the slave quarters. The slave grapevine was effective in passing on instructions, while the lexicon in slave spirituals often gave vital clues. Sometimes all they knew was that if they followed the North Star at the end of the Little Dipper they would eventually reach free Northern territory. On cloudy or starless nights, the forest guided them, for they knew that moss only grew on the north side of trees. In addition, directions and information were sometimes secretly encoded in patchwork quilts hung outside a home. Quilts were specifically sewn with the intent of displaying known visual symbols, designs, and patterns. These encoded quilts provided a substitute for written words and directed the runaways to Safe Houses and Routes. For example, the distance between knots on the quilt indicated the distance between Safe Houses, while a bright star or drinking gourd represented the North Star. Lit lanterns on house porches also gave signs to passing fugitives. Special gestures, handshakes, and behavior also formed part of this intricate, complex system of signs and codes that developed over the years into a unique Railroad language.

The upper Southern states supplied a high proportion of the fugitives, due to their obvious proximity to free territory. Family flights were rare. Escapees were usually highly skilled young unattached male adults; enslaved women generally stayed behind with their children. Fugitives most often traveled by night to avoid detection and used the stars for guidance. They escaped by any means possible, including by foot, cart, rafts, and ship. Usually they sought isolated Stations such as farms, or small villages where sympathizers could effectively hide them. When possible, Conductors met them at border points or crossroads, like the city of Wilmington, Delaware. The city of Cincinnati, in the hilly southwest corner of Ohio, was another major location on the Underground Railroad. The city's strategic location on the westward-flowing Ohio River made it a focal point for American migration in the 1800s, and it was considered the gateway to the West. It was in Cincinnati that Harriet Beecher Stowe gained firsthand knowledge of fugitive slaves through her contact with the Underground Railroad. It is estimated that half of all fugitives heading north crossed the Ohio River.

The town of Sandusky, Ohio was a key port on Sandusky Bay, an arm of Lake Erie in the northern part of the state, near Cleveland. The town was a busy training ground for runaways to learn new working skills from the large resident free Black population. Upon arrival in Sandusky, fugitives immediately felt safe as they blended in amongst the many free Blacks. The apparent disappearance or vanishing of escapees in Sandusky resulted in the well-known saying, "I guess that's gone by way of Sandusky".

Other important American Stations included: America's first integrated co-educational institute Oberlin College in Oberlin, Ohio; Ripley, Ohio, along the Ohio river; the town of Milton, Wisconsin; Ashtabula city on Lake Erie, also in Northeastern Ohio at the mouth of the Ashtabula River; the city of Battle Creek in Southern Michigan, at the junction of the Battle Creek and Kalamazoo rivers; Alliance, Ohio, a city in Northeastern Ohio at the headwaters of the Mahoning River; Carlisle, Southern Pennsylvania, near Harrisburg; Longside, New Jersey; the city of Lawrence in Eastern Kansas; and, the town of Quincy, an important station in western Illinois on bluffs of the eastern bank of the Mississippi River.

Many Canadian communities on the border served, at one time or another, as Terminals for the Underground Railroad. Escaped slaves crossed the border from Northern New York and Vermont states, and the cities of Chicago, Milwaukee, and Cleveland. Cleveland was an especially active hub where no less than five Lines converged. They used open boats to cross the Great Lakes to land at the small ports in Ontario. By the 1830s, the Underground Railroad had brought the first permanent settlements of fugitive slaves to the small town of Sandwich in Southwestern Ontario. Others traveled eastward towards the Maritimes and the city of Halifax, with some moving overland to Montreal, Quebec. The cities of Erie, Pennsylvania and Buffalo, New York were other key Stations for quick escape to freedom in Canada. Communities such as Saint Catharines and Niagara-On-The-Lake, two border cities in Southern Ontario, harbored many runaways. In fact, Niagara was ten percent Black in the early 1800s. Many Blacks settled northwards in Prescott, Brantford, Kingston, Hamilton, and Toronto. The narrow passage across the Detroit river to Canada made the cities of Detroit, in Southeastern Michigan, and Windsor, in Southern Ontario, major stops on their way to the important points of arrival in the cities of Amherstburg, Colchester, and Chatham in Southeastern Ontario. Southern Ontario was described as the Canadian Canaan. Chatham, in particular, quickly flourished into a Black Canadian settlement on the Thames River and was soon promoted by its residents as a "Mecca" with plenty of business and employment opportunities.

The fugitive slaves arriving in Canada usually found friends, protection, and freedom under the British flag. Once in Canada, slaves were free from the prosecution mandated by the Fugitive Slave Acts. These statutes, passed by the American Congress in 1793 and 1850, provided for the capture and return of slaves who escaped into free states or territories.

Several Canadian publications were devoted to anti-slavery causes and general issues faced by the recently settled African Canadians. For example, two Black owned newspapers, *Voice of the Fugitive*, founded in 1851, and *The Provincial Freeman*, founded in 1853, attacked racism, advocated the cause of human liberty, created a more sympathetic climate for African Canadians, and provided helpful advice to new arrivals. A fierce and competitive rivalry emerged between the two newspapers and their dedicated editors. The newspapers had similar goals but different opinions on how to reach them.

The *Voice of the Fugitive* was edited by Henry Bibb [1815, Shelby County, Kentucky, USA; 1854] a former American mulatto slave who escaped to Detroit in 1842. He spent the next several years advocating the anti-slavery cause in the border area of Ohio and New York. In 1849, he published in New York his autobiography: *Narrative Of The Life And Adventures Of Henry Bibb, An American Slave, Written By Himself.* That same year, Bibb and his wife, Mary, settled in Southern Ontario and became local representatives of the Refugee Home Society. During his years as a journalist, Bibb worked and lived in Sandwich and then Windsor, Ontario from 1851-53. The Voice of the Fugitive, under his direction, consistently called for the immediate and unconditional abolition of slavery everywhere, but especially on American soil. It attempted to persuade every oppressed Black person in the United States to settle in Canada. It claimed that Canadian laws made no distinction among people, based on skin complexion, and the government did not tolerate the institution of human bondage. It also vehemently opposed any calls for the annexation of Canada to the United States. Bibb strongly supported Canada's Black sponsored settlements and saw Canada as a temporary respite for the fugitives before an eventual return to the United States.

The Provincial Freeman was founded by Mary Ann Shadd and Black American abolitionist Samuel Ringgold Ward [1817, Maryland, USA; 1866, St. George Parish, Jamaica] in 1853. Born to slave parents, Ward escaped in 1820 with his family to New York City and grew up in New York State. He was educated there and later became a teacher in free-Black schools. In 1839 he became an agent of the American Anti-Slavery Society. Licensed the same year by the New York Congregational Association, he served as minister to an all-White congregation in South Butler, New York from 1841 to 1843. His second pastorate, from 1846 to 1851, was in Cortland, New York. It was as a compelling orator, however, that Ward achieved prominence in antebellum America. During the 1840s he joined the Liberty Party and lectured for abolition in nearly every Northern state. For his eloquence, he was called the "Black Daniel Webster", but in 1850 he criticized Webster for his acquiescence concerning the Fugitive Slave Act. By 1851, he was forced to move to Ontario, Canada with his wife because of his participation in the rescue of a runaway slave. During his two years in Canada, he served as an agent of the Anti-Slavery Society of Canada and assisted the escaped American slaves who had taken residence north of the border. In 1853, Ward went to England on a fund-raising mission in support of abolitionist activities. During his two-year stay, he gave many lectures and published, in 1855, a narrative of his life entitled *Autobiography of a Fugitive Negro: His Anti-Slavery Labors in the United States, Canada and England*. In that same year, he settled in Kingston, Jamaica. Until 1860, he served as pastor to a small group of Baptists there, and later moved to St. George Parish.

Under the firm editorship of Mary Ann Shadd, the *Provincial Freeman* described the American policies towards Blacks as despotic and oppressive. In 1857, it depicted Canada as a government without castes in its political system, where all men stood on the broad platform of equality before the laws and were alike cared for by Her Majesty's government. In addition, it boldly proclaimed that no matter what skin color men or women carried upon them, the moment they set foot upon Canadian soil, they would be free. Shadd, however, did not support the Black settlement programs. She felt such communal experiments delayed the ultimate goal of integration. Unlike Bibb, she wished to instill a sense of Canadian permanence in the newly arrived fugitives.

The Underground Railroad extended across fourteen Northern states from Nebraska to Maine, but its greatest activities were concentrated in Indiana, New York, Ohio, Pennsylvania, and the New England states. Fugitives were aided from one Station to another until they reached Canada. Hundreds of slaves avoided the overland journey by traveling to New England as stowaways on boats from Southern ports. From New England, they made their way to New Brunswick. Those who were most active in aiding fugitives to escape by way of the Railroad were Northern abolitionists, American Indians, and other anti-slavery groups. These included members of several Protestant denominations, especially Quakers, Mennonites, Baptists, and Methodists. Many former slaves were active in the system. Members of interracial abolitionist societies added their efforts to the work of Black churches and other Black organizations. Participants in this vast informally organized network risked imprisonment, financial ruin, and jeopardized their personal safety and the safety of their families. In some cases, apprehended conspirators were branded with the letters "SS" for "slave stealer".

Professional slave catchers and vigilant agents often captured refugees to earn rewards. The negative publicity accorded to this clandestine activity helped to make Northern Whites aware of the evils of slavery. The federal Fugitive Slave Law of 1793 became difficult to enforce as Northern judges and legislators restricted owners' rights of recovery. A new law, part of the Compromise of 1850, was more severe, but the activities of the Underground Railroad continued. Alarmed at Northern defiance of the law, Southerners grew increasingly outraged and provoked. Antagonism over runaways and the publicity accorded them were crucial in fanning the flames of sectional mistrust that eventually led to the Civil War. When the War started in 1861, the Railroad's activities stopped.

The Underground Railroad was long in operation and development. Understanding it requires a broad perspective, one that reaches beyond borders, as the institution of slavery itself did. Canada's place and role in this dynamic period is in many ways unequaled and highlights important differences between Canada and the United States. Canada's participation was central to the success of the Railroad and provided dramatic intrigue and excitement, highlighted by extraordinary individuals who overcame incredible odds. The great efforts and deeds involved in harboring escaped slaves in Safe Houses and sending them through the intricate links that made up the network quickly grew into legend. In Canada, the mythology surrounding the Underground Railroad grew as the United States failed to abolish slavery. The belief that Canada was a sanctuary of liberty provided much needed hope to many distraught slaves, especially in the Deep South. Canada filled the need for a Promised Land. In the minds and hearts of slaves, it provided a promise of safe haven and a sustained example of racial cooperation. If it and its promises had not existed, either in fact or in myth, for those determined to escape and begin new lives, a similar myth would have been created as a means of sustaining hope.

The Southern slavocracy countered the growing Canadian myth with stories of the harsh living conditions and weather. They even went so far as to tell Blacks that Canadian Abolitionists were cannibals who liked nothing better than to boil runaways. Slaveholders also applied pressure on their federal government to request the extradition of escaped slaves harbored in Canada. Canada's position on this matter was clear. Escaped slaves would be extradited back to the United States only if found guilty of a crime as defined by Canadian law. Very few fugitives suffered this fate. Canada based its policy on various Canadian criminal court cases, the extradition provisions of the Webster-Ashburton Treaty of 1843 signed by Canada and the United States, and the Canadian extradition law of 1849. In the end, the extradition issue's real consequence was its threat and not necessarily its successful application. For example, Solomon Moseby was a runaway slave who reached Ontario from Kentucky by horse. He was seized by a slave-catcher but prevented from being sent back to the United States when hundreds of free African Canadians rioted and freed him from a jail at Niagara-On-The-Lake where he was being held before being deported.

Estimates of the number of Black slaves who gained their freedom via the Railroad vary greatly. Numbers range from forty thousand to one hundred thousand. It is estimated that about thirty thousand Blacks reached Canada. Although only a small minority of Northerners participated in the Underground Railroad, its existence did much to arouse Northern sympathy for the plight of the slave in the antebellum period. At the same time, it convinced many Southerners that the North as a whole would never peaceably permit the institution of slavery to remain unchallenged. Publicity in the North concerning African American rebellions and the influx of fugitive slaves helped to arouse wider sympathy for those still in bondage and support for the anti-slavery movement.

Underground Railroad heroes quickly emerged to encourage and inspire both the slave and abolitionist communities. One such charismatic hero was Henry "Box" Brown who in 1848 engineered one of the more fantastic slave escapes. Brown, a Virginia slave who worked in a Richmond tobacco factory, vowed to escape following the sale of his wife and three children to a Methodist minister in North Carolina. Sympathetic accomplices, including White shoemaker Samuel A. Smith, sealed Brown into a three-foot packing crate in Richmond, Virginia, and shipped him by train to Philadelphia, Pennsylvania. Brown's successful and daring twenty-six hour journey as human cargo made him a darling to abolitionist societies and compelling print in Northern newspapers. He had traveled upside down and was soaking wet when awaiting abolitionists finally opened his crate. Brown used his sudden celebrity by recounting his exciting escapade to White Northern audiences. He even used his famous shipping crate as a prop during these performances. Ironically, he was one of the few Underground Railroad fugitives to actually escape by rail. Samuel A. Smith later packed and sent others to freedom until he was caught and imprisoned for seven years.

Thousands of men and women risked everything for a taste freedom, including a young woman by the name of Ann Maria Weems [circa 1841, Maryland, USA;]. Ann Maria was born into slavery and lived in bondage with her parents on her master's farm in Unity, Maryland. Ann Maria, her mother, and siblings were all owned by Charles and Carole Price. Her father, John Weems, was a free Black who worked for the Price family in exchange for room and board. The Price's small family farm held twelve slaves that cultivated tobacco, wheat, and corn. They also ran an inn and tavern on the farm. Hard times forced the Price family to sell Ann Maria's brothers south to Alabama. In order to prevent any further sale of family members, John Weems contacted the Washington Vigilante Committee, which offered to purchase freedom for his wife and daughters. Charles Price agreed to the sales but refused to sell Ann Maria because he considered her a valuable slave since she was in her early child bearing years. Later, the Price family moved to Rockville, Maryland and brought Ann Maria as a house servant. In 1855, at the approximate age of fourteen, Ann Maria escaped with the help of the Washington Vigilante Committee. The Committee made sure to stage the escape as a kidnapping so that if caught, Ann Maria could claim she had no part in the affair. Disguised as a young teenage boy and using several aliases, Ann Maria traveled the Underground Railroad north with a five hundred-dollar bounty on her head. She hid in Washington for two months and then fled to Philadelphia, passing through William Still's house. She then moved on to New York City, Albany, and finally Canada, where she became a free woman and settled with her aunt and uncle at the Buxton Settlement in Dresden, Ontario. In 1861, Ann Maria's parents joined her in Canada, but moved back to the United States ten years later. Ann Maria took a husband in Buxton and was married by the Reverend King.

Canadian Alexander Milton Ross [; 1897, Detroit, Michigan, USA], a White doctor and amateur ornithologist from Belleville, Ontario, traveled the Southern plantations studying birds and, when the moment seemed right, supplied slaves with information on secret routes out. During a five-year period, he himself was directly instrumental in the escape of over thirty slaves. Ross became so well known for his anti-slavery deeds that President Abraham Lincoln invited him to the White House and asked him to help break a Confederate spy ring based in Montreal.

The network of anti-slavery Northerners who risked their property, their lives, and the lives of their families in helping fugitive slaves reach places of safety, included courageous abolitionist from all walks of life. One of these dedicated individuals was White abolitionist and feminist Lucretia Coffin Mott [1793, Nantucket Island, Massachusetts, USA; 1880, near Abington, Pennsylvania]. At the age of thirteen, Lucretia entered Nine Partners, a Quaker boarding school near Poughkeepsie, New York. In 1811 she married James Mott, a teacher at the school who later would help found Swarthmore College in 1864. Together they had six children. For a time, Lucretia ran a small school in Philadelphia, Pennsylvania. After 1817, she became more active in the church and began speaking at Quaker meetings. In 1821, she became an official Quaker minister. When the Quakers split over the slavery question in 1827, she and her husband joined the Hicksites; an antislavery liberal faction led by Quaker minister Elias Hicks [1748,

Hempstead, Long Island, New York, USA; 1830, Jericho]. As a young man in his twenties, Hicks had already become widely known as a pastor. As of 1775, his vigorous preaching during his tours of Canada and the United States, his attacks on slavery, and his inclination toward Unitarianism gained him a wide following. He worked for ridding the Quakers of slavery, and urged a boycott of the products of slave labor. In addition, he advocated establishment of an area in the Southwest as a home for freed slaves, and helped secure legislation that ended slavery in New York State. In 1811, he published his book, *Observations on the Slavery of the Africans and Their Descendants*. It was his liberal religious views and opposition to his preaching which caused the Religious Society of Friends to divide into two sects, the Orthodox and the Hicksite, or Liberal. The Hicksites became increasingly isolated from other Quakers until the twentieth century, when cooperation began to prevail.

In Philadelphia, a center of the anti-slavery movement during the mid-1800s, Lucretia Mott and other citizens, including African American Philadelphia businessmen James Forten and Robert Purvis, helped form the American Anti-Slavery Society and the Philadelphia Female Anti-Slavery Society in 1833. Four years later, Mott helped organize the Anti-Slavery Convention of American Women. Lucretia became a prominent abolitionist and was widely known for her eloquent speeches against slavery. In 1840, she and her husband were delegates to the London Anti-Slavery Convention, where she met noted American feminist Elizabeth Cady Stanton [1815, Johnstown, New York, USA; 1902, New York City]. She and Stanton would later, in 1848, organize the Women's Rights Convention in Seneca Falls, New York and launch the first woman suffrage movement in the United States.

During the first half of the nineteenth century, American social reformers with different goals such as abolition, temperance or women's suffrage often pooled resources and worked hand in hand for the general advancement of various social issues. Advocates of one cause often strongly supported the views and activities of another. For example, pioneer suffragists like Elizabeth Cady Stanton and Susan B. (Brownell) Anthony [1820, Adams, Massachusetts, USA; 1906] were also staunch abolitionists. Suffragists worked mainly through the abolitionist and the temperance movements, but antifeminist prejudices severely limited the role of woman members. A notable instance of such prejudice occurred at the London Anti-Slavery Convention of 1840 attended by Lucretia

Mott. For several days, the convention debated acrimoniously the right of eight American women to take part in the proceedings. Internationally famous pastors argued during the debate that equal status for women was not in accordance with the will of God. Eventually two of the women, Mott and Stanton, were seated behind a curtain, effectively hidden from view and denied the right to speak. William Lloyd Garrison supported the women by removing himself to the balcony.

Following the enactment of the second Fugitive Slave Law in 1850, the Motts helped African Americans escape to freedom by making their home a Station of the Underground Railroad. During the Civil War, however, Lucretia lived in retirement. She opposed slavery, but because of her pacifist convictions, she could not approve of the War. After slavery was abolished in the United States, she supported the movement to give Blacks the right to vote. For the rest of her life, she traveled extensively, attending meetings and conventions on women's rights, temperance, and the securement of world peace.

Another famous rescuer was White abolitionist Levi Coffin [1789, New Garden (now in Greensboro), North Carolina, USA; 1877, Cincinnati, Ohio]. Coffin opposed slavery despite a Southern upbringing. He moved to Newport (now Fountain City), Indiana in 1826 and, with his wife Catherine, made his house into a Station of the Underground Railroad. He induced his neighbors to contribute food and supplies for fugitive slaves. Thousands of African Americans were helped to pass through Indiana by route of the Underground Railroad. The state was just across the river from the slave state of Kentucky. Indiana had roads, highways, and canal towpaths that conveniently ran north and south, and had many residents who were outraged by the harsh federal Fugitive Slave Law of 1850. A particularly active route was the one through Wayne County, which was largely populated by Quakers. Coffin's house in Wayne County sheltered over three thousand fleeing slaves on their way north to freedom. For his many deeds, he became known as the "President of the Underground Railroad". Harriet Beecher Stowe based her fictional characters Simeon and Rachel Halliday in *Uncle Tom's Cabin* on Levi and his wife.

Throughout his life, Levi Coffin remained dedicated to the cause of freedom and equality. In 1847, he moved to Cincinnati and opened a store selling goods made exclusively by free Black labor. He aided freed slaves after the Civil War and in 1864 raised funds for freedmen in Britain. He was a delegate to the 1867 International Anti-Slavery

Conference held in Paris, and in that same year, he published his autobiography, *Reminiscences of Levi Coffin*.

The role of Northern Whites leading slaves from Station to Station has often been overstated. In fact, members of the free Black community most actively assisted slaves to escape by way of the Railroad.

The majority of fugitive slaves found help from the Underground Railroad only when they crossed into the North. Some Conductors, however, ventured into the South. One such Conductor was former slave Harriet Ross Tubman (originally named Araminta Ross) [circa 1820, Bucktown, Dorchester County, Maryland, USA; 1913, Auburn, New York]. Tubman was the most famous Conductor and an icon of the Underground Railroad. Among Blacks, she came to be known as Moses, after the Biblical hero who led the Hebrews out of thralldom in Egypt. Tubman and other abolitionists established a secret network of Safe Houses after the Fugitive Slave Act of 1850 made it illegal to harbor runaway slaves. The Act enabled slave hunters to pursue runaways onto free soil thus making it dangerous for runaways to remain in the Northern states. Tubman guided runaway slaves to freedom with stealth-like precision for more than a decade prior to the Civil War.

Harriet Tubman was one of eleven children born to slaves Harriet Greene and Benjamin Ross on a Maryland plantation. She later adopted her mother's first name. Harriet was put to work at the age of seven and served as a maid and children's nurse before becoming a field hand when she was twelve. A year later, her overseer struck her on the head with a heavy weight. Because of the blow, she suffered permanent neurological damage, experienced unexpected blackouts, and fell asleep suddenly several times a day throughout the rest of her life. Hard work, however, toughened her and made her as strong as the men with whom she labored.

In 1844, she received permission from her owner to marry John Tubman, a free Black man. For the next five years Harriet lived in a state of semi-slavery – that is she remained legally a bondwoman but her owner allowed her to live with her husband. Things changed for Harriet with the death of her owner in 1847, followed by the death of his young son and heir in 1849. These events made her status uncertain. Amid rumors that the family's slaves would be sold to settle the estate, Harriet herself escaped slavery at night via the Underground Railroad to the

North. Her husband remained in Maryland. Having reached freedom, she moved to Philadelphia, Pennsylvania, and later to Cape May, New Jersey, where she worked as a maid in clubs and hotels. By December 1850, she had saved enough money to make the first of her many daring journeys back into the South to lead other slaves out of bondage. In 1851, she returned to Maryland hoping to persuade her husband to come North with her. By this time, John Tubman had remarried. Harriet did not marry again until after John's death.

In Philadelphia, Harriet Tubman had joined the anti-slavery cause and vowed to return south to help other slaves escape. She decided to become a Conductor on the Underground Railroad. On her first trip in 1850, Tubman brought her own sister and her sister's two children out of slavery in Maryland. In 1851 she rescued her brother, and in 1857 returned to Maryland to guide her aged parents to freedom. The Fugitive Slave Law of 1850 had created federal commissioners in every county to aid in the return of escapees and provided severe punishments for those convicted of helping fugitive slaves. Harriet Tubman was a likely target of the law, so in 1851 she moved to Saint Catharines, Ontario, where she resided for seven years. Saint Catharines was the final destination of many fugitive slaves. By the late 1850s, several Northern states enacted personal liberty laws that guaranteed the rights of escaped slaves. In 1857, Tubman was able to buy land and move back to the United States with her parents to Auburn, New York, an active hub of abolitionist sentiment.

Over a period of ten years and despite overwhelming odds and hardships, Tubman, by then reverently known as the Black Moses of her people, ran a secret escape system to places of safety in northern communities, including Niagara, Canada. This complex network of Safe Houses and friendly individuals protected Tubman and her Passengers on their perilous journeys. With a pistol in one hand and a Bible in the other, Tubman, steely-eyed, determination bordering on the maniacal, made an estimated nineteen rescue trips into the South, including eleven return trips to Canada. Tubman faced great danger guiding slaves to freedom, as Southerners offered large rewards for her capture. Slave-owners were constantly on the lookout for her and at one point, she carted a bounty of $40,000 on her shoulders. Despite this, she personally spirited three hundred persons out of slavery by following the North Star to the Land of Freedom, without ever being caught.

To avoid suspicion when traveling in slave states, Tubman used disguises, sometimes posing as an old man or old woman. She brought along a sleeping powder to stop babies from crying and always had a handgun to prevent any runaways from backing out once the journey had begun. She usually began her escapes on Saturday night for specific reasons. First, many owners did not make their slaves work on Sundays and thus might not miss them until Monday, when the fugitives had already traveled approximately thirty-six hours. Second, newspapers advertising the escape would not be published until the beginning of the week, so by the time copies reached subscribers, Tubman and the runaway slaves were likely to be near their destination in the North. Often she left runaways in the care of other Conductors after leading them part of the way herself.

Tubman constantly modified her route and her method of operation. She and her Passengers usually moved only at night, sheltering in cellars, barns, haystacks, and chimneys. She allowed no dropping out or turning back. She never lost any of her Passengers and had an uncanny ability to find food and shelter during these hazardous missions. These amazing feats quickly established her as one of the most famous guides and leaders of the Underground Railroad.

During this period, Tubman supported her parents and worked to raise money for her missions into the South. She spoke at abolitionist assemblies and at women's rights meetings, often concealing her name for protection from slave catchers. Her forceful leadership led John Brown to refer to her admiringly as "General" Tubman. She consulted with Brown on his plan to start an armed rebellion against slavery in the South, and helped plan his attack at Harpers Ferry. She also promised that many of the slaves she had freed would join him. Illness prevented her from joining the ill-fated raid itself.

During the Civil War, Tubman served as a scout, spy, and nurse for the Union Army in South Carolina. She nursed and cooked for White soldiers as well as for sick and starving African Americans who sought protection behind Union lines. She helped prepare food for the 54th Massachusetts Regiment before its heroic but futile attack on Fort Wagner in 1863. She often bravely led Union raiding parties into Confederate territory. For this, she won the respect of many grateful Union officers. She later received an official commendation, but no pay for her efforts. She spent many decades trying to collect back pay from the federal government, which refused to recognize her wartime services. In 1899 she was finally granted a pension, but it was given to her not for her own service but because she was the widow of Nelson Davis, an African American War veteran of the 8th Colored infantry whom she had married in 1869. He was twenty years her junior and died of tuberculosis in 1888.

Tubman spent the years after the War in Auburn, where she continued her work to improve the lives of African Americans. She fed, sheltered, and nursed any Blacks who came to her home for aid. She raised money to help former slaves with food, shelter, and education. She also established a care facility for the elderly at her own home in Auburn. Although she was in poor health, she worked to support two schools for freedmen in the South and continued to provide a home for her parents. She often had to borrow money for food from friends who gratefully remembered her heroic deeds in the crusade against slavery. After many years of effort, she was able to sponsor a home for needy African Americans in Auburn, which was opened in 1908.

During the latter part of her life, Tubman became active in promoting the rights of women, particularly of African American women. She also became a strong supporter of woman suffrage. In 1895 she was a delegate to the first and only meeting of the National Conference Of Colored Women In America, an organization formed to address attacks, made by the press and others, on the morality and civic pride of Black American women. The group evolved into the National Association Of Colored Women in 1896, although Tubman had only limited involvement in this group.

Harriet Tubman spent her long and productive life in the service of others. She was illiterate, but in 1869, her friend Sarah Hopkins Bradford had helped her publish her first biography, *Scenes from the Life of Harriet Tubman*. In subsequent editions, the title was changed to, *Harriet Tubman: The Moses of her People*. With these biographies, Tubman raised money for her various charitable causes, and hoped her accomplishments could be an inspiration to others. When Harriet Tubman died, while in her nineties, she was buried in Auburn with military honors. A year later the city unveiled a tablet in her memory.

During her lifetime, Harriet Tubman served as a model to both White and Black anti-slavery activist. She worked closely with many outstanding individuals dedicated to freedom, justice, and equality. In Philadelphia, she collaborated with prominent African American abolitionist William Still [1821, New Jersey, USA; 1902, Philadelphia,

Pennsylvania]. Born a free man, William Still worked tirelessly against slavery between 1840 and 1861 and harbored over two thousand seven hundred fugitives. He was an active Conductor and leader of the Philadelphia Vigilante Committee, which had been founded by a group of Blacks and Whites determined to help runaway slaves and shield them from recapture. He was present when the crate containing Henry "Box" Brown was opened. In 1872, he wrote a classic work entitled *The Underground Railroad*, which gave daily descriptions of his activities and documented interviews with runaways who passed through Philadelphia. He wrote numerous letters on behalf of fugitives and arranged for the smuggling of the letters to worried family members down South. He was a wealthy coal merchant and helped found the first African American YMCA. On his death, he was eulogized as the "Father of the Underground Railroad".

Harriet Tubman also worked with Underground Railroad Conductor Thomas Garrett [1789, Pennsylvania;]. Garrett was a Quaker and White church leader who settled in Wilmington, Delaware in 1822. He became one of the principle organizers of the Underground Railroad in the Mid-Atlantic region of the United States. He ran a clearinghouse for runaways and is reputed to have helped almost twenty-seven hundred escape to freedom. In 1848 Garrett was arrested, tried, and found guilty of aiding fugitive slaves. He was fined five thousand dollars, which forced him to sell all his belongings.

Harriet Tubman also gained the respect and admiration of Frederick Douglass, who himself was an active participant in the Underground Railroad's success. Douglass's autobiography demonstrated the importance of the Railroad network to his own freedom. In his 1845 account, he described the complexities of his decision to flee, and is noteworthy for how little it says about the actual workings of the Underground Railroad. His silence revealed much about the continuing danger faced by those who sought freedom for themselves and others. Douglass rejected the philosophy that slaves must not actively resist their oppression. He believed in the right of slaves to revolt and the right of runaways to resist re-enslavement. He acted on these beliefs by making his home in Rochester, New York a station on the Underground Railroad. He thus became part of the intricate network of abolitionists who helped smuggle slaves from the South. He joined other anti-slavery activists in helping many of these runaway slaves reach safety and freedom in Canada.

The Underground Railroad was famous for delivering runaway slaves to freedom and a better life in Canada. The actual extent of that freedom, and the true quality of life experienced by the new arrivals was an epic struggle in itself.

The first organized attempt on the part of free Blacks to resettle in Canada met with great difficulties and eventually failed. In 1829, Blacks from Cincinnati, Ohio, fleeing the restrictions of Ohio's Black Code, founded the Wilberforce refugee colony near Lucan, in Middlesex County, Southern Ontario. The community was built with the aid of several leading White American abolitionists who mismanaged the finances they themselves had raised. These financial problems greatly contributed to the settlement's failure.

Another Canadian Black resettlement community was established in 1842 in the colony of Dawn, near Dresden, Ontario. The Dawn colony project germinated in 1834 in Cincinnati. It was first instigated by former slave Hiram Wilson [1803, Acworth, New Hampshire, USA; 1864] who left Cincinnati's racially restrictive atmosphere for Ohio's abolitionist center at Oberlin College. Oberlin turned out some of America's first Black professionals. Wilson, a member of the American Missionary Association, traveled to Canada with the intention of opening several integrated schools within the free Canadian Black communities. In doing so, he borrowed heavily and accumulated large debts that put his plans at risk of failure. During this time he met Reverend Josiah Henson [1789, Port Tobacco, Charles County, Maryland, USA; 1883, Dresden, Ontario, Canada], an illiterate freed American slave. According to legend and fact, Henson's early life in slavery was the inspiration and provided much of the material for Harriet Beecher Stowe's *Uncle Tom's Cabin*.

Henson was born a slave in the border state of Maryland, and as a youth toiled under three different owners. His arm was permanently handicapped by the sever beating from one of his owner's enemies. At age eighteen he became a Christian and at twenty-two he married. His marriage lasted over forty years and produced a large family of twelve children. He remained loyal to his owner despite several opportunities for escape. As a preacher in the Methodist Episcopal Church, he collected enough money to purchase his freedom. When his owner reneged on the deal, Henson fled to Canada with his family in 1830. Near Colchester in Southern Ontario, he rented land that had already

203

been cleared and learned to farm tobacco and wheat. As a preacher, he quickly became a proud community leader and was respected for his independence, unique ability to solve problems, and intelligence. It was in 1836 that he met Hiram Wilson. Together, they called a convention in 1838 to determine how and where White abolitionist money, targeted for Southern Ontario, would be spent. For example, Wilson had attracted the attention of James Cannings Fuller, a Quaker philanthropist from Skaneateles, New York. Fuller wished to finance the building of missions on Canadian soil and accordingly raised much of the money to establish the British-American Institute, an integrated vocational school and refuge for fugitive slaves in Southern Ontario. Around the Institute grew the community of Dawn. Wilson was its instigator and Gerrit Smith agreed to serve on the school's administrative board. In 1842, Henson moved to the new community, purchased two hundred acres of land, and built businesses. He was active on the executive committee for almost three decades. Judged by some to be a poor administrator constantly engaged in disputes over finance and management, Henson nevertheless served as Dawn's spiritual leader and patriarch and made numerous fundraising trips in the United States and England.

In 1846, Canadian Blacks met to discuss their common concerns at the Convention Of The Colored Population at Drummonville, Quebec. The Convention addressed the issue of financial mismanagement plaguing the Dawn project. The delegates appointed a committee to audit the books and attacked Dawn's leadership, including Henson and Wilson. Soon after, Wilson resigned from Dawn and in 1849 opened a new refuge for fugitives in St. Catharines, Ontario. Henson stayed on until 1868 when the Institute closed and sold its assets.

In 1849, Henson's slave narrative was published in Boston under the title – *Josiah Henson, Formerly a Slave, Now an Inhabitant of Canada: Narrated by Himself*. Three years later his life was forever changed with the appearance of *Uncle Tom's Cabin*. He was increasingly identified as the real Uncle Tom and quickly became a leading spokesman for Canadian Blacks.

Henson's leadership, in part, led to another Dawn-type enterprise, with similar results, near the town of Amherstburg, Ontario. This resettlement project arose from a Black convention held in Windsor in 1846. White philanthropists in Detroit, Michigan, launched the Sandwich Mission, later called the Fugitives' Union Society, with Henson as President. In 1852, this body merged with and took the name of another newly formed Michigan-based group called The Refugee Home Society. The project was plagued with internal disputes and improper administration, but struggled on into the Civil War years.

After the War, Henson was received by Queen Victoria in England at Windsor Castle and, on a return visit to the United States in 1877, by President Rutherford B. Hayes at the White House. Henson continued thereafter as a Canadian resident and Black spokesman until his death at ninety-four years of age.

In 1849, Louisiana educator Reverend William King [1812, Londonderry, Ireland; 1895, Chatham, Ontario, Canada] brought fifteen slaves from the United States to Canada where they received their freedom, land, fair treatment in court, and the right to vote. These Blacks were mostly slaves the Presbyterian Reverend inherited on the death of his wife, Mary Phares. Mary had herself previously inherited the slaves from her father on his death. Reverend King freed his slaves and brought them to Canada in 1848. With the strength of his leadership, convictions, determination, and political connections, he founded the Elgin Settlement in North Buxton; located in Raleigh Township and Kent County in Southern Ontario, near the town of Chatham. White Baptists had settled the surrounding area before 1840.

The settlement, named in honor of the reigning Governor General Lord Elgin, grew out of Reverend King's dream to establish a refuge for African Americans escaping slavery. His methodical and vigorous structuring of the community enabled former slaves to become self-sufficient landowners and successful business people. Elgin was the most successful of all the organized Black communal experiments in Canada and transformed King into a well-respected figure. Although less successful than *Uncle Tom's Cabin*, Harriet Beecher Stowe's 1858 novel entitled *Dred, A Tale of the Great Swamp*, was directly based on the Elgin Settlement and it's founder Reverend King.

Before establishing the Elgin settlement, King had attended the University of Glasgow and had been rector at a prominent college in Louisiana. There he married Mary, the daughter of a plantation owner, and purchased slaves as house servants. He returned to Scotland with his family to study theology at Edinburgh and then worked as a welfare agent in the city's slums. Following the death of his son, wife, and daughter, he traveled to Ontario to do missionary work for the Free Presbyterian Church. Although his church did not consider slave ownership in itself as sinful, King was uncomfortable with the concept, and, having briefly returned to Louisiana to settle his affairs, returned with his inherited slaves. At Elgin, he built a home and remarried in 1853. Missionary work within the settlement was headed by King and centered at the newly created Presbyterian Buxton Mission.

The Elgin Settlement was the last of four organized Black settlements to come into existence in Canada. The colony was composed of nine thousand acres. The land was purchased by the Elgin Association, a Canadian stock company that raised the money and acted as agent for the community. The Association had been organized in 1849 and legally incorporated the following year with one hundred and twenty-six stockholders. The purchase of land by the Association was locally opposed by business, political, and racial motivations. Opponents included competing landholders and a segment of public opinion hostile to the idea of importing Blacks into Canada. Despite these obstacles, land was purchased by the Association, divided into fifty-acre lots, and sold for $2.50 per acre. Land could only be bought by Blacks and resold to Blacks. Settlers had ten years to pay for it in annual installments, with six-percent interest. Each family of settlers had to clear the land with their own tools and build a log house according to minimum standards. Crops were planted as soon as small clearings were made in the dense forests. The felled trees were sold as lumber. The economy evolved primarily around agriculture. The early Black pioneers brought with them the farming skills that they had acquired on Southern plantations and in some cases on farms in Northern states and in other areas of Canada.

Sensing various sources of opposition to Black settlement within the White population, Reverend King responded by quickly organizing Black voting-blocs to elect officials sympathetic to Black concerns. In 1857, approximately three hundred African Canadians, most of them former slaves from Southern plantations, walked the streets of Chatham to vote in the courthouse. They had traveled ten miles from Elgin settlement; the area settled only six years previously by freed slaves. When the voting ended, the area's incumbent provincial parliament member, who had won his seat two years previously on an anti-Black immigration platform, had been defeated. This was the first effective display of political Black power on the North American continent.

Through the Civil War years, North Buxton prospered, enjoying an economic and social advancement almost miraculous for people who until a few years prior had been forcibly denied the basic rights of marriage and education. Although many slaves who fled to North Buxton did so to escape physical abuse and cruel punishment, they primarily came with the hope to enjoy the many opportunities freedom offered. Unlike White immigrants who had come to Canada from Scotland, Ireland, or the United States, Blacks regarded the opportunity to have and raise families as the most precious opportunity offered by settlement in Canada. As slaves, they had little hope of this. An owner could at any time sell the children of his slaves. In Canada, they would know life as spouses and parents of families, a totally new experience to many of these former slaves. In the early days of the colony, many of the fugitive slaves who arrived at the settlement were children. Families in the community gladly took these children in and made them members of their family. In addition to these adopted members, it was common for women in Buxton to give birth to well over ten or fifteen children.

Having gained freedom and control of themselves and their children, the former slaves, along with the free Blacks who joined them in Canada, demonstrated a vigorous energy and fierce will to succeed. They worked tirelessly throughout the year, clearing and farming their land or helping to build the Great Western Railroad, which was being extended through the area. Using three thousand dollars invested by Blacks from Toronto and Buffalo, the Buxton settlers formed a cooperative to build several businesses, including a factory for making a type of refined potash called pearl ash, and a brickyard and a saw-and-grist mill. The fact that a large amount of the land in the Elgin settlement was marshy presented a major obstacle for agriculture. A system of drainage ditches was developed to abate the problem. This allowed for the cultivation of a variety of crops. Two runaway slaves from Kentucky were credited as having introduced the growing of tobacco into Ontario at Elgin.

The settlement produced hay, lumber, barrel staves, and selling crops such as potatoes, corn, oats, wheat, tobacco, turnips, cabbage, raspberries, plumbs, crabapples, wild gooseberries, and all kinds of nuts. The harvests were better than expected. The weather was thought less cold than the settlers had originally imagined. Whatever they successfully planted in the ground, they were able to sell in Chatham, six miles away. Many walked up and down the distance once or twice a week in order to sell their produce. Livestock also flourished in Elgin. By 1855, there were large numbers of farm animals, including oxen, cows, hogs, sheep, horses, geese, chickens, ducks, and all kinds of game, such as deer, raccoon, ground-hogs, black squirrels, hens, pheasants, quails, wild turkey, wild duck, woodcock and red-headed woodpeckers, and sapsuckers. Within ten years after Elgin was founded, some of the former slaves had paid in full the government price for their land and some had enough money left to send their children to college. Frederick Douglass visited the Settlement in 1854 on his way to Toronto and later declared how impressed he was with its achievements.

The Elgin Settlement's influence on United States history extended beyond its function as a refuge for slaves. During the Civil War, seventy of its young men went south to fight slavery in various Union Army regiments. One of Buxton's sons, Anderson Ruffin Abbott [1837, Toronto, Ontario, Canada; 1913] was among the doctors, along with fellow Elgin settler John Rapier, who in 1863 set up Freedmen's Hospital in Washington, D.C., the first public hospital for Blacks in the United States. Anderson's father, Wilson Ruffin Abbott [1801, Richmond Virginia, USA; 1876, Toronto, Ontario, Canada] had been born of a White father and a free Black mother. Married and prosperous, Wilson moved to Toronto in 1835 and committed himself entirely to Canada, never returning to the United States. He became a successful Toronto businessman and local politician. He supported the Anti-Slavery Society of Canada and taught his nine children to think of themselves as Canadians. Anderson was the second oldest son and was of a more militant persuasion than his father. He was educated at Toronto Academy and graduated from Oberlin College. He then attended the University of Toronto's medical school and became, in 1861, the first Canadian-born Black to obtain a license to practice. In 1863, Anderson joined the Union army and was appointed an army surgeon. Following the War, he returned to Southern Ontario and practiced medicine in Chatham. He eventually moved to Toronto and was accepted by all levels of local society. He was a strong proponent of Black rights and opposed discrimination. As an editor and writer he championed Black education and Canadian patriotism.

The United States government took interest in the Canadian Black settlements. American doctor, educator, and first director of the Perkins School For The Blind, Samuel Gridley Howe [1801, Boston, USA; 1876], was commissioned by President Abraham Lincoln and the Freedmen's Enquiry Commission to travel throughout Ontario and report on the condition of refugees from slavery. It was believed that the information from these findings would be helpful in preparing to deal with the newly emancipated slaves in the United States following the Civil War.

Howe, an abolitionist and financial supporter of John Brown, had previously escaped to Canada in 1859 after Brown's raid on Harpers Ferry. He returned to the United States shortly thereafter when tensions calmed. In 1843 he had married Julia Ward (famous as Julia Ward Howe) [1819, New York City, New York, USA; 1910, Newport, Rhode Island], who later wrote the Civil War's "Battle Hymn of the Republic". Both were ardent anti-slavery crusaders and members of the Free-Soil Party.

In 1863, Howe visited Buxton and reported his positive impressions. He lauded the community's good highways laid out in all directions through the forest, and its two hundred cottages built on the same pattern, all looking neat and comfortable. Around each cottage, he described a cleared space, of several acres, which was well cultivated. He noted that the fences were of good order, the barns appeared well filled, while cattle, horses, pigs, and poultry abounded. He was struck by signs of industry, thrift, and comfort, everywhere. He identified no signs of intemperance, idleness, or want. He noticed no tavern, but did note the school building and St. Andrews's Church. Most interesting of all, he noted, were the inhabitants. He marveled at how twenty years prior, most of them were slaves and owned nothing, including their children. Since there manumission, they now owned themselves, houses and farms, and had their wives and children with them. He concluded his report by noting that they were now enfranchised citizens of a government that protected their rights, and possessed great essentials for human happiness.

Howe's 1864 report on the colony of Dawn was quite different. A witness to the missionary efforts and their self-help philosophy, he was also made privy to their controversial system of sending agents to literally beg for money and provisions. He concluded that self-segregated communities were not to be recommended since they encouraged and prolonged dependence on Whites and their institutions.

Buxton continued to grow and to prosper until the period after the Civil War. Following the War, there was a great exodus back to the United States. Buxton's population, which had reached well over one thousand, declined sharply as people returned to the land of their youth for many reasons. Families returned to their former homes to find loved ones that may have been left behind years before, and young people journeyed back south to find better job opportunities and to use their education and skills to help with the South's reconstruction.

James Thomas Rapier [1839, Alabama, USA; 1883] was one Buxton resident that chose to return to the United States. In 1856, Rapier and his brother John, a future doctor, had been sent from Alabama to Buxton to live with their Uncle Henry K. Thomas. Rapier's father, a free Black, was a wealthy planter who hoped his sons would take advantage of the educational opportunities offered in Buxton. Henry K. Thomas had emigrated from Buffalo, New York in 1852, to avoid the Fugitive Slave Laws. He purchased one hundred acres of land and settled down to live in the Buxton for the rest of his life.

Up until his arrival in Canada, James Rapier had led an unproductive life of ill repute, including gambling and drinking. He agreed to continue his education at the Buxton School and started out well, but soon returned to his old habits. He experimented with several business projects and became involved in local politics. In 1857, he had a religious experience that caused a complete change in his lifestyle. He became a member of the Methodist Church, repented his youthful indiscretions, and began his studies at the Buxton School. In 1860, he moved to Toronto to continue his education at the Toronto Normal School. In spite of having little money, he obtained a teaching certificate, graduating with honors in 1863. He returned to Burton and took a position teaching in the Buxton School. While in Buxton, he joined the local Militia and bought fifty acres of land.

After the Civil War, James Rapier returned to Florence, Alabama and became a successful cotton planter. He also helped Blacks during the reconstruction of the South. He began a career in public life by serving as a delegate to Alabama's first Republican state convention, and was a member of the platform committee. In 1867, he participated in the convention called to rewrite the state constitution. After losing a campaign in 1870 to become Alabama's secretary of state, he won a congressional seat in 1872 and served in the United States Congress. In Washington, he worked for the passage of the Civil Rights Act of 1875, although he was defeated for reelection in 1874. Except for service as collector of internal revenue in Alabama's second district, Rapier did not again hold public office. He continued, however, as an active labor organizer, seeking to unite poor urban workers and rural sharecroppers, and he wrote pro-labor editorials for the *Montgomery Sentinel*, of which he was the publisher.

Another Buxton resident, Thomas W. Stringer, returned to the United States after the War and became general superintendent of the African Methodist Episcopal Church in Mississippi, establishing thirty-five churches in that state. Stringer also helped develop Negro Masonry in Mississippi and organized the Fraternal Life Insurance Benefit, which became the most successful Black cooperative business in the state.

In 1851, Abraham Doras Shadd [1801, Wilmington, Delaware, USA; 1882, Buxton, Ontario, Canada] and his wife Harriet Parnell Shadd came to and settled in the North Buxton area. Both were active abolitionists. In 1859, Abraham was the first Ontario Black to be elected to a political office as Counselor of Raleigh Township. Before his arrival in Canada, he had established himself as a prominent free African American with many accomplishments, including his role as a Conductor on the Underground Railroad at his homes in both Wilmington, Delaware and West Chester, Pennsylvania. Together, he and his wife had provided aid to fugitives and helped to provide educational opportunities to the African Americans of the surrounding area. In 1833, he was an active participant in the founding of the American Anti-Slavery Society and was elected president of the National Convention For The Improvement Of Free People Of Color.

In Canada, the Shadds continued to help runaways and worked to make educational opportunities available to everyone. A schoolhouse was built on their property for that purpose. Their three daughters were adults by the time they made the move to Raleigh. Mary Ann Camberton Shadd Cary (known as Mary Ann Shadd) [1823, Wilmington, Delaware, USA; 1893, Washington, D.C.], the eldest, was the first of the daughters to make a home in Canada.

Born a free African American in the slave state of Delaware, Mary Ann Shadd moved to Windsor, Ontario to set up a school for slaves who had escaped to Canada. A staunch opponent of slavery, she had been an active abolitionist in the United States and written articles for Frederick Douglass' *North Star* newspaper. From 1839 to 1851, she taught in and established schools for African Americans in Delaware, New York, and Pennsylvania. In Canada, she edited an anti-slavery newspaper, *The Provincial Freeman* (1853-58), for the Canadian Black community. In doing so, she became the first Black woman publisher and editor in North America. In 1852, she authored a pamphlet entitled *Notes on Canada West*, and lectured against slavery in the mid-1850s. During the Civil War, she was a recruiting officer for Blacks in the

Union Army. By the end of the War, the Shadd family had become very prominent in Chatham and in Raleigh Township.

In 1856, Mary Ann had married Thomas F. Cary, an African Canadian barber and small businessman and abolitionist from Toronto. She became stepmother to Cary's three children. They were married for five year until Thomas' death in 1860. They had two children of their own.

Mary Ann Shadd was an intelligent, fiery, hard-working, successful, and experienced woman when she returned to the United States after the War. She was the first female admitted to Howard Law School and received a law degree in 1881. She became an attorney at the age of fifty-eight. She also became the first Black woman to be allowed to vote in a federal election in Washington, D.C. During the latter part of her life, she pursued her work as a social reformer, wrote articles for *The People's Advocate* and Frederick Douglass' *New National Era*, and joined the National Woman's Suffrage Association.

Another noted member of the Shadd family was Israel Shadd, who, along with his wife, had worked on a large, wealthy slave-plantation in the Mississippi River Valley. Following the Civil War in 1865, when the owner of the plantation was captured and imprisoned, some of his former slaves requested his release from jail because of the kindness that he had shown to them while in bondage. The jailed owner's name was Jefferson Davis [1808, Kentucky, USA; 1889, New Orleans, Louisiana], president of the Confederate States of America.

In addition to Mary Ann Shadd, another Elgin Settlement woman left her mark. Harriet Rhue Hatchett [circa 1850 Elgin Settlement, Ontario, Canada;] attended the Buxton School and eventually was one of the Black girls of the settlement who became qualified to teach school. She became a talented musician because of her early training in piano, which she learned from Reverend King's wife. After the Civil War, Harriet along with many other young men and women of the settlement returned to the South to help recently emancipated slaves. She taught school in Kentucky where she married Millard Hatchett. Years later, they returned to Buxton where Harriet used her talents to write music, and to work with the young people of Buxton to develop their musical talents. Hattie was credited with composing the song adopted by the Canadian military as the World War I official marching song, "That Sacred Spot".

Former Black slave William Parker and his wife Eliza Ann Elizabeth Howard Parker, also a former slave, arrived in Raleigh Township in 1852. There, they settled and raised their family as residents of the Elgin Settlement in Buxton. William and Eliza were leading figures involved in the Christiana Riots, and consequently are credited with having helped bring about changes in Pennsylvania's attitude toward fugitive slaves. In addition, Eliza was one of the remarkable people in the forefront of the crusade for women's rights.

During the Parker's first escape from bondage in Maryland, a neighbor was entrusted to drive the wagon in which they and other fugitives were hidden. After driving all night, the wagon should have traveled far away from their owner's estate. As the slaves witnessed the first dawn light, however, they discovered they were only a few miles away from the scene of their enslavement. The driver had betrayed them. Compensated for delivering fugitives into the hands of slave catchers, the driver had driven in a circle all night and was on the point of accomplishing his deed when he was discovered by the angry and desperate escapees. Enraged, they killed him and continued on their flight. The Parkers eventually settled in the town of Christiana, in the free state of Pennsylvania.

In 1851, a United States Marshall with a posse of about twenty men rode into Christiana to recapture two runaway slaves. There, they met the Negro Vigilance Committee led by William Parker who was hiding the fugitives in his home. The Parkers, their fellow runaways, and sympathetic White Quakers were besieged in their home by the slave catchers. Eliza joined the men in using a gun in their defense. Together they took arms in a futile resistance that killed and wounded members of the posse. During the fight and rioting that followed, Eliza's husband and another male rioter escaped to Rochester, New York, and stopped at the home of Frederick Douglass for help. There they received food, shelter, and assistance in making their escape to Canada.

Eliza was among those who remained. She was caught, arrested, and put on trial for treason against the United States. In all, thirty Blacks and Quakers were arrested. The participants stood trial for treason against the federal government – for the Christiana Riots were being considered an act of war against the United States. What followed was the most important trial held in the United States relative to the Underground Railroad Passengers. United States Congressman Thaddeus Stevens [1792, Danville, Vermont, USA; 1868, Washington,

D.C.] acted as the principle defense lawyer for those arrested. The defendants were all eventually released or found not guilty. The lives of Eliza and the other rioters had been spared. Stevens was hailed as a hero to the accused but suffered a backlash in public opinion for his role in the affair. He lost his nomination for Congress for the next election.

The outcome of the Christiana treason trial helped to change Pennsylvania's laws. Slave catchers were, from then on, legally prevented from capturing runaways anywhere in the state. William Still had attended the trial in support of the jailed participants. The defendants were given red, white, and blue scarves to wear around their necks as a symbol of the miscarriage of American justice.

After the trial, Eliza traveled via the Underground Railroad into Canada and eventually joined her husband in Raleigh Township. In 1852, they settled in the Elgin Settlement where they bought land and raised their family. William Parker attended night classes at the Buxton School. He was soon elected to the Raleigh Township Council and served on the Settlement's court of arbitration. Although William returned to the United States in later years, Eliza decided to live out her life in Buxton.

Following the post Civil War exodus, the Black population of Buxton never again reached its earlier numbers. The African Canadian population in and around the Buxton settlement had once approached two thousand people, but after the War numbers decreased dramatically. The lands that were exclusively owned by Blacks were sold, or in some cases, abandoned. Whereas almost the entire population had once been involved in agriculture, only a few families remained on farms. Despite this, the Elgin Settlement was the most completely realized of the several attempts in Canada at planned, utopian communities of Black refugees. A few descendants of the original settlers still live in Buxton today, including the Robbins and Prince families.

Canada's relationship with the Underground Railroad influenced the course of North American history. Its role as a sanctuary for thousands of defenseless human beings cannot be underestimated. However, in many ways, Canada only partly lived up to its promise and cherished reputation. Although free communities, work, and land ownership were made available for the new arrivals, discrimination, prejudice, and segregation were nevertheless omnipresent throughout Canadian society. Anti-Black immigration sentiments were prevalent in many areas. Even the promise of safety was made tenuous by the constant threat of extradition, and, Southern slave catchers illegally crossing the mostly unguarded national border and forcibly returning runaways to slavery. In the end, however, Canada did provide an enslaved people with a true, albeit imperfect, hope of freedom and a fresh beginning.

Contemporary White and Black authors forever immortalized the epic journey to freedom in Canada in song and verse. For example, American poet Walt Whitman's [1819, West Hills, Long Island, near Huntington, New York, USA; 1892, Camden, New Jersey] famous "Song of Myself" addressed the great hardship that fugitive slaves faced. They risked injury, exhaustion, starvation, and were rarely certain who would give them shelter and who would turn them in to the authorities.

Canadian bound runaways often sang inspirational songs. A version of the song "The Free Slave" by the American abolitionist George W. Clark illustrates this well:

"I'm on my way to Canada
That cold and distant land
The dire effects of slavery
I can no longer stand –
Farewell old master,
Don't come after me.
I'm on my way to Canada
Where colored men are free."

Crossing the border Suspension Bridge into Canada at the Niagara frontier, fugitive slaves allegedly sang these famous words, which in many ways captured the spirit of their personal heroic journey, while at the same time rendering homage to the many great escape stories that marked the Black experience in North America.

"I'm now embarked for yonder shore,
Where a man's a man by law.
The iron horse will bear me over,
To shake the lion's paw;
Oh, righteous Father, wilt thou not pity me,

And help me on to Canada, where all the slaves are free.
Oh I heard Queen Victoria say,
That if we would forsake,
Our native land of slavery,
And come across the lake,
That she was standing on the shores,
With arms extended wide,
To give us all a peaceful home,
Beyond the rolling tide."

In 1967, over a century after the Underground Railroad ceased to operate, Doctor Martin Luther King, Jr.'s words expressed the thoughts of many: "Canada is not merely a neighbor of Negroes. Deep in our history of struggle for freedom Canada was the North Star."

Frederick Douglass

EPILOGUE

The Compromise of 1850 was the last great attempt at reconciling the two nations within the United States. Since the birth of the Republic, a chasm had slowly expanded to a point of no return. The decade to follow would witness two opposing forces stubbornly positioning themselves for the oncoming storm of discontent. Meanwhile, Canada prepared to choose sides and protect its still loosely knit and largely undefined identity and precarious sovereignty, from the threat of things to come.

In the United States, the decade preceding the Civil War would bear witness to growing tensions between the North and South and provide ominous signs of the horrors forthcoming. Dramatic events unfolded with lightning speed and unleashed dire consequences. – The bloody Kansas Border War and the shocking arrival of abolitionist John Brown onto the North American stage; the Dred Scott Supreme Court decision; the true consequences of the 1850 Compromise and its Fugitive Slave Law; the creation of the new national Republican Party in 1856; the great Lincoln-Douglas debates of 1858 and the emergence of Abraham Lincoln as a national political figure; the violent raid at Harpers Ferry; the contentious Presidential election of 1860; the secession of Southern States into a new Confederate nation; and, the inauguration of President Lincoln in early 1861. As Canada witnessed these events, it faced increasing tensions within its borders as it struggled to define an uncertain domestic and international future. Canada too had to contend with two nations within its borders. English Canadian and French Canadian relations were tenuous at best. Its de facto leaders – English Canada's John A. Macdonald and French Canada's George Etienne Cartier – were still years away from finding the compromise solution of Canadian Confederation; a solution in part derived from the shock waves generated by the great Civil War that tore apart its southern neighbor. On the eve of the first shots fired at Fort Sumter, the United States appeared beyond any peaceful reconciliation. Canada waited with anticipation and nervously watched the fledgling American juggernaut take its last climatic steps on a historic path that led tragically down the road to secession and civil war.

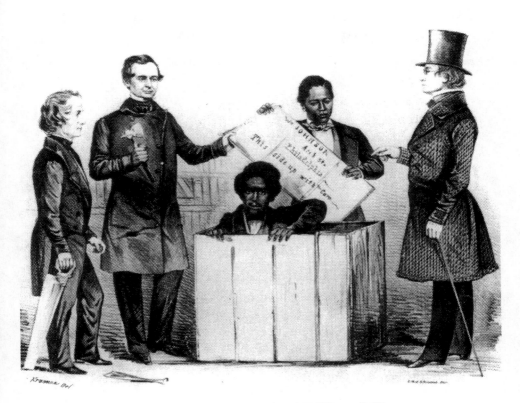

Henry "Box" Brown and William Still

CHRONOLOGY OF EVENTS

Seven or Nine Years' War / French and Indian War, 1754-63
American Revolution, 1775-83
U.S. Constitution protects slavery, 1788
U.S. Fugitive Slave Act of 1793
Foreign slave trade outlawed in Canada, 1807
Foreign slave trade outlawed in U.S., 1808
War of 1812, 1812-15
Missouri compromise of 1820
Slavery outlawed in Canada, 1834
Mexican-American War, 1846-48
Canada achieves responsible government, 1848
U.S. Fugitive Slave Act and Compromise of 1850
Publication of *Uncle Tom's Cabin*, 1852
Kansas-Nebraska Act, 1854
Dred Scott Decision, 1857
John Brown Raid, 1859
Abraham Lincoln wins U.S. Presidential Election, 1860
American Civil War, 1861-65
Emancipation Proclamation, 1863
13th Amendment U.S. Constitution abolishing slavery, 1865
Canadian Confederation, 1867

Levi and Catherine Coffin

BIBLIOGRAPHY and SOURCES

Adams, John R. Harriet Beecher Stowe. Rev. ed. Twayne, 1989.

African American Biography. 4 vols. Gale Research, 1994.

Africans in America: America's Journey Through Slavery. Educational Foundation, 1998.

Alexander, Stella, comp., Quaker Testimony Against Slavery & Racial Discrimination: An Anthology. 1958.

Alexis, Stephen. The Life of Toussaint L'Ouverture: Black Liberator. Macmillan, 1949.

Allin, Cephas D. and Jones, George M. Annexation, Preferential Trade and Reciprocity: An Outline of the Canadian Annexation Movement of 1849-50, with Special Reference to the Questions of Preferential Trade and Reciprocity. Reprint Services Corporation, 1991.

Alvin D. McCurdy Collection, Preserving Black History. Archives of Ontario. Toronto, Canada.

Anthony, Katharine, Louisa May Alcott. 1938; repr. 1977.

Aptheker, Herbert. Abolitionism: A Revolutionary Movement. Twayne, 1989; Nat Turner's Slave Rebellion & full text of the so-called "Confessions" of Nat Turner made in prison in 1831. Humanities Pr. 1966.

Archives nationales du Québec. Montreal, Quebec, Canada.

Archives of Ontario. Toronto, Ontario, Canada.

Arvin, Newton. Longfellow: His Life and Work. 1963. Reprint. Greenwood, 1977.

Association of Canadian Archivists. Ottawa, Ontario, Canada.

Atlantic Monthly Press, One Hundred Nineteen Years of the Atlantic. 1977.

Bacon, Margaret H. The Quiet Rebels: The Story of the Quakers in America. Rev. ed. New Society, 1985.

Bailyn, B., The Peopling of British North America. 1986.

Ball, Edward. Slaves in the Family. Farrar, Straus & Giroux, 1998.

Barbour, Hugh, and Frost, J. W. The Quakers. Rev. ed. Friends United, 1994.

Barman, Jean. The West Beyond the West: A History of British Columbia. Univ. of Toronto Pr., 1991.

Bartlett, I. H., Wendell Phillips. 1961; repr. 1973; and, Wendell and Ann Phillips. 1982.

Baym, Nina, and others, eds. The Norton Anthology of American Literature. 2 vols. 4th ed. Norton, 1995.

Bearden, Jim and Linda Jean Butler. Shadd. Toronto: NC Press Limited 1977.

Beatty, Richmond C. James Russell Lowell. Shoe String, 1969. First published 1942.

Beecher, Lyman, Autobiography, ed. by Charles Beecher, 2 vols. 1864; repr. 1976.

Bell, David G. Early Loyalist Saint John. New Ireland Pr., 1983.

Bell, Winthrop P. The "Foreign Protestants" and the Settlement of Nova Scotia. Acadiensis, 1992.

Bercovitch, Sacvan, ed. The Cambridge History of American Literature. Cambridge, 1994.

Bergeron, Leandre. The history of Quebec: A Patriot's Handbook. NC Press, 1971.

Berlin, Ira, and others, eds. Free at Last: A Documentary History of Slavery, Freedom, and the Civil War. New Pr., 1992; Slaves Without Masters: The Free Negro in the Antebellum South.1974; 1981.

Bernard, Jacqueline, Journey toward Freedom: The Story of Sojourner Truth. 1967; repr. 1990.

Bertley, Leo W. "Canada and Its People of African Descent." Pierrefonds: Bilongo Publishers, 1977.

Bibliothèque nationale de France. Paris, France.

Bilodeau, R., Comeau, R., Gosselin, A., Julien, D., Historie Des Canadas, Hurtubise HMH.

Bilotta, James D., Race and the Rise of the Republican Party, 1848-1865. 1993.

Birney, William. James G. Birney and His Times. 1890, reprinted 1969.

Black Canadian Studies, Dalhousie University Libraries. Halifax, Nova Scotia, Canada.

Blassingame, John W. The Slave Community: Plantation Life in the Ante-Bellum South. Oxford Pr. 1979.

Blight, David W. Frederick Douglass' Civil War: Keeping Faith in Jubilee. 1989.

Bliss, Michael. Northern Enterprise: Five Centuries of Canadian Business. 1987.

Bloch, Marc, Slavery and Serfdom in the Middle Ages, trans. by W. R. Beer. 1971.

Blockson, Charles L., Hippocrene Guide to the Underground Railroad. New York: Hippocrene Books, 1994; The Underground Railroad, First Person Narratives. N.Y.: Prentice Hall, 1987. Berkley Pubs., 1994.

Bolger, Francis W. P. (ed.) Canada's Smallest Province: A History of P. E. I., Nimbus (Halifax), 1973; 1991.

Bontemps, Arna. Free at Last: The Life of Frederick Douglass. Dodd, 1971.

Borome, Joseph, Toussaint L'Ouverture: A Life with Letters. 1993.

Borst, Raymond R. The Thoreau Log: A Documentary Life of Henry David Thoreau. G. K. Hall, 1992.

Boston African American National Historic Site. Boston, Massachusetts, USA.

Botkin, B. A., editor. Lay My Burden Down: A Folk History of Slavery. Reprint, Delta, 1994.

Bourne, Kenneth. Britain and the Balance of Power in North America, 1815-1908. London, 1967.

Boyd, Melba J., Discarded Legacy: Politics & Poetics in the Life of Frances E. W. Harper, 1825-1911. 1994.

Bradford, Sarah, Scenes in the life of Harriet Tubman, 1886; reprint 1995.

Bradley, Keith R. Slaves and Masters in the Roman Empire: A Study in Social Control. 1984, reissued 1987.

Braithwaite, William Charles. The Beginnings of Quakerism, 2nd ed. rev. by Henry J. Cadbury. 1955, re. 1970; and, The Second Period of Quakerism, 2nd ed. rev. by Henry J. Cadbury. 1961, re.1979.

Brandt, N. H., Jr., The Town that Started the Civil War. 1990.

Bridgman, R., Dark Thoreau. University of Nebraska Press, 1982.

Bristow, Peggy et al, "We're Rooted Here and They Can't Pull Us Up,"Essays in African Canadian Women's History. 1994.

British Columbia Archives. Victoria, British Columbia, Canada.

Britton, Karen G. Bale O'Cotton: The Mechanical Art of Cotton Ginning. Texas A & M Univ. Pr. 1992.

Brooks, Tom W. "British North Americans (Canadians) in the American Civil War – 1861-1865." Camp Chase Gazette, June 1991; with Trueman, Robert. "Anxious for a little war: the involvement of Canadians in the Civil War of the United States". Toronto: WWEC, c1993; with Milligan, Edward. "Black Canadians Who Fought For The Freedom of Black Americans."; and, with Jones, Michael Dan. Lee's Foreign Legion: A History Of The 10th Louisiana Infantry.

Buckland, William W. The Roman Law of Slavery: The Condition of the Slave in Private Law from Augustus to Justinian. 1908, reprinted 1970.

Buckner, Phillip A., and Reid, J. G., eds. The Atlantic Region to Confederation. Univ. of Toronto Pr., 1994.

Bumsted, J. M. Land, Settlement, and Politics on Eighteenth Century Prince Edward Island. McGill-Queens Univ. Pr., Montreal, 1987; Peoples of Canada. 2 vols. Oxford, 1992, 1993; A History of Canada. 1992.

Burns, James M. The American Experiment. 3 vols. Knopf, 1981-1989.

Bush, Michael, ed., Serfdom and Slavery: Studies in Legal Bondage. 1996.

Buxton National Historical Site and Museum. North Buxton, Ontario, Canada.

Cain, William E., ed., William L. Garrison & the Fight against Slavery: Selections from The Liberator. 1995.

Canadian Heritage, Parks Canada. Ottawa, Ontario, Canada.

Canadian National Edition. McClelland & Stewart Inc. 1999.

Canadian War Museum. Ottawa, Ontario, Canada.

Canby, Henry Seidel. Thoreau. 1939, reprinted 1965; The Correspondence of Henry David Thoreau, ed. by Walter Harding and Carl Bode. 1958, reprinted 1974.

Cannon, Devereaux D. Jr. The Flags of the Union: An Illustrated History. Pelican Publishing Co. 1994; The Flags of the Confederacy: An Illustrated History. Pelican Publishing Co. 1997.

Carbone, Elisa. Stealing Freedom (Ann Maria Weems). Random House, 1998

Careless, J.M.S. ed., Colonists & Canadiens, 1760-1867, 1971, repr. 1980.; Brown of The Globe, 2 volumes.1959-63; The Union of the Canadas. 1967; ed, The Pre-Confederation Premiers. 1980.

Catton, Bruce. The Civil War. Houghton Mifflin Company. 1960, 1988.

CBC Massey Lectures, 1967, Doctor Martin Luther King Junior.

Chapman, John J. William Lloyd Garrison.1921. Reprint. Beekman Pubs., 1974.

Chapple, William. The Story of Uncle Tom. Uncle Tom's Cabin Museum, Dresden, Ontario, Canada.

Chatham Kent Museum, Chatham, Ontario, Canada.

Clairmont, Donald and Magill, Dennis. Africville: The Life & Death of a Canadian Black Community, 1987.

Clark, Clifford E., Jr., Henry Ward Beecher. 1978.

Clifford, Deborah D., Crusade for Freedom: A Life of Lydia Maria Child. 1992.

Clinton, Catherine. Fanny Kemble's Civil Wars: The Story of America's Most Unlikely Abolitionist. Simon & Schuster, 2000.

Coil, Suzanne M. Harriet Beecher Stowe. Watts, 1993.

Cole, Donald B. Martin Van Buren and the American Political System. 1984.

Conrad, Earl. Harriet Tubman. Eriksson Press, 1970. First published in 1943.

Conrad, Margaret, History of the Canadian Peoples, 2 vols. 1993.

Cottman, Michael H. The Wreck of the Henrietta Marie: An African-American's Spiritual Journey to Uncover a Sunken Slave Ship's Past. Random House, 1998.

Cougle, Jim. Canadian Blood American Soil: The Story of Canada's Contribution to the American Civil War. The Civil War Heritage Society of Canada, 1994.

Coupland, Reginald. Wilberforce. 1923, reprinted 1968.

Cowper and Newton Museum. Olney, Buckinghamshire UK England.

Cratin, Michael, Roots and Branches: Current Directions in Slave Studies. 1980.

Critical Essays on John Greenleaf Whittier. Edited by Jayne K. Kribbs. G. K. Hall, 1980.

Cromwell, Otelia, Lucretia Mott. 1958; repr. 1971.

Cross, M.S. and Fraser, R.L. The Waste that Lies Before Me: The Public and the Private Worlds of Robert Baldwin," Historical Papers 1983.

Crowder. N. K., Early Ontario Settlers. 1993.

Crowe, Keith J. A History of the Original Peoples of Northern Canada. Rev. ed. McGill-Queens Pr., 1991.

Crozier, Alice C., The Novels of Harriet Beecher Stowe. 1969.

Curtin, Philip D., The Atlantic Slave Trade: A Census. 1969.

Curtis, James C. The Fox at Bay: Martin Van Buren and the Presidency, 1837-1841. 1970.

Dahlstrand, F. C., Amos Bronson Alcott. 1982.

Dandamaev, Muhammad A. Slavery in Babylonia: From Nabopolassar to Alexander the Great (626-331 BC), rev. ed. 1984; originally published in Russian, 1974.

Darroch, G., and Soltow, L., Property and Inequality in Victorian Ontario. 1994;

Davies, Norman. Europe: A History. Oxford University Press, 1996.

Davis, David Brion. The Problem of Slavery in Western Culture. 1966, reissued 1971; The Problem of Slavery in the Age of Revolution, 1770-1823. 1975; and, Slavery and Human Progress. 1984.

DeJong, N. J., and Moore, M. E., Shipbuilding on Prince Edward Island: Enterprise in a Maritime Setting, 1787-1920. 1994.

Delamar, G. T., Louisa May Alcott and "Little Women". 1990.

Diedrich, Maria. Love across Color Lines: Ottilie Assing & Frederick Douglass. Farrar, Straus & Giroux, 1999; and, Gates, Henry Louis ed., Pedersen, Carl ed. Black Imagination and the Middle Passage. Oxford University Press, 1999.

Dillman, Richard. Essays on Henry David Thoreau: Rhetoric, Style, and Audience. Locust Hill, 1993.

Dillon, Merton L., Benjamin Lundy and the Struggle for Negro Freedom. 1966.

Dion, Leon, Quebec, trans. by T. Romer, rev. ed. 1976.

Dobard, Raymond G., and Tobin, Jacqueline L. Hidden in Plain View: The Secret Story of Quilts and the Underground Railroad. Random House, 1999.

Documenting the American South (DAS). Academic Affairs Library, The University of North Carolina at Chapel Hill. Chapel Hill, North Carolina, USA.

Douglass, Frederick. Narrative of the Life of Frederick Douglass: An American Slave. Viking Penguin, 1997; My Bondage and My Freedom. Dover Pub., 1977; Autobiographies, ed. Henry L. Gates, Jr. 1994.

Drew, Benjamin, editor. The Refugee or a North-Side View of Slavery: Narratives of Fugitive Slaves in Canada Related by Themselves. Boston: John P. Jewett and Co., 1856. Rep. 1968, Negro Univ. Press.

Du Bois, W. E. B., The Suppression of the African Slave-Trade to the U.S.A. 1638-1870. 1896; repr. 1973.

Duberman, Martin B. James Russell Lowell. Houghton, 1966.

Eccles, W. J. The Canadian Frontier, 1534-1821, rev. ed. 1983; and, France in America. 1972.

Edgar, Walter. South Carolina: A History. University of South Carolina Press, 1998.

Egerton, Douglas R., Gabriel's Rebellion: The Virginia Slave Conspiracies of 1800 and 1802, 1993.

Elbert, Sarah. A Hunger for Home: Louisa May Alcott's Place in American Culture. 1987.

Eltis, David. The Rise of African Slavery in the Americas. Cambridge University Press, 1999.

Feldman, Eugene Pieter Romanyn. Black Power in Old Alabama: The life and Stirring Times of James T. Rapier, Afro-American Congressman from Alabama, 1839-1883. Chicago, 1968.

Filler, Louis, Crusade against Slavery, ed. by Keith Irvine, 2d rev. ed. 1986.

Finkelman, Paul. Slavery and the Founders: Race and Liberty in the Age of Jefferson.

Finley, Moses I. Ancient Slavery and Modern Ideology 1980; and (ed.), Classical Slavery. 1987.

Fladeland, Betty. James Gillespie Birney: Slaveholder to Abolitionist. 1955, reissued 1969.

Fogel, Robert W., and Engerman, Stanley, Time on the Cross: The economics of American Negro slavery. 2 vols. 1974; University of America Press, vol. 1, repr. 1985.

Foner, Philip, ed., The Life and Writings of Frederick Douglass, 5 vols. 1950-55, repr. 1975; and, Frederick Douglass. 1964; ed., Frederick Douglass: Selected Speeches and Writings. Chicago Review Pr., 1999.

Foner, R. Eric, Free Soil, Free Labor, Free Men: The Ideology of the Republican Party before the Civil War. 1996; and, Reconstruction. 1988. repr. 1989; and, The Story of American Freedom. 1998.

Forbush, Bliss, Elias Hicks, Quaker Liberal. 1956.

Forsey, Eugene. Trade Unions in Canada 1812-1902. 1982.

Forster, Ben and Forster, Jakob J.B. A Conjunction of Interests: Business, Politics, and Tariffs, 1825-1879. University of Toronto Press, 1986.

Foster, Frances Smith, A Brighter Coming Day: A Frances Ellen Watkins Harper Reader. 1990; and, as ed., "Minnie's Sacrifice," "Sowing and Reaping," and "Trial and Triumph": Three Rediscovered Novels by Frances Ellen Watkins Harper. 1996.

Fox, William, Regimental Losses in the American Civil War 1861-1865, 1889.

Franklin, John Hope, Schweninger, Loren. Runaway Slaves: Rebels on the Plantation. Oxford University Press, 2000; Franklin, and Alfred Moss. From Slavery to Freedom: A History of African Americans. Reprint, McGraw-Hill, 1997.

Frederick Douglass National Historic Site. Washington, D.C., USA.

Freeman, D. C., et al., eds., Whittier and Whittierland. 1987.

Friends World Committee for Consultation, Handbook of the Religious Society of Friends, 5th ed. 1967.

Friesen, Gerald. The Canadian Prairies: A History. 1984. Reprint. Univ. of Toronto Pr., 1987.

Furneaux, Robin. William Wilberforce. 1974.

Garlan, Yvon. Slavery in Ancient Greece. 1988; originally published in French, 1982.

Garrison, Wendell P. and Francis J. William Lloyd Garrison, 1805-1879: The Story of His Life Told by His Children, 4 vol. 1885-89. Ayer Company Publishers, 1970.

Garrison, William Lloyd. The Letters of William Lloyd Garrison. 6 vols. Harvard Univ. Press, 1971-1981.

Gates, Henry Louis, Jr., editor. The Classic Slave Narratives. New American Library, 1987; with Appiah, Kwame Anthony, eds. Africana: The Encyclopedia of the African and African American Experience. Basic Civitas Books, 1999; Wonders of the African World. Random House, 1998; with West, Cornel. The African-American Century: How Black Americans Have Shaped Our Century. Free Press, 2000.

Genovese, Eugene D. Roll, Jordan, Roll: The World the Slaves Made. Random House, 1976; The Political Economy of Slavery. University Press of New England 1990; 1965.

224

Gerson, Noel B. Harriet Beecher Stowe. Praeger, 1976.
Gilbert, Olive, Narrative of Sojourner Truth. 1878; repr. 1968.
Gilder Lehrman Institute of American History. The Gilder Lehrman Collection, Pierpont Morgan.
Goodman, Paul, Of One Blood: Abolitionism and the Origins of Racial Equality. 1998.
Gould, B.A., Investigations in the Military and Anthropological Statistics of American soldiers, 1869.
Grant, Mary H. Private Woman, Public Person: An Account of the Life of Julia Ward Howe from 1819 to 1868. Carlson Pub., 1994.
Greaves, Ida. "The Negro in Canada", McGill University Economic Studies, no. 16. Orillia, Ontario, 1930.
Green, Constance McLaughlin. Eli Whitney & the Birth of U.S. Technology. Scott, Foresman, 1956; 1987.
Green, J. A., Wendell Phillips. 1943; repr. 1964.
Greene, Dana, ed., Lucretia Mott. 1980.
Greenslet, Ferris, James Russell Lowell, His Life and Work. 1905; repr. 1973.
Griffith, C. E., The African Dream. 1975.
Gutman, Herbert G. The Black Family in Slavery and Freedom, 1750-1925. 1976.
Gwyn, Julian, Excessive Expectations: Studies in Nova Scotia's Business and Economic History, 1740-1870. McGill-Queens University Press, 1998.
Halliburton, Warren J., comp. Historic Speeches of African Americans. Watts, 1993.
Hamilton, Virginia. Many Thousand Gone: African Americans from Slavery to Freedom. Knopf, 1993.
Hamm, T. D., The Transformation of American Quakerism: Orthodox Friends, 1800-1907. 1988.
Harding, Walter. The Days of Henry Thoreau: A Biography. 2nd ed. Princeton University Press, 1982, 1992.; and, with Meyer, Michael. The New Thoreau Handbook. 1980.
Hare, Lloyd C., Greatest American Woman, Lucretia Mott (1937; repr. 1970).
Harriet Beecher Stowe Center. Hartford, CT, USA.
Harriet Tubman Home. Auburn, NY, USA.
Harris, L., Newfoundland and Labrador, rev. ed. (1968).
Hawkins, Hugh, The Abolitionists, 2d ed. (1972).
Heartman, C. F., Phillis Wheatley (1992).
Hedrick, Joan D. Harriet Beecher Stowe: A Life. Oxford University Press, 1993.
Heilbroner, R. L., and Singer, A., The Economic Transformation of America: 1600 to Present, 2d ed. 1984.
Henson, Josiah. Josiah Henson, Formerly a Slave, Now an Inhabitant of Canada: Narrated by Himself. Uncle Tom's Cabin Museum, 1984.
Hentz, Caroline L. Collected Works of Caroline Lee Whiting Hentz. Reprint Services Corporation. 1992.
Heymann, Clemens D. American Aristocracy: The Lives and Times of James Russell, Amy, and Robert Lowell. Dodd, 1980.
Hicks, Elias, The Journal of the Life and Religious Labors of Elias Hicks. 1832; repr. 1991.
Hidy, Ralph W. The House of Baring in American Trade and Finance, covering 1763-1861. 1949, rep. 1970.
Higginson, T. W., John Greenleaf Whittier. 1992.
Hilen, Andrew, ed., The Letters of Henry Wadsworth Longfellow, 4 vols. 1966-72.
Hill, Daniel G. The Freedom Seekers, Blacks in Early Canada, Stoddart, 1992.
Hiller, J., and Neary, P., eds., Newfoundland in the Nineteenth and Twentieth Centuries. 1980.
Historical Atlas of Canada. Univ. of Toronto Pr., 1987. Multivolume work.
Historical Atlas of the United States. Rev. ed. National Geographic Soc., 1993.
Hochschild, Adam. King Leopold's Ghost: A Story of Greed, Terror, and Heroism in Colonial Africa. Houghton Mifflin Company, 1999.
Hodgetts, J.E. Pioneer Public Service: An Administrative History of the United Canadas, 1841-1867. 1955.
Hogue, C. and Fauteux, M. (eds.), Hommage à LaFontaine, Le Comité Du Monument LaFontaine, 1931.
Holmes, E.M., Harriet Beecher Stowe. 1992.
Holland, Josiah Gilbert. History of Western Massachusetts: The Counties of Hampden, Hampshire, Franklin, & Berkshire, Embracing an Outline, or General History, of the Section, an Account of Its Scientific Aspects & Leading Interests, & Separate Histories of Its 100 Town Histories. Heritage Bks, 1994.
Hoobler, Dorothy and Thomas. The African American Family Album. Oxford, 1995.
Hopkins, Keith. Conquerors and Slaves. 1978.
Hornsby, Alton, and Straub, D. G. African American Chronology. 2 vols. Gale Research, 1993.
Houston, Susan E., and Prentice, Alison. Schooling and Scholars in 19th Century Ontario. U of T Pr., 1988.
Howard, Leon, Victorian Knight-Errant: Study of the Literary Career of James Russell Lowell. 1952; 1971.
Howarth, William. The Book of Concord: Thoreau's Life as a Writer. 1982.
Huggins, Nathan Irvin. Slave and Citizen: The Life of Frederick Douglass, ed. Oscar Handlin, Little, 1980.
Innis, Harold A. The Fur Trade in Canada: An Intro to Canadian Economic History, rev. ed. 1956, re.1973.
Innis, M. Q., ed., Mrs. Simcoe's Diary. 1965.
Irwin, Graham, Africans Abroad: A Documentary History of the Black Diaspora in Asia, Latin America and the Caribbean. Columbia University Press,1977.
Isaac, Robert. Wilberforce and Samuel Wilberforce, The Life of William Wilberforce, 5 vol. 1838, repr.1972.
Isichei, Elizabeth. Victorian Quakers. 1970.
Jacobs, Harriet A., Child, L. Maria (eds.), Yellin, J.F. (eds.). Incidents in the Life of a Slave Girl: Written by Herself. Harvard University Press, 1987.

James, Cyril Lionel Robert. The Black Jacobins: Toussaint L'Ouverture and the San Domingo Revolution. 2nd ed. Vintage, 1989.
John Freeman Walls Historic Site and Underground Railroad Museum, Maidstone Township, Ontario, Canada. Proverbs Heritage Organization, Windsor, Ontario.
Johnson, F. Roy. The Nat Turner Slave Insurrection. 1966.
Johnson, J. K., and Wilson, B. G., eds. Historical Essays on Upper Canada. Carleton Univ. Pr., 1989.
Johnson, Oliver. William Lloyd Garrison and His Times. 1879.
Jones, Howard, Mutiny on the Amistad. 1986; repr. 1997.
Jones, Rufus M. The Quakers in the American Colonies. 1911, reissued 1966; and, The Later Periods of Quakerism, 2 vol. 1921, reprinted 1970.
Kein, Sybil ed. Creole: The History and Legacy of Louisiana's Free People of Color. Louisiana Press, 2000.
Keir, D. Lindsay. The Constitutional History of Modern Britain 1485-1937 (1966).
Kennedy, W. P. M., Lord Elgin. 1926.
Kimball, G., The Religious Ideas of Harriet Beecher Stowe. 1982.
Klein, Herbert S., African Slavery in Latin America and the Caribbean. 1986.
Klein, Martin A. Breaking the Chains, Wisconsin: University of Wisconsin Press, 1993.
Kolchin, Peter. American Slavery, 1619-1877. Hill & Wang, 1993.
Korngold, Ralph, Citizen Toussaint. 1949; repr. 1979.
Kraditor, A. S., Means and Ends in American Abolitionism. 1989.
Lampe, Gregory P. Frederick Douglass: Freedom's Voice, 1818-1845. Michigan State Univ. Press, 1998.
Landon, Fred. Abolitionist Interest in Upper Canada, Ontario History, 44, 1952.
Lawson, A. and H., The Man Who Freed the Slaves. 1962.
Leacock, Stephen B., Mackenzie, Baldwin, LaFontaine, Hincks, rev. ed. 1926.
Lean, Garth. God's Politician: William Wilberforce's Struggle. 1980.
Lebeaux, Richard. Young Man Thoreau. 1977, repr. 1989; and, Thoreau's Seasons. 1984.
Ledoux, Tom. Vermont in the Civil War. www.vermontcivilwar.org 1996-2001 by VTCW150.
Levine, Robert S., Martin Delany, Frederick Douglass, and the Politics of Representative Identity. 1997.
Lewis, Bernard, Race and Slavery in the Middle East: An Historical Enquiry. 1990.
Lewis, David Levering. W.E.B. Du Bois: The Fight for Equality and the American Century, 1919-1963. Henry Holt & Company, 2000.
Library of Congress. Washington D.C.
Library of Parliament. Ottawa, Canada.
Litwack, Leon F. North of Slavery: The Negro in the Free States, 1790-1860. 1961, reprinted 1970; eds. with Meier, August. Black Leaders of the Nineteenth Century. University of Illinois Press, 1988.
Lobb, John (ed.). Josiah Henson, An Autobiography of the Rev. Josiah Henson ("Uncle Tom") from 1789 to 1881. rev ed. 1881, repr 1969.
Lofton, John, Insurrection in South Carolina: The Turbulent World of Denmark Vesey. 1964; and, Denmark Vesey's Revolt. Kent State University Press, 1990.
Logan, Rayford W. Haiti and the Dominican Republic. 1968.
Longfellow, Samuel, The Life of Henry Wadsworth Longfellow, 3 vols. 1891, repr. 1985.
Lonn, Ella. Foreigners in the Confederacy, University of North Carolina Press, 1942; Desertions During The Civil War, Gloucester, Massachusetts, 1966.
Lovejoy, Paul E., ed., Africans in Bondage. 1987.
Lovett, Bobby L. The African-American History of Nashville, Tennessee, 1780-1930: Elites and Dilemmas. University of Arkansas Press, 1999.
Loving, Jerome. Walt Whitman: The Song of Himself. University of California Press, 1999.
Lowance, M. I., Jr., et al., eds., The Stowe Debate. 1994.
Lower, Arthur R.M. Colony to Nation, Toronto: McClelland and Stewart Ltd., 1977.
Mabee, Carleton, and Newhouse, S. M. Sojourner Truth: Slave, Prophet, Legend. N.Y. Univ. Press, 1993.
MacDonald, Ruth K. Louisa May Alcott. Twayne, 1983.
MacNutt, W. S., New Brunswick: A History, 1784-1867. 1963; New Brunswick and Its People. 1966; The Atlantic Provinces: The Emergence of Colonial Society, 1712-1857. 1965.
MacPherson, A. G., ed., The Atlantic Provinces. 1972.
Magdol, Edward, The Antislavery Rank and File. 1986.
Maison Louis-Hippolyte-LaFontaine. Boucherville, Quebec, Canada.
Malcomson, Scott L. One Drop of Blood: The American Misadventure of Race. Farrar, Straus-Giroux, 2000.
Marietta, Jack D. The Reformation of American Quakerism, 1748-1783. 1984.
Martin, Chester. Foundations of Canadian Nationhood. 1955.
Martin, Gaston. Histoire de l'esclavage dans les colonies française. Paris, 1948.
Martin, Waldo E., Jr. The Mind of Frederick Douglass. North Carolina, 1985.
Martyn, C., Wendell Phillips: The Agitator. 1890; repr. 1979.
Mason, Julian D., Jr., The Poems of Phillis Wheatley. 1966.
Matthews, Geoffrey J. (ed.), Historical Atlas of Canada, 3 vol. 1987-93.
May, Samuel J. Some Recollections of Our Antislavery Conflict. 1869.
Mayer, Henry. All on Fire: William Lloyd Garrison and the Abolition of Slavery. St. Martin's Press, 2000.

McCalla, Robert J. The Maritime Provinces Atlas. Rev. ed. Formac, 1991.
McConnell, W.H. Commentary on the British North America Act . 1977.
McDougall, W. A., Promised Land, Crusader State: The U.S. Encounter with the World since 1776. 1997.
McFeely, William S. Frederick Douglass. Simon and Schuster, 1991.
McKissack, Frederick and Patricia C. Sojourner Truth: Ain't I a Woman? Scholastic, 1992.
McLoughlin, W. G., The Meaning of Henry Ward Beecher. 1970.
McNaught, Kenneth. The History of Canada. 1970.
McPherson, James M. Battle Cry of Freedom. Oxford University Press, 1988.
Mellon, James, editor. Bullwhip Days: The Slaves Remember. Reprint, Avon.
Meltzer, Milton, and Holland, P. G., eds., Lydia Maria Child: Selected Letters, 1817-1880. 1982.
Mendelsohn, I. Slavery in the Ancient Near East: A Comparative Study of Slavery in Babylonia, Assyria, Syria, & Palestine, from the Middle of the 3rd Millennium to the End of the 1st Millennium. 1949;1978.
Merrill, Walter M. Against Wind and Tide: A Biography of William Lloyd Garrison. Harvard Press, 1963.
Merritt, Susan E. Her Story : Women from Canada's Past, Vanwell Publishing, 1993.
Middleton, Joyce. The women of the Elgin settlement and Buxton.
Middletown, J. E., and Landon, F., The Province of Ontario: A History, 4 vols. 1927.
Milbauer, Richard J. Lewis Tappan & the Evangelical War Against Slavery, Southern Honor, & Yankee Saints and Southern Sinners. Louisiana State University Press, 1997.
Miller, Douglas T. Frederick Douglass and the Fight for Freedom. Facts on File, 1988.
Miller, James E., Jr. Walt Whitman. Rev. ed. Twayne, 1990.
Miller, Randall M., and Smith, J. D., eds. Dictionary of Afro-American Slavery. Greenwood, 1988.
Mills, David. The Idea of Loyalty in Upper Canada, 1784-1850. McGill-Queens Univ. Pr., 1988.
Milner, C. A., II, et al., Oxford History of the American West. 1994.
Miriam Schneir, Writer; Editor, Feminism: The Essential Historical Writings.
Mirsky, Jeannette and Nevins, Allan. The World of Eli Whitney. 1952; repr. 1962.
Morrison, Samuel E. The Oxford History of the American People, Vol. 2, N.Y.: Oxford University Press, Inc., 1972; with Commager, H. S., The Growth of the American Republic, 2 vols., 7th ed. 1980.
Morton, Desmond. A Military History of Canada. Rev. ed. McClelland, 1992.
Morton, William L. The Kingdom of Canada: A General History from the Earliest Times, 2nd ed. 1969.
Myerson, Joel, ed., The Cambridge Companion to Henry David Thoreau. 1995; with Shealy, D., eds., The Selected Letters of Louisa May Alcott. 1987; and The Journals of Louisa May Alcott. 1997.
National Archives of Canada. Ottawa, Ontario, Canada.
National Archives, Washington, D.C., USA.
National Assembly of Quebec. Quebec City, Quebec, Canada.
National Gallery of Canada. Ottawa, Ontario, Canada.
National Library of Canada. Ottawa, Ontario, Canada.
National Park Service. U.S. Department of the Interior, Washington, D.C. USA.
National Underground Railroad Freedom Center, Cincinnati, Ohio, USA.
National Underground Railroad Museum, Maysville, Kentucky, USA.
Neilson, Hubert. "Slavery in Old Canada Before and After the Conquest", Transactions of Literary and Historical Society of Quebec, ser. 2, no .26, 1906.
New York Public Library, New York City, New York, USA.
Newfoundland and Labrador Provincial Archives Division. St-John's, Newfoundland, Canada.
Nieboer, H.J. Slavery as an Industrial System: Ethnological Researches, 2nd rev. ed. 1910, reprinted 1971.
Niven, John. Martin Van Buren: The Romantic Age of American Politics. 1983.
North American Black Historical Museum. Amherstburg, Ontario, Canada.
Norval Johnson Heritage Library. Niagara Falls, Ontario, Canada.
Nye, Russell B. William Lloyd Garrison and the Humanitarian Reformers. 195).
O'Connor, Tony. Vermont Civil War Enterprises. vermontcivilwar.org/vtcwe.htm Newport, Vermont, USA.
Oates, Stephen B. The Fires of Jubilee: Nat Turner's Fierce Rebellion. 1975, reissued 1990.
Oliphant, Laurence, Narrative of the Earl of Elgin's Mission to China and Japan. 1859.
Olmsted, Denison, Memoir of Eli Whitney, Esq. 1846; repr. 1972.
Ontario Black History Society Archives. Toronto, Ontario, Canada.
Ontario Legislative Library. Toronto, Ontario, Canada.
Ortiz, Victoria, Sojourner Truth, a Self-made Woman. 1974.
Ouellet, Fernand. Lower Canada 1791-1840. 1980; Economic & Social History of Quebec, 1760-1850. translation, 1980.
Painter, Neil Irvin. Sojourner Truth: A Life, a Symbol. 1996.
Palmer, Bryan D. Working Class Experience: Rethinking the History of Canadian Labour, 1800-1991, 2nd edition 1992.
Parini, Jay, ed. The Columbia History of American Poetry. Columbia Univ. Pr., 1993.
Parish, Peter J., Slavery, History and Historians. 1989.
Parkinson, Wenda. "This Gilden African': Toussaint L'Ouverture. Quartet Bks., 1978.
Patterson, Orlando. Slavery and Social Death: A Comparative Study. 1982.
Paul, Sherman. The Shores of America: Thoreau's Inward Exploration. 1958, reissued 1972.

Payne, Alma J. Louisa May Alcott. 1980.

Pickard, John B. John Greenleaf Whittier: An Introduction and Interpretation. Barnes & Noble, 1961.

Pickard, Samuel T. Life and Letters of John Greenleaf Whittier. 2 vols. Haskell House, 1907; Reprint 1969.

Pollock, John. Wilberforce. 1977, reissued 1986.

Potter, Joan, and Claytor, Constance. African-American Firsts. Pinto Pr., 1994.

Powell, William S. North Carolina: Through The Ages. University of North Carolina Press, 1989; North Carolina: A History. University of North Carolina Press, 1977, 1988.

Prentice, Alison et al., Canadian Women: A History. 1988.

Preston, Dickson J. Young Frederick Douglass: The Maryland Years. Johns Hopkins, 1985.

Prince Edward Island Public Archives and Records Office. Charlottetown, PEI, Canada.

Public Archives of Canada. Ottawa, Canada.

Public Archives of Nova Scotia. Halifax, Nova Scotia, Canada.

Purvis, Thomas L. A Dictionary of American History. Blackwell, 1995.

Quarles, Benjamin, Frederick Douglass. 1960; repr. 1997.

Quist, John W. Restless Visionaries: The Social Roots of AnteBellum Reform in Alabama and Michigan. Louisiana State University Press, 1998.

Ray, Arthur J. Indians in the Fur Trade: Their Role as Trappers, Hunters, and Middlemen in the Lands Southwest of Hudson Bay, 1660-1870. 1974, and The Canadian Fur Trade in the Industrial Age. 1990.

Reilly, Linda C., Slaves in Ancient Greece. 1978.

Remini, Robert V. Martin Van Buren and the Making of the Democratic Party. 1959, reissued 1970.

Reynolds, David S. Walt Whitman's America: A Cultural Biography. Vintage Books, 1996.

Richards, Laura E., and Elliott, Maud Howe. Julia Ward Howe, 1819-1910. Cherokee Pub. Co., 1990.

Richardson, H. E., Cassius M. Clay. 1987.

Richardson, Patrick. Empire and Slavery, New York: Harper and Row, 1974.

Richardson, Robert D., Jr. Henry Thoreau: A Life of the Mind. University of California Press, 1986.

Riddell, William Renwick. "Le Code Noir", JNH, 10, 1925; "The Slave in Canada", JNH, 5, 1920; "An Official Record of Slaves in Upper Canada", OHS, Papers and Records, 25, 1929; "Additional Notes on Slavery", JNH, 17, 1932; The Life of John Graves Simcoe, First Lieutenant-Governor of the Province of Upper Canada, 1792-96, Toronto, 1926.

Ripley, C. Peter et al. editors, The Black Abolitionist Papers: Vol. II: Canada, 1830-1865. University of North Carolina Press, 1992.; and, Witness for Freedom: African American Voices on Race, Slavery, and Emancipation. University of North Carolina Press, 1993.

Robbins, Arlie C. Women of North Buxton and the Elgin Settlement: Eliza Ann Elizabeth Howard Parker. North Buxton Labour Day book, 1978; Legacy to Buxton. Ideal Printing, 1983.

Robinson, Gwendolyn and John W. Seek the Truth: A Story of Chatham's Black Community, 1989.

Robinson, Randall N. The Debt: What America Owes to Blacks. Dutton/Plume, 1999.

Rogers, Al. Amazing Grace: The Story of John Newton. July-August 1996 issue of "Away Here in Texas".

Ros, Martin. Night of Fire: The Black Napoleon and the Battle for Haiti. Sarpedon, 1993.

Rugoff, Milton, The Beechers. 1981.

Russell, E., The History of Quakerism. 1942; repr. 1980.

Ryerson, Stanley B., Unequal Union: Confederation and the Roots of Conflict in the Canadas, 1815-1873, 1968.; The founding of Canada: Beginnings to 1815. Progress Books, 1975.

Sadlier, Rosemary. Leading the Way: Black Women in Canada. Toronto: Umbrella Press, 1994; Tubman: Harriet Tubman and the Underground Railroad. Toronto: Umbrella Press, 1997; Mary Ann Shadd. Toronto: Umbrella Press, 1995.

Sandwich Baptist Church. Windsor, Ontario, Canada.

Saxton, Martha, Louisa May Alcott. 1977; repr. 1995.

Scherman, Katharine, Slave Who Freed Haiti: The Story of Toussaint L'Ouverture. 1964.

Schneider, Richard J. Henry David Thoreau. Twayne, 1987.

Schor, J. A., Henry Highland Garnet. 1977.

Schuyler, G. W., Saint John. 1984.

Scott, D. C., John Graves Simcoe, rev. ed. 1926.

Scott, Foresman. Eli Whitney: A standard work on Whitney's influence and significance. 1956; 1987.

Scudder, Horace E., James Russell Lowell, A Biography, 2 vols. (1901; repr. 1973).

Sears, Richard D., The Kentucky Abolitionists in the Midst of Slavery. 1854-1864. 1993.

Shepard, Edward M. Martin Van Buren, rev. ed. 1899, reprinted 1983.

Shreve, Dorothy Shadd. The AfriCanadian Church: A Stabilizer. Paideia Press, 1983.

Siebert, William H., Underground Railroad from Slavery to Freedom. NY, 1898; repr. 1968.

Smeaton, William, Longfellow and his Poetry. 1992.

Smiley, D. L., The Lion of Whitehall: The Life of Cassius M. Clay. 1963.

Smith, Leonard H., Nova Scotia Immigrants to 1867. 1994.

Smith, Theodore Clark, The Liberty and Free Soil Parties in the Northwest. 1897; repr. 1967.

Sochen, June Herstory: A Record of the American Woman's Past.

Soderlund, Jean R., Quakers and Slavery. 1985.

228

Stampp, Kenneth M. The Peculiar Institution-Slavery in the Ante-Bellum South. Random House, 1989, first pub. 1956; The Causes of the Civil War. N.Y.: Simon and Schuster. 1974.

Stanley, G.F.G. A Short History of the Canadian Constitution. 1969; New France. 1968.

Starobin, Robert S., ed., Denmark Vesey: The Slave Conspiracy of 1822. 1970.

Statistics Canada Library, Ottawa, Ontario Canada.

Stern, Madeleine B. Louisa May Alcott: A Biography, University of Oklahoma Press, 1985. First published in 1950; ed., Critical Essays on Louisa May Alcott. 1984.

Stetson, Erlene, and David, Linda. Glorying in Tribulation: The Lifework of Sojourner Truth 1994.

Stewart, James Brewer, Holy Warriors, rev. ed. 1997; Wendell Phillips: Liberty's Hero. 1986; William Lloyd Garrison and the Challenge of Emancipation. Harlan Davidson, 1992.

Still, William. The Underground Railroad. Chicago: Johnson Publishing Co., 1970.

Stouffer, Allen P., The Light of Nature and Law of God: Antislavery in Ontario, 1833-1877. Montreal, 1992.

Stowe, Harriet Beecher. eds. Ammons, Elizabeth. *Uncle Tom's Cabin*. Norton, 1994.

Styron, William. The Confessions of Nat Turner. Random House, 1993.

Suite, Benjamin. "L'esclavage en Canada", La revue Canadienne, n.s., 8, 1911.

Sundquist, Eric J., ed., Frederick Douglass: New Literary and Historical Essays. Cambridge, 1990.

Tappan, Lewis, The Life of Arthur Tappan. 1870; repr. 1970.

Taylor, Bob Pepperman. America's Bachelor Uncle: Thoreau and the American Polity. Univ. Kansas, 1996.

Taylor, M. W. Harriet Tubman. New York: Chelsea House Publishers, 1991.

Terborg-Penn, Rosalyn. African American Women in the Struggle for the Vote, 1850-1920. Indiana Pr.1998.

Tharp, Louise Hall, Three Saints and a Sinner: Julia Ward Howe, Louisa, Annie, and Sam Ward. 1956.

The first black power town." Ebony Vol.XXVII No. 4, 1972.

The Latest Word: Buxton National historic site & museum, Volume 1 Issue 1, August, 1998.

The Society of Architectural Historians. Chicago, Illinois.

Thomas, Hugh. The Slave Trade: The Story of the Atlantic Slave Trade; 1440-1870. Simon&Schuster, 1997.

Thomas, John L. *The Liberator*, William Lloyd Garrison. 1963.

Thompson, Lawrance, Young Longfellow. 1938; repr. 1969.

Thoreau, Henry David. Simplify, Simplify and Other Quotations from Henry David Thoreau. Ed. K. P. Van Anglen. Columbia University Press, 1996.

Tragle, Henry I., The Southampton Slave Revolt of 1831. 1971.

Trayer, Paul. Étude historique sur la condition légale des esclaves dans les colonies françaises. Paris, 1887

Trudel, Marcel. L'esclavage au Canada français : Histoire et conditions de l'esclavage. Quebec, 1960; "L'attitude de l'Église catholique vis-à-vis l'esclavage au Canada français'", CHA, Report, 1961; The Beginning of New France. 1972.

Trueblood, D. Elton. The People Called Quakers. 1966, reissued 1971.

Turner, Nat T. Confessions of Nat Turner, Leader of the Late Insurrection in Southampton, Virginia, as Fully and Voluntarily Made to Thomas R. Grey. Ayer Co. 1961.

Underground Railroad Museum, Flushing, Ohio, USA.

Underground Railroad Network, African-Canadian Heritage Tour. Chatham, Ontario.

United States Census Bureau, Washington DC, USA.

Van Buren, Martin. 1833, The Autobiography of Martin Van Buren, ed. by Fitzpatrick, John C. 1920, repr. in 2 vol., 1973, and Inquiry into the Origin and Course of Political Parties in the United States, ed. by Abraham Van Buren and John Van Buren. 1867, repr. 1967.

Van Steen, Marcus, Governor Simcoe and His Lady. 1968.

Vann, Richard T. The Social Development of English Quakerism, 1655-1755. 1969.

Viger, Jacques, and LaFontaine, Louis Hippolyte, eds., "De l'esclavage en Canada", La Société Historique de Montréal, Mémoires et documents relatifs à l'histoire du Canada 1, 1859.

Von Frank, Albert J., The Trials of Anthony Burns: Freedom and Slavery in Emerson's Boston. 1998.

Voss, Frederick S., Majestic in His Wrath: A Pictorial Life of Frederick Douglass. 1995.

W.I.S.H. Centre, Woodstock institute Sertoma Help Centre, African-Canadian Heritage Research Facility. Chatham, Ontario, Canada.

Wade, Mason. The French Canadians, 1760-1967, 2 vols. Macmillan, 1968.

Wagenknecht, Edward C. Henry Wadsworth Longfellow: His Poetry & Prose. Ungar, 1986. Henry Wadsworth Longfellow: Portrait of an American Humanist. Longfellow: A Full-Length Portrait. 1955; Harriet Beecher Stowe: The Known & the Unknown. 1965; James Russell Lowell, Portrait of a Many-Sided Man. 1971.

Walker, James. The Black Loyalists (rev ed. 1992); Racial Discrimination in Canada: The Black Experience, Canadian Historical Association, Ottawas, 1985; A History of Blacks in Canada. 1980.

Walser, Richard, The Black Poet (George Moses Horton). 1967.

Walters, Ronald G., The Antislavery Appeal. 1977; repr. 1984.

Walvin, James, The Quakers: Money and Morals. 1998.

Ward, W. Peter Courtship, Love, and Marriage in Nineteenth-Century English Canada. 1990.

Warner, Oliver M. William Wilberforce and His Times. 1962.

Watson, Alan. Roman Slave Law. 1987.

Watson, James L., Asian and African Systems of Slavery. 1980.

Weatherford, W. D. "The Attitude of the Roman Catholic Church toward the Negro During Slavery", American Churches and the Negro, Boston, 1957.

Westermann, William L. The Slave System of Greek and Roman Antiquity. 1955.

Whiper, Rollin, Life of Martin R. Delany by Frances Anee. 1991.

Wiedemann, Thomas, Greek and Roman Slavery. 1981.

Wiencek, Henry. The Hairstons: An American family in Black and White. St. Martin's Press, 2000.

Williams, Cecil Brown. Henry Wadsworth Longfellow. Twayne, 1964.

Willis, Deborah. Reflections in Black: A History of Black Photographers, 1840 to the Present. Norton, 2000.

Wilson, G. E., The Life of Robert Baldwin. 1933.

Wilson, Major L. The Presidency of Martin Van Buren. 1984.

Winks, Robin W. The Blacks in Canada, second edition, McGill-Queen's University Press 1997; The Civil War Years: Canada and the United States. McGill-Queen's University Press 1998; ed., Slavery: A Comparative Perspective. 1972; Canadian Historical Review, "The Creation of a Myth: Canadian Enlistments in the Northern Armies during the American Civil War" Vol. XXXIX, No.1, March, 1958.

Woloch, Nancy. Women and the American Experience. 2nd ed. McGraw, 1994.

Woodwell, R. H., John Greenleaf Whittier. 1985.

World Bk., McClelland and Stewart, Funk & Wagnalls, Microsoft, Learning company, Grolier, Britannica. Broderbund, Interactive multimedia.

Wright, E.C. The Loyalists of New Brunswick. 1955.

Wyatt-Brown, Bertram, Lewis Tappan and the Evangelical War against Slavery. 1968.

Wynn, Graeme. Timber Colony: A Historical Geography of Early Nineteenth Century New Brunswick. University of Toronto Press, 1981.

Yavetz, Zvi, Slaves and Slavery in Ancient Rome. 1988.

Yee, Shirley J., Black Women Abolitionists. 1992.

Ziegler, Philip. The Sixth Great Power. 1988, covering 1762-1929.

Zweig, Paul. Walt Whitman: The Making of the Poet. Basic Bks., 1985. First pub. 1984.

Sojourner Truth

INDEX